SHADRACH MINKINS

SHADRACH MINKINS

From Fugitive Slave to Citizen

Gary Collison

Harvard University Press
Cambridge, Massachusetts
London, England 1997

Library of Congress Cataloging-in-Publication Data

Collison, Gary Lee, 1947–
    Shadrach Minkins : from fugitive slave to citizen / Gary Collison.
    p. cm.
    Includes bibliographical references and index.
    ISBN 0-674-80298-5 (alk. paper)
    1. Minkins, Shadrach. 2. Slaves—Virginia—Norfolk—Biography.
    3. Fugitive slaves—Massachusetts—Boston—Biography. 4. Afro-
    Americans—Québec (Province)—Montréal—History—19th century.
    5. Norfolk (Va.)—Biography. 6. Boston (Mass.)—Biography.
    7. Montréal (Québec)—Biography. I. Title.
E450.M653 1997
973.7'115'092—dc20
[B]
96-35555

For Linda

Contents

Illustrations

SHADRACH MINKINS

Prologue

On the afternoon of Saturday, February 15, 1851, a dreary, rain-swept day in the middle of a late-winter thaw, the Boston Court House was the center of great excitement and tension. The corridor outside the U.S. Court Room on the second floor was jammed with people, the atmosphere electric. Inside the courtroom, flanked by two rough-looking deputies, sat a husky, copper-colored man wearing a waiter's apron. Papers filed by the U.S. district attorney referred to him merely as Shadrach. His full name was Shadrach Minkins, although he had been calling himself Frederick Wilkins or Jenkins since arriving in Boston nine months before. Evidence presented to the U.S. commissioner that morning appeared to show that he was an escaped slave, the property of John DeBree of Norfolk, Virginia, a purser in the U.S. Navy. Thus a hitherto-obscure black man was caught up in the great currents of American history.

In 1851 the nation was prospering. New territories were being settled in the Midwest and Far West. Great factories all along the East Coast were thundering with giant machinery, turning out everything from shoes to nails to chairs to cloth—especially cotton cloth. Spurred by the development of the cotton gin and power looming, a swath of new plantations had sprung up across the Deep South to supply the tremendous demand for this fiber. A commercial revolution was under way, and fortunes were being made from Texas to New Hampshire.

This growth and prosperity were threatened by increasingly bitter division between the North and the South. While much of the South remained steadfastly agrarian, homogeneous, and elitist, the North grew increasingly industrial, heterogenous, and democratic. Southern fire-eaters and Northern abolitionists called loudly for disunion. Positions hardened, and the future of the United States seemed doubtful.

In 1850, to stem the rising fear, anger, and hatred, Henry Clay, Daniel Webster, and other like-minded men had pushed a series of compromises through Congress. The Fugitive Slave Law, the final piece of the package of laws known as the Compromise of 1850, provided owners of fugitive slaves with the full support of the federal government in recovering their property. For African-Americans the next ten years would be filled with persecution. Black communities throughout the North would be disrupted, and more than a thousand black men, women, and children would be hunted down. Hundreds of fugitives would be captured and sent back into slavery. Many families would be broken up and many lives changed forever as thousands fled to Canada for safety.

Once the new Fugitive Slave Law was enacted in mid-September, it was only a matter of time until Boston, the center of the antislavery movement, was tested. Many Southerners yearned to see Boston abolitionists humiliated, and Northern supporters of the Compromise yearned equally for a demonstration that even in Boston the new law could be effective. After a Georgia slaveowner failed to secure the arrest of a famous fugitive couple, William and Ellen Craft, these yearnings grew ever more insistent.

On the morning of February 15, 1851, federal officers arrested Shadrach Minkins while he was serving breakfast at the Cornhill Coffee House, in the commercial heart of the city. With that arrest, Minkins became the first fugitive slave to be seized in New England under the Fugitive Slave Law, and national attention immediately focused upon him and upon Boston. The news was immediately broadcast in papers throughout the country. On Shadrach Minkins, briefly, rested the contradictory hopes and fears of the nation. His arrest was expected to furnish the test of the Compromise and the Fugitive Slave Law that its supporters and critics had been anxiously awaiting. Daniel Webster, the aging secretary of state and former senator from Massachusetts, hoped the event would help carry him on a pro-Union ticket into the White House in the 1852 election. For Boston's blacks, however, Shadrach Minkins' arrest called forth their deepest fears and determination.

Despite the notoriety of his case, Shadrach Minkins' life has remained shrouded in obscurity. Beyond the few court records and his few hours in the national spotlight, he would remain unknown. Even his name—variously reported as Frederick or Sherwood or Shadrach Wilkins or Minkins or Jenkins—remained uncertain.

Before the nation could learn more about him, a small band of Boston's black citizens burst into the courtroom, shoved the deputies aside, and seized the startled fugitive. Their footsteps thundered through the corridor, down the stairs, and out into Court House Square. The air filled with shouting and cheering. Then Shadrach Minkins' rescuers raced with him through the streets to Boston's West End—and disappeared.

Afterward little was heard of Shadrach Minkins. Stories circulated that he had passed through Concord, Massachusetts, and, later, that he had reached safety in Montreal, had married, and was operating a small restaurant. For the next few years there were occasional reports that someone had visited and talked with him. Then the reports stopped. There was only silence.

The silence continued. Of four famous Boston fugitive slave cases between the passage of the Fugitive Slave Law of 1850 and the outbreak of the Civil War, the 1851 arrest and rescue of Shadrach Minkins has been the most neglected by historians. One obvious reason for this neglect is that the case was a very brief affair: less than three hours after being arrested, Minkins was rescued from the custody of federal officers and was never recaptured. Boston's other fugitive slave cases, by contrast, were drawn out for days and even weeks and provoked sustained protest and controversy. The Anthony Burns case in 1854 even resulted in an ill-fated abolitionist attack on the Boston Court House and the death of a federal deputy marshal. Both Thomas Sims (who was captured in 1851) and Anthony Burns were sent back into slavery, dispatched from Boston with elaborate military displays.

Another reason for the silence about Shadrach Minkins is that his rescue was accomplished entirely by blacks, and no black Bostonian wrote extensively about black involvement in aiding fugitive slaves. White abolitionists, when they wrote about the incident at all, tended to give credit to the antislavery movement in general and to recount their own participation in that movement. And most of the white abolitionists who helped fugitives directly lost all contact with them afterward.

* * *

This book, like many, I imagine, is the outgrowth of a footnote. The key event occurred one evening in the summer of 1986, at the end of a long day in the McGill University library spent squinting at microfilm frames of the Montreal segment of Canada's 1861 house-to-house census. I was looking for checkmarks in column 13, headed "Colored Persons Mulatto or Indian." Hour after hour in the darkened room, the images of the census slips flashed on the screen before me. Sometimes the handwriting was so faded, so faint, or such a hasty, illegible scrawl—and often it was all these things together—that no matter how long I peered at the screen I couldn't make out the names or the information. Beside me was a pad with a short list of black residents of Montreal. By drawing up this list I was uncovering an African-American equivalent of a lost tribe of Israel. The birthplaces—Maryland, Delaware, Virginia—implied a long journey, hardship, and exile.

But where was Shadrach Minkins? It was getting late, and there was little microfilm left on the final spool. Then a new record flashed onto the screen with a mark in column 13. I glanced at the family name and wrote it down: "Nichols." Then I looked back to the screen and made out the first name—"Shadrach." For a moment the information did not register. Then a shot of adrenalin swept through me. The census taker had misheard the respondent and had written down "Nichols" instead of "Minkins." There were the names of his wife and his two children. There were his age, his occupation. There was his birthplace, Virginia. The census taker had found him, and I was looking over his shoulder.

It has taken another decade to gather up other pieces of the puzzle and to break the near silence of almost a century and a half, to tell the story of Shadrach Minkins' life as a slave in Norfolk, Virginia, as a fugitive slave in Boston, Massachusetts, and as a free citizen in Montreal, Canada. Shadrach Minkins, illiterate all his life, died with his thoughts and experiences unrecorded. The core of his story comes from contemporary newspapers, especially those in Boston, with their remarkably detailed records of the trials that followed his rescue, and thus of the rescue itself. Many gaps remain, along with many unanswered questions. But with the addition of each new fragment filling in the outline of his story, Shadrach Minkins emerged both as an individual and as a representative of the struggles of African-Americans before and after Emancipation. It is a story that reveals much about the frustrations and the triumphs of African-Americans in the nineteenth century. It is a story of those who renounced their enslavement, who found the promise of the North unfulfilled, who left the country that they felt had betrayed them, and who found in Canada a measure of freedom and security. It was not a paradise free from racial prejudices, but nevertheless it was an environment in which Shadrach Minkins and his fellow refugees could create new lives, find new identities, and build a new community.

NORFOLK

1   "Han't Got No Self"

Many years before the Civil War, an abolitionist met a black woodchopper along a bank of the Ohio River in what is now West Virginia. They had the following conversation:

"Halloo, there! Where are you going?" I called to him.
"Gwine chopping in de woods!"
"Chopping for yourself?"
"Han't got no self."
"Slave, are you?"
"Dat's what I is."[1]

Perhaps no words have ever captured the estrangement of slavery so succinctly: "Han't got no self." In 1850 Shadrach Minkins and more than three million other slaves in the United States had no self, no *own*, no *my*.

Shadrach Minkins also had no history. Because of the African diaspora and his classification as property, he was cut off from his family and his communal heritage. Numerous recent studies of slavery, particularly in archaeology and social history, help us understand, in a general way, Shadrach Minkins' place in history and the circumstances that surrounded him. A rich portrait of African-American culture has been emerging from the study of fabric, buildings, pottery, and musical instruments and from song, story, and dance.[2] Still, these elements provide only background. Trying to tell the story of an individual who had no self is exceedingly difficult. Shadrach Minkins, an illiterate all his life, left no narrative of his life in slavery. No friends told his story for him. He has not even a stone to mark his grave.

For the basic outline of the life of any obscure person in the nineteenth century, white or black, there are a few standard resources—the federal census taken every decade from 1790 on, local tax rolls, court records, and so-called vital records of births, marriages, deaths. But as any black genealogist will testify, the documentary trail into the past usually stops abruptly at the slavery period. The 1850 federal census, for example, recorded slaves not by name but merely as numbers in various sex and age categories: such-and-such an owner had so many male slaves between ages five and ten, so many between ten and twenty, and so on. Local records, like the federal censuses, also focused on the owner. The vast majority of slaves lived and died without leaving an identifiable trace.

However, pieces of the history of some slaves survive precisely because they were regarded as property; records of births and deaths, purchases and sales kept by owners preserve at least an outline of their lives. Although in Shadrach Minkins' case there is no known owner's ledger, the barest sketch of his life survives for a reason equally connected with the matter of ownership. Under the Fugitive Slave Law of 1850, before an owner could recover a slave from the North, ownership had to be proved before a federal judge or commissioner. The documents delivered to the Boston federal court in 1851 by Shadrach Minkins' owner, John DeBree, attest that DeBree had purchased Shadrach Minkins from one John Higgins, a trader, in 1849, and that earlier in the same year Higgins had purchased him from Martha Hutchings, the proprietor of a grocery store. The records also show that some years previously Martha Hutchings had purchased Minkins from Thomas Glenn, owner of the Eagle Tavern, and that Glenn had apparently owned Minkins' father, David, and his mother, name unknown.

DeBree, Higgins, Hutchings, Glenn—these names on his bills of sale are Shadrach Minkins' slavery genealogy. They take us back to Norfolk, Virginia, during the early decades of the nineteenth century.

After the Revolutionary War, which left Norfolk and the Gosport Navy Yard across the river in charred ruins, the town recovered slowly. Because of its strategic position in southeastern Virginia near the mouth of Chesapeake Bay and adjacent to the great natural harbor of Hampton Roads, it was poised to be a leading East Coast port—a New York or Boston of the South. Although direct trade with Europe was small, Norfolk served as a key transfer point between shallower-drafting inland vessels and deep-hulled ships of the Atlantic trade. In 1792, when Britain became too enmeshed in European conflicts to enforce its monopoly on West Indian trade, Norfolk merchants suddenly had the opportunity they had longed for. The port was soon crammed with ships. Norfolk shipbuilding, in the doldrums since before the Revolution, suddenly rebounded. Every creek and inlet became an impromptu shipyard.[3]

By the beginning of the nineteenth century Norfolk had become Virginia's largest city, with a population of nearly 7,000 persons, of whom more than 3,000 were black. In 1806, 120 Norfolk-owned vessels were engaged exclusively in foreign trade, and Thomas Jefferson predicted a glorious future for the city. The docks were piled high with Indian corn, tobacco, naval stores, and produce, much of it bound for the sugar plantations in the West Indies. Ships also carried goods to the thriving interregional East Coast markets. The booming business climate made Norfolk exceedingly attractive to such men as the lawyer William Wirt, later attorney general under two presidents. Wirt admitted being "drawn to Norfolk by the attractions of her bank" and the ready availability of cash, a scarce commodity in many parts of the infant nation.[4]

Norfolk in these years just before Shadrach Minkins' birth had a cosmopolitan air. Native Virginians were the majority, but Scotch, English, and Irish immigrants were numerous, and there were lesser numbers of French, Portuguese, Spanish, and Dutch. By far the largest non-English-speaking population was of French origin. Following the slave insurrection in Santo Domingo in 1793, thousands of refugees had arrived in Norfolk, many with their bondsmen (despite laws against importing slaves). Hundreds had stayed. Other Frenchmen and slaves were arriving around the same time from Haiti. Frenchmen were so numerous that they had their own fraternal organization, and their language was often heard in shops and on streetcorners.[5]

Norfolk's 2,614 slaves and 352 free blacks played a vital role in turn-of-the-century prosperity. They performed some of the skilled and much of the unskilled labor, and prosperity fueled the demand for their services on the docks and in Norfolk businesses and homes. Many of the men worked as stonecutters, plasterers, blacksmiths, painters, coopers and carpenters, barbers, shoemakers, domestic servants, stable hands, chimney sweeps, canal diggers, and porters, while black women commonly worked as seamstresses, laundresses, housekeepers, nurses, nannies, and cooks. On the wharves and in the harbor, slaves and free blacks performed a great variety of tasks.[6] Some slaves, especially those skilled in building and maritime trades, could even save enough of their premium wages to purchase freedom for themselves and family members.[7] Most, however, faced a lifetime of servitude.

Norfolk whites like the indefatigable local promoter William S. Forrest believed Norfolk's blacks to be among the most "happy and contented" people on the face of the earth, a condition that Forrest attributed to their "having, generally, liberal, kind and indulgent owners, who allow them many privileges and who look anxiously to their welfare."[8] Even Norfolk blacks, who must necessarily have had far less rosy views, commonly believed their condition enviable. In comparison with slaves from farming districts, slaves in urban environments like Norfolk had easier lives. Norfolk ex-slave Peter Randolph remembered that Norfolk slaves "do not fare so hard as on the plantations," and Jane Pyatt of Portsmouth remembered in old age that as a girl she had had "everything a person could wish for except an education."[9] Urban slaves often had better food and rarely wore the coarse Negro cloth or cheap Negro brogans of the rural field hand.[10] Their labor tended to be less arduous and their punishments less severe. Frederick Douglass, who labored for several years as a field hand on the nearby Eastern Shore of Maryland, thought that in comparison with a plantation slave, "a city slave is almost a free citizen."[11] Douglass attested that many of the advantages by which he lifted himself out of slavery were derived from the years he spent in Baltimore.

If slavery was softened in cities like Norfolk, Richmond, Baltimore, and New Orleans, it still was slavery, and the protective veneer of sophisticated town life could be exceedingly thin. Sales broke up city families no less than country families. In his autobiography Douglass told of Baltimore slaves horribly beaten or forced to contend with pigs for scraps.[12] At the beginning of the nineteenth century, M. L. E. Moreau de Saint-Méry, a leading spirit of the French Revolution who fled from its excesses, was astounded by the "state of debasement" in which he found Norfolk slaves living. Slaves "are beaten for the slightest faults with whips made of rawhide and cord," he wrote, "and a slave-owner can always find constables willing to execute his desires in this respect." Noting that Virginia law required every free black "to carry a certificate from the Governor, certifying to his liberty," he concluded with disgust: "Free Men of Color are no better treated than the slaves, except for the fact that no one is allowed to beat them."[13] The slave jail, the auction block, and the constable's whipping post were the constant urban reminders of the violent force that held all blacks in subjugation.

We do not know with certainty when Thomas Glenn first owned Shadrach Minkins, who was apparently called Sherwood as a child and young man, but it appears that Glenn owned Minkins' mother and so had come into possession of her son on the day of his birth. No record of Minkins' date of birth survives, if it ever existed. Like Frederick Douglass, Minkins probably did not know either the day or even the year of his birth. Lack of such knowledge reminded many a slave that in the eyes of the dominant society, he or she had been born a thing.

If newspaper advertisements are any indication, some slaves appear to have had no idea of their ages. One Norfolk woman who was offered for sale was vaguely described as "between 30 and 40 years of age."[14] Other slaves were advertised as being "about" such-and-such an age. Owners themselves sometimes did not know the ages of their slaves, but because young adults brought higher prices than older ones, owners' memories were likely to be purposefully inaccurate. Owners who shaved five or ten years from a slave's age pocketed a handsome dividend. Shadrach Minkins himself may have unwittingly participated in such a deception. An 1849 newspaper advertisement announcing that he was to be sold reported his age as twenty-seven.[15] This claim would put the year of his birth somewhere around 1822. But in 1861 Minkins would report his age as forty-seven, which would mean that he was born about 1814.[16]

By the time of Shadrach Minkins' boyhood, Norfolk's boom had gone bust. British laws prohibiting American vessels from engaging in the immensely profitable trade with the British West Indies, combined with the U.S. Embargo Act of 1807 and the Navigation Law of 1820, shut off much of Norfolk's commerce. By the 1830s new shallow-draft steamships from Baltimore, New York, and Philadelphia could bypass Norfolk altogether and deliver their cargoes directly to Richmond, Petersburg, and Alexandria. Although Norfolk maintained a thriving trade with North Carolina via the Dismal Swamp Canal, which opened in 1828, unsuccessful efforts to develop effective railroad links further hampered Norfolk's prospects.[17]

Norfolk in 1830 contained just under 10,000 persons, roughly half black and half white.[18] Although one visitor in the 1830s described it as a "bustling, active" town of "well filled shops" and streets "lined with hampers, barrels, crates, and all the usual pavement impediments of a commercial port," another found "little of hope or energy" in Norfolk commerce and, visiting the docks, was astonished to see "only four square-rigged vessels."[19] In 1844 a traveler from Massachusetts found "everything . . . in a dilapidated condition," for which he blamed slavery, and a decade later Frederick Law Olmsted, in one of his dispatches to the *New-York Daily Times,* disparaged Norfolk as "a dirty, low, ill-arranged town . . . [with] all the immoral and disagreeable characteristics of a large seaport, with very few of the advantages": it had "no lyceum or public libraries, no public gardens, no galleries of art, . . . no 'home' for its seamen; no public resorts of healthful and refining amusement, no place better than a filthy tobacco-impregnated bar-room or a licentious dance-cellar for the stranger of high or low degree to pass the hours unoccupied by business."[20]

The Eagle Tavern (and hotel) where Shadrach Minkins worked had long been regarded as a fashionable establishment. In 1794, when the French frigate *Normandie* visited the port, the Americans hosted a dinner for its officers at the tavern. By 1830 Shadrach Minkins' owner, Thomas Glenn, a native of New Kent County, Virginia, had been operating the Eagle Tavern for at least a decade and a half.[21] Contemporaries testified that the establishment was "neatly conducted" and its host always "kind" and "liberal." A later local historian characterized it as "the best hotel in the Borough."[22] Conveniently located near the waterfront, it was a favorite haunt of officers from the Gosport Navy Yard in Portsmouth, just across the Elizabeth River. According to his obituary, Glenn was often "the happy instrument of reconciling disagreements" between the officers. "A more feeling and benevolent heart never inhabited a human bosom," his obituary would boast.[23]

The location of the Eagle Tavern near the foot of Market Square (and later close by on Commerce Street) put young Shadrach Minkins at the center of Norfolk life. A constant traffic of ferry passengers crossing the

A view of the natural harbor of Hampton Roads, looking south toward the Elizabeth River. Norfolk appears on the left, Portsmouth on the right.

Elizabeth River from Portsmouth and the adjoining Gosport Navy Yard landed just a few steps from the tavern door. The shops of grocers, dry-goods merchants, clothiers, auctioneers, druggists, tailors, and stationers, together with boardinghouses and the offices of physicians and commission merchants, lined Market Square, attracting a large clientele.[24] One side of the square was a favorite location for slave auctions.

On market days the squat, rectangular market building, its roof supported by brick pillars "almost big enough to support the dome of St. Peter's," bustled with activity.[25] The square itself was filled with carts of slave and free black vendors. Gentlemen in top hats, ladies in crinolines, sailors, and children of both races crowded the square. Black vendors of fish, poultry, and produce sat beside carts, wagons, and wheelbarrows.[26] One visitor in the 1820s remembered particularly that the vendors' horses were "about the size of a two year old cow, and nothing but skin and bone."[27]

The Eagle Tavern, together with other hotels, tavern-inns, and boardinghouses scattered about the town, provided accommodations of greatly varying quality to travelers, sailors, and itinerant laborers passing through Norfolk. Although no description of the Eagle has been preserved, we know from the 1830 census that Thomas Glenn owned Shadrach Minkins and a dozen other slaves, and all of them, presumably, were employed about the hotel.[28] Visitors' comments on the differences between Northern

Norfolk's Market Square, 1836 (author).

and Southern hotels hint at what the Eagle must have been like. Northern travelers were constantly irritated by the superfluity of "help" but the dearth of real assistance at Southern hotels and inns. Anne Royall, who visited Norfolk in the 1820s, complained that even the smallest inn had ten to thirty black servants. "This is taxed on the traveller, which is petty robbery!" she sputtered.[29] When Olmsted stayed at hotels in Richmond, Petersburg, and Norfolk in the 1850s, he complained of an "utter want of system and order." To get even the simplest task accomplished, according to Olmsted, required time and tenacity. Once, discovering that his room lacked water, towels, and a basin for washing up, he rang and rang the front desk, and the front-desk clerk rang and rang for service, all to no avail. Later two slaves suddenly appeared at his door, listened politely to his requests, and disappeared. A quarter of an hour later one of them returned with a pitcher of water, but no towels.[30]

Like slaves everywhere, those in Norfolk, though restricted on many fronts, constructed a world for themselves in bondage. In their songs and dances, their food, their manner of speech and modes of dress, their manner of worshipping, their superstitions, their celebrations and ceremonies, their patterns of thought and sense of such basic coordinates as time, space, home, family, and duty, slaves both resisted and reacted to the dominant white culture, forging a separate, distinctive identity and culture no longer African, but neither totally American.[31] They resisted their bondage more directly by refusing to work, by working slowly, or by sabotaging their work; they lied, feigned illness, hid, or ran away. They stole food, clothing, and livestock, destroyed property, and even murdered.[32]

Norfolk slaves apparently never participated in the small-scale slave plots in Virginia in 1663, 1672, 1687, 1723, and 1781–82, but at the turn of the century they came close to revolting. In 1800, during what became known as Gabriel's Rebellion, an estimated 150 slaves from around Norfolk gathered near the city to join in a general Virginia revolt but disbanded when they learned that the main group in Richmond had failed.[33] In 1802 Norfolk blacks were suspected of conspiring to set fire to the town at Easter. Many white men of the town armed themselves and patrolled the streets. Ultimately two Norfolk slaves, supposed conspirators, were tried and convicted. One was later released, but the other, named Jeremiah, went to the gallows "with a declaration of his innocence, leaving a wife and two children." Although all the evidence against him had come from a slave whom many considered unreliable, nervous Norfolk whites, more worried about making a strong impression on their slaves than about niceties of law, applauded the execution.[34]

When Shadrach Minkins was still a young man, an event occurred that would have a profound impact on him and his fellow blacks, both slave and free. Although it took place more than forty miles away, in Southampton County, it shook not merely all Virginia but the entire slaveholding South. This event was the famous Nat Turner slave insurrection. It began on the morning of August 22, 1831, when Turner, a self-styled preacher, led his handful of followers toward the farmhouse of Joseph Travis, the owner of Hark Travis, called "General Moore" by his fellow slaves. Within minutes they had murdered the Travis family. The band pressed on through the countryside to nearby farms, killing whites and adding recruits and horses along the way, including several free blacks, until their numbers had swelled to more than sixty. By dawn of the first morning, Turner's band had raided fifteen houses and had killed more than sixty white men, women, and children.[35]

Turner's revolt set off an explosive retaliation that spread quickly beyond the borders of Southampton County. Using the slave revolt as a license to terrorize blacks, murderous white vigilantes swept into Tidewater Virginia, in the southeast, where most of the slaves and most of the wealth were concentrated. In the first frenzied days at least a hundred free blacks and slaves were lynched, shot, tortured, burned to death, or decapitated. Some of the bodies were horribly mutilated.[36] Blacks as far away as North Carolina suffered under the vigilante terror. Harriet Jacobs, then a young slave in Edenton, North Carolina, saw "country bullies and poor whites" descend on Edenton like "a troop of demons, terrifying and tormenting the helpless." The homes of blacks were looted with impunity. "Everywhere men, women, and children were whipped till the blood stood in puddles at their feet."[37]

When inevitably inaccurate accounts of Nat Turner's revolt first reached Norfolk, the mayor, frightened that the rebellion might spread, begged federal troops at Fort Monroe to rush to Southampton County, which they did without waiting for official orders. Ignorant of the mayor's action, Virginia governor John Floyd ordered Norfolk militia units to join the Southampton County forces, leaving the city virtually undefended.[38] Norfolk citizens organized armed patrols to guard their streets and to capture suspects, but the impromptu volunteer force was hardly equipped to handle anything serious.[39]

Norfolk blacks were spared from the worst outrages by distance from Southampton County and by white sympathizers. No blacks were murdered, and meandering white patrols generally contented themselves with bullying and with firing their pistols and rifles in the streets, much to the dismay of local authorities.[40] Although a dozen Norfolk blacks suspected of involvement were arrested, local authorities insisted on waiting for substantial evidence. "There have been some idle rumors of its having been known to our blacks here, but the general impression is that they were ignorant of it," wrote Norfolk resident Susan Selden confidently.[41] All those arrested were eventually released.

Free blacks in Norfolk's outlying districts did not fare so well. Even before Turner's rebellion, harassment had been nearly intolerable. *Free Man of Color: The Autobiography of Willis Augustus Hodges* recounts in hair-raising detail the constant invasions of the Hodgeses' family home by vigilante bands in neighboring Princess Anne County in the late 1820s. Sometimes hiding behind masks and paint, the invaders beat the Hodgeses, stole their food and possessions, and destroyed their property with impunity. Several literate members of Willis Hodges' family, accused of forging passes and free papers for slaves, were jailed, tried, and sent to prison. Turner's rebellion brought a new wave of "trouble, sorrow, and death" upon the Hodges family and other free blacks in Tidewater Virginia. Hundreds of families "suffered severely," wrote Hodges. "Many lost their property and were completely broken up, and had to leave Virginia and seek homes in the free states or Canada."[42]

After Norfolk troops returned from Southampton with the reassuring news that all but a handful of the rebels had been captured or killed, something like normalcy returned to the city. Norfolk's volunteer guard eventually grew tired of patrolling the streets.[43] Yet Turner's rebellion left a permanent legacy of suspicion, soon embodied in legislation, against all of Virginia's black population, especially its free blacks. Initially legislators actually considered a proposal for the gradual emancipation of Virginia's slaves, but under intense opposition from the Tidewater regions the proposal withered.[44] Over the next few years the Virginia legislature passed laws further tightening the restrictions on free blacks, making them even more (in historian Ira Berlin's phrase) "slaves without masters." All blacks were prohibited from owning firearms (previously permits had been granted in individual cases), selling liquor, and preaching or holding religious services except those conducted by white ministers. Stiffer penalties were enacted for crimes committed by free blacks, and for the first time free blacks were denied the right to attend school. Blacks who attended any gathering where reading or writing was taking place could receive as many as twenty "stripes," as lashes were known for the lines of raw welts and sores left on the skin. Northampton County whites even attempted to persuade the legislature to remove their entire free black population of over 1,300 persons.[45]

Moses Grandy, who had purchased his freedom and left Norfolk for Boston before Nat Turner's insurrection, ran up against the new restrictions when he revisited Norfolk to negotiate for the freedom of one of his sons. At first denied permission to go ashore, Grandy was eventually granted nine days in which to transact his business. If he remained any longer, he was told, he faced arrest, physical violence, and even reenslavement.[46]

During the next three years Shadrach Minkins and Norfolk's other slaves and free blacks faced new levels of white suspicion, fostered in part by the emancipation of blacks in the British West Indies in 1833 and in part by the strident rhetoric of Bostonian William Lloyd Garrison, chief spokesperson of the heretofore tame antislavery movement. Under Garrison's leadership, Southerners found their institutions under violent attack by a host of Northerners clamoring for the immediate and total abolition of slavery. Garrison's *Liberator* attacked colonization schemes with a vengeance, and antislavery petitions flooded Congress. As a result, the South's paranoia doubled. Abolitionist literature seemed to be everywhere, and every stranger was suspected of attempting to run off slaves or of inciting them to bloody deeds.

By 1835, only a few years after Virginians themselves had debated the gradual abolition of slavery, no words questioning slavery were tolerated. In that year the panic over what Southerners called the "aggressions" of Northern abolitionists reached a peak in Norfolk after a series of incidents throughout Virginia and a barrage of threatening news reports and rumors from other states. At a series of meetings, furious Norfolk whites demanded action against the "desperate and lawless gang of atrocious Fanatics" who, they claimed, threatened to "desolate the land with all the horrors of a servile war." A committee of vigilance was formed to patrol the neighborhoods and to question strangers closely. Officers were directed to arrest slaves going at large and to see that they and their owners were "prosecuted as the law directs."[47]

Another committee was appointed to see that laws regulating free blacks were "rigidly enforced." Free blacks who had remained in the state contrary to the 1806 law now found it more and more difficult to escape expulsion or reenslavement.[48] Forty free blacks in Norfolk were notified that they were in violation of the law against remaining in the state. Within two years, all but six had left the borough.[49] Those remaining found themselves increasingly excluded from trades and increasingly confined to a life in poverty and squalor. Owners were discouraged from emancipating their slaves.[50] Driven by what one white writer euphemistically called the "rigid treatment of the Patrols," nearly a hundred Norfolk County free blacks signed a written agreement stating their intention to emigrate to Liberia. "Thousands are anxious to embark," one Norfolk reporter claimed, although the actual number of emigrants sponsored by the Colonization Society was never very large.[51]

Although white fears of incendiary abolitionist propaganda and black rebellion eventually tapered off, the message to young Shadrach Minkins and other Virginia blacks in that period of intense suspicion could not be forgotten. It was a painful civics lesson. It reminded them forcibly that the world of Norfolk was not their world. For more than two centuries they had shared the homes of whites, tended their crops, raised their children, fed and nursed them. They had shared their tragedies and their joys. Their blood was mingled with the blood of white Virginians. Yet more than half a million Virginia blacks, the vast majority of whom were slaves, remained an alien race in an alien land. They inhabited the Commonwealth of Virginia at the will and the whim of whites. In the aftermath of events of the early 1830s, their slim opportunities for power and freedom and economic comfort had narrowed even further and were not likely to expand ever again.

In this unpromising Virginia world a slave named Shadrach Minkins quietly came of age. As a boy he would have ambled along Norfolk's magnolia-scented streets. In the summer he would have swum in the

Elizabeth River with other boys and hunted turtles and crabs and sala-
manders along the banks and mudflats. He would have heard the songs of
slaves with their strange, haunting mixture of joy and sorrow, hope and
despair. He would have learned about slavery—about the invisible wall
that separated him from every person with white skin. And he would have
learned to practice the protective slave mannerisms—the averted eyes,
the wide smile, the tentative gait and bent stance—that made whites
comfortable. In the evenings he would have listened to stories of beatings
and brutality and of the selling of fathers and mothers, brothers and
sisters. All slaves learned about these things, talked about them, worried
about them.

Young Shadrach Minkins would have heard also the whispered, celebrated stories of those who had fled to the North—the husbands and
wives, the aunts and uncles, the sons and daughters and cousins, friends
and acquaintances who had stolen away to freedom. And at the docks, he
would have watched the great white sails fill with wind and the ships glide
silently toward the horizon, freed from the land, free to drift wherever the
wind would take them.

2 "Horses and Men, Cattle and Women, Pigs and Children"

"AUCTION SALE," read a typical notice in an antebellum Norfolk newspaper:

> WILL BE SOLD on WEDNESDAY NEXT, 29th inst., on the Farm (Sewill's Point—recently occupied by Wm. Wilkins, dec'd), All his Household and Kitchen Furniture, a Negro Woman and child, a Horse, Cow and Calf, the crops of the present year, the Farming Utensils, &c. Sale to commence at 12 o'clock. Terms cash. By order of Administrator. JH & J Nash, Auct'rs.[1]

Nearly every issue of local newspapers from Norfolk to New Orleans carried such notices, the slaves listed indiscriminately with the furniture and animals. "There were horses and men, cattle and women, pigs and children, all holding the same rank in the scale of being, and all subjected to the same narrow examination," wrote Frederick Douglass of his own participation, at the age of ten, in the valuation of his master's estate. The experience, Douglass said, provided "a new conception of my degraded condition."[2]

For Shadrach Minkins, Frederick Douglass, and many other slaves, the main defense against their "degraded condition" lay in the sustaining powers of family and community and culture, or else in sabotage or flight, two stratagems that brought with them tremendous risks. Like Frederick Douglass, Shadrach Minkins would finally risk all to assert his humanity.

In the summer of 1832, barely a year after Nat Turner's bloody abortive rebellion had cast a broad shadow over blacks throughout the South, Thomas Glenn died, leaving a wife, Ann, and five children.[3] His death cast its own small but ominous shadow over the lives of Shadrach Minkins and his other slaves.

For slaves, the death of their master was an event fraught with faint hopes and dark possibilities. Perhaps Minkins hoped that Glenn's will would give him his freedom, but such an outcome was unlikely and, moreover, would have provided very little security. Being granted freedom in Virginia meant being required to leave the state within a short time. A more likely scenario was that Glenn's widow Ann might sell off the assets, including the slaves. If the Glenn slaves were divided among the heirs, as commonly occurred after the death of a master, Minkins and the others could easily find themselves sold at auction. If he was not sold, there would still be little guarantee against separation from friends and family members. About the best that Minkins could hope for was to be given to one of the Glenn family or to be sold to a local resident who needed his services.

Although we know that Ann Glenn did not immediately sell Shadrach Minkins and the other slaves, we do not know what happened to them during the next four years.[4] But on December 28, 1836, "after a painful illness," Ann Glenn died.[5] She left five underage children and an estate consisting of a house and lot on Bermuda street, the tavern building (on leased ground), some furniture and miscellaneous possessions, and at least eight slaves, including Shadrach Minkins.[6] Her will directed that the estate be sold and the proceeds divided equally among the five orphaned children.

With the court's indulgence, until the children came of age management of the Glenn estate fell to Norfolk businessman Elijah P. Goodridge, probably the Goodridge of Anderson & Goodridge, purveyors of "men's coarse Brogans" and "Negro's coarse Shoes" together with hats, soap, tobacco, whiskey, salt, nails, and other miscellaneous supplies.[7] Because Goodridge was an indifferent recordkeeper (the court officer was later to complain of being given a "confused mass of bills and receipts"), exactly how faithfully he executed his responsibilities to the young Glenns is difficult to determine.[8] Yet the surviving accounts and court notes suggest that he fulfilled them conscientiously: he saw that the children were well clothed and had school supplies, lessons, and spending money. Initially he boarded the children with a Mrs. Fitzhugh, but after the tavern building lost its tenant at the end of 1837, Goodridge solved the problem of the vacant building and the children's care by persuading Adeline Mills, Ann Glenn's sister, to move in with the five orphans. Sometime during the first days of 1838 the children's belongings arrived at the tavern, and they set up housekeeping with their aunt.[9]

In the meantime Shadrach Minkins and the other Glenn slaves were "hired out." This arrangement, a kind of leasing, was a common practice with a long history in the slaveholding South, particularly the urban South. Owners of excess slaves (owners "overcapitalized" in slaves, to use the economist's terminology) rented or leased them out for a specified term—a day, week, month, or, most commonly, a year. Norfolk hired slaves worked as domestics, laborers, carpenters, bakers, cooks, oystermen, carriage drivers, masons, and in many other occupations. In other parts of Virginia large numbers worked in factories and mines. Around Norfolk, the Dismal Swamp Canal Company hired many slaves for the backbreaking labor of maintaining existing channels and digging new ones.[10] The Gosport Navy Yard also employed many slaves. Hired slaves provided owners with steady income, ranging from around $10 per year for young children to $100 a year or more for skilled adult workmen. Widows and orphans were so often supported entirely by slave labor in this way that Southerners sometimes condemned abolitionists on precisely these grounds; the Northern abolitionists who encouraged slaves to run off, so the Southern argument went, were leaving widows and orphans to starve.[11]

E. P. Goodridge's accounts for the Glenn estate in 1838, the first full year of records, reveal little about the arrangements under which the slaves worked. The accounts merely list the names of the slaves, their eight different Norfolk white hirers, and the yearly wages of each, amounting to $342 altogether.[12] Shadrach Minkins appears in the accounts as "Sherwood":

By Cash of Mrs Gamm	hire Maria 1838	40
By " " Williams	" Letty	40
By " " F Milhado	" Charles	72
By " " Owens	" Richard	30
By " " Hutchings & Co.	" Sherwood	80
By " " P. Nimmo	" Isaac	80
By " " Smith	" Mary	40
By " " Miss Mills	" Susan	40

By 1839 the income to the estate from Minkins and the others had increased to $459, largely because of rising wages for the men.[13] Both Shadrach (Sherwood) and Isaac earned $100 each. Charles's hire inched up to $85, and Richard's to $40. The women's annual hire, on the other hand, changed little or not at all or else decreased. While Letty's hire remained the same, $40, Susan's fell from $40 to $25. Maria's earnings for 1839 are given as $50 for "Maria & boy."

R. S. Hutchings & Company, where Shadrach Minkins worked during these years, had been founded many years before by Londoner Richard S. Hutchings, a "much esteemed and respected" citizen, according to the Norfolk *American Beacon*.[14] After his death in 1828 the business was operated by his widow, Martha. Although the establishment was called a grocery, liquors were its main commodity (in the jargon of the time, grocery businesses that did not sell hard liquors were called "family groceries"). The store and warehouse stood on Newton's Wharf at the foot of Market Square only a few steps from the Eagle Tavern, and one would guess that Martha Hutchings knew Shadrach Minkins well long before she first hired him.

The inventory of Richard Hutchings' estate shows an apparently prospering business. In 1828 the stock on hand included more than a hundred barrels of rum, whiskey, gin, and other spirits; dozens of boxes of teas, bags of coffee, and kegs of tobacco; together with smaller supplies of pepper, sugar, nutmeg, writing paper, "shot" chocolate, raisins, lard, and other miscellaneous supplies. The total was valued at more than $7,000.[15] Hutchings' personal property included two houses and six slaves: Max (age fifty), Tempy (thirty-three, "disabled"), Elsey (twenty-three, listed as a runaway), Sukey (eighteen), Jack (fourteen), and Charlotte (six).[16] In 1834, to effect the final division among the heirs, Max, Jack, "Suchy and child," and Charlotte were sold for $1,465.[17]

Shadrach Minkins and the other Glenn slaves had little more security or certainty in their arrangements than the Hutchings' slaves had had. In 1840 Shadrach Minkins would be the only one of the Glenn slaves still working for his original hirer. The others were shuttled from employer to employer nearly every year, and it was a roll of the dice whether they found themselves in worse or better circumstances.

Notwithstanding the uncertainty of each year's arrangements, being hired out had important advantages: it usually kept slaves close to friends and family, and it also kept them out of the hands of the traders who supplied slaves for the lucrative Deep South market. In the first half of the nineteenth century, the second great black migration in American history was under way. The earlier migration had brought Africans to the shores of America; the second, equally involuntary and equally massive, shifted large numbers of blacks to the new cotton and sugar cane country westward from South Carolina and Georgia to Arkansas, Missouri, and the Gulf Coast states of Alabama, Mississippi, Louisiana, and Texas.[18] Slave brokers in Richmond, Petersburg, and Norfolk continually sought more slaves to supply to this seemingly inexhaustible market. "I will give the highest Cash price for likely young Negroes, of both Sexes, from the age of 10 to 30 years . . . I also attend to shipping Negroes to the Southern States," read a typical notice in April 1850 in the Norfolk *Southern Argus*.[19] One visitor in the 1830s noted that sales to the Deep South were "practised largely here at Norfolk, without censure or reproach":

> In sight of French's hotel, in which we resided, and so near as to enable us to hear their occasional shoutings and cries, is a slave-depot, in which the slave-dealers of the town, collect and confine such slaves as they can pick up by purchase, till they have a gang sufficiently large to transport . . . Here they are kept, with as little food and clothing as is compatible with bare existence: for, regarding them as articles of traffic, they spend no more upon them than will suffice to keep them alive, and in travelling condition.[20]

Fifty-five-year-old fugitive slave Philip Younger, recounting his own odyssey and those of many thousands of others, recalled being sent from Virginia "at ten, to Tennessee; at twelve, to Alabama."[21] Other fugitive slaves who traced their origins to Norfolk testified to having followed similar routes.[22]

Shadrach Minkins and other young, healthy Virginia slaves had to fear this fate acutely. Every Virginia and Maryland slave knew many who had vanished into the raw plantation country opened after Eli Whitney's famous ginning machine made cotton farming the source of many a Southern fortune. Portsmouth slave George Teamoh could do nothing to prevent his wife and three children, owned by a different Portsmouth white, from being delivered to a Richmond slave jail pending sale, probably to the Deep South market.[23] While Frederick Douglass was growing up on the Eastern Shore of Maryland during the third and fourth decades of the century, fifteen relatives, including a sister and two aunts, were sold "down South," together with dozens of Douglass' acquaintances.[24] Freed Norfolk black Moses Grandy, although he worked as hard as he could to purchase his many children, had to watch helplessly as six of them were sold to the New Orleans market.[25]

Even Norfolk free blacks were vulnerable to slave traders, who seldom asked questions. Solomon Northup, a Washington, D.C., free black, was kidnapped and loaded onto a ship bound for New Orleans. While the ship lay at anchor in the Norfolk harbor, he saw a man being dragged aboard. "His face was swollen, and covered with wounds and bruises, and . . . one side of it was a complete raw sore," Northup remembered. During the voyage to New Orleans Northup learned that this man, a free black mason named Arthur, had been seized at night in the streets of Norfolk, "gagged and bound with ropes, and beaten until he became insensible." Luckily for Arthur, when the ship reached New Orleans two Norfolk men appeared on the dock bearing papers attesting to his freedom. When Arthur recognized them, Northup wrote, he went "almost crazy with delight" and "could hardly be restrained from leaping over the brig's side." Once on the dock, Arthur "grasped them by the hand, and clung to them a long, long time."[26] Northup was not so lucky; he spent twelve years in slavery before being rescued and returned to his family in Washington.

We have no way of knowing what the lives of Shadrach Minkins and the other Glenn slaves were like in the years in which they were hired out. Their treatment may have been kind, indifferent, or cruel. E. P. Goodridge's accounts consist only of dollars and cents. Occasionally, however, there are hints about the patterns of the slaves' lives. Numerous entries show that Goodridge probably collected the slaves' wages directly from the hirers and paid the bills for unusual expenses: "blanket for negro $2.50," "clothes for Isaac $3.75," and "shoes for [Isaac] & Louisa $2.25" are typical entries. Another entry, for "Dr. Hoages bill for Negro $3.50," shows that Goodridge, not the hirer, apparently was responsible for medical expenses during the term of the hire.[27]

A few entries provide more ominous evidence about the power that the executor wielded over Shadrach Minkins and the other slaves as well as about the tensions generated by enslavement. The very first page in Goodridge's records contains the entry "Constable for whipping Negro $1.50." What slave received this punishment, and for what crime, is not explained. Entries two years later hint that the object of the constable's scourge may have been the slave named Richard. In August 1840 Goodridge wrote in his ledger: "Jail fees, boy Richard $1.76." Then in December Goodridge recorded paying $2.50 to merchant J. H. Robertson "to sell boy Richard for bad conduct." In 1842 Goodridge sent Louisa to jail and had her whipped by the constable. "Officer for whipping &c. $2.05" was entered into the account.[28]

Although Richard and Louisa were the only transgressors identified in the records, and Richard the only one sold for misbehavior, good conduct gave Shadrach Minkins and the others no assurance against sale and separation but merely delayed the inevitable fall of the auctioneer's gavel when the five Glenn children reached adulthood and the estate would need to be settled. In 1839 Robert Glenn was working for the railroad, and William Glenn had found employment at a local store, where he also roomed. Each traveled to Washington separately that year, William first in an attempt to join the U.S. Navy, and Robert in July to seek a commission in the Marine Corps. Both returned to Norfolk, apparently having been rejected for being too young. In December the two set off together for Texas, where they hoped to enlist in the infant navy of the self-proclaimed independent republic. This time William, at least, succeeded. By then a third son, George, had begun to work at a countinghouse and, according to the report of the court commissioner, was "probably" able to support himself.[29]

In 1843 a crucial change occurred in the arrangements for the Glenn slaves: the slave dealers Nash & Company took charge of hiring their time on a month-to-month basis, an indication that they were being kept available should an interested buyer come along. By March Susan had been sold at auction for $200.[30] At the end of the year the list of slaves in the Glenn estate accounts had dwindled to five adults: Isaac, Maria, Louisa, and two slaves mentioned for the first time, Beverly and Dick (Charles had died the previous November).[31] For part of the year Maria worked for Constable John Caphart, a man who was feared by all the slaves and who would later play a dramatic part in Shadrach Minkins' life.[32] Court records concerning the Glenn estate end shortly thereafter, so it is likely that the remaining slaves were sold early in 1844.

Shadrach Minkins' name simply vanishes from the accounts of the Glenn estate after 1840, when the records show that he was hired again by R. S. Hutchings & Company for $100. Several notations in the court records make it fairly clear that he was given to the oldest Glenn, Robert, at the beginning of 1841. In December 1840, preliminary to selling Richard for bad conduct, Goodridge had paid twenty dollars to the court commissioner to draw up a plan for dividing the slaves.[33] Another note reveals that Robert Glenn had reached the age of twenty-one and received his portion of slaves. In all likelihood Shadrach Minkins was included in Robert's portion.[34] Robert may have sold Minkins to Martha Hutchings outright or continued to hire him to her. We do know from the court proceedings in Boston that by 1849 Martha Hutchings had purchased him. Probably Minkins worked for her throughout the decade.

At the Hutchings store, where Shadrach Minkins lived at least part of the time, he may have done little more than carry stock and clean. There was always plenty of menial work to do in a grocery. However, slaves who proved to be bright and willing could assume many additional responsibilities in such a setting. One such local slave was "Uncle Dick," who clerked in a Portsmouth store for most of his adult life. After his death in 1860 the *Argus* devoted half a column to him at a time when only a few prominent white citizens rated an obituary. "Fidelity and honesty, mingled with great politeness," the *Argus* explained, had earned Uncle Dick a "position in the community of which any man might feel proud." He was given complete freedom with the money drawer, and "in no instance or under any circumstances, with the amplest opportunities, did his account current exhibit error." His funeral, too, attracted unusual attention. Uncle Dick's owner closed his store for the day, and his entire family, together with a handful of prominent Norfolk white citizens and a great portion of the black community, attended the funeral.[35]

Even if the life of Uncle Dick seemed an attractive model to Shadrach Minkins, it represented a life out of his reach. Minkins' fate, like the fate of all slaves, was tied to his owner's fortunes, and Martha Hutchings' were not the sort to permit a lifelong relationship. Like Harriet Beecher Stowe's fictional Little Harry and like tens of thousands of real slaves, Shadrach Minkins was to become a casualty of the economic misfortune of his owner. Under Martha Hutchings, R. S. Hutchings & Company did not prosper. Whether this failure was her fault, the fault of Norfolk's economic malaise, or some combination is not clear. Court records for the 1840s show Hutchings and a succession of partners struggling against mounting unpaid bills and lawsuits. A judgment against the company for over $15,000 apparently finished the business. Martha Hutchings' creditors agreed to take $7,000 plus interest in settlement for the whole debt, but even that amount was too much for Hutchings and her current partner to pay.[36]

Exactly when R. S. Hutchings & Company defaulted is unknown, but in July 1849 the Norfolk *American Beacon* carried a telltale announcement:

WILL BE SOLD

At Public Auction, before the Court House, at 12 o'clock, on Monday, the 23d inst.; Negro Man Shadrach, and Negro Woman Hester and her children Jim and Imogene, by virtue of a writ of fieri facias against the goods and chattels of Martha Hutchings and Edward DeCormis, at suit of Joseph Cowperthwaite, assignee of the President, Directors & Co. of the Bank of the United States.

WM. B. LAMB, Serg't.[37]

On July 23, 1849, Shadrach Minkins began a new life. His purchaser, John A. Higgins, was a young commission agent who kept an office on

SALES THIS DAY.

PURSUANT to an advertisement affixed to the door of the Court House of the city of Norfolk,

WILL BE SOLD,

At Public Auction, before the Court House, at 12 o'clock, on MONDAY, the 23d inst.,

Negro Man Shadrach and Negro Woman Hester and her children Jim and Imogene, by virtue of a writ of fieri facias against the goods and chattels of Martha Hutchings and Edward DeCormis, at suit of Joseph Cowperthwaite, assignee of the President, Directors & Co. of the Bank of the United States.

jy 18—tds   WM. B. LAMB, Serg't.
(Beacon copy.)

Advertisement of sheriff's sale of Shadrach Minkins, *Norfolk and Portsmouth Herald*, July 23, 1849.

Widewater Street opposite the market. Higgins, his wife, Mary, and their infant child were then living with Mary's father, John DeBree, a career Navy man from New Jersey. By the end of November Higgins had sold Minkins to DeBree for $300.[38] The low price, barely one-third of the market value of a healthy young man, may have represented the payment of a debt, perhaps Higgins' share of expenses in the DeBree household.

Minkins' new owner, John DeBree, a native of New Jersey, had long been a resident of Norfolk. He had joined the Navy in 1817 and shortly thereafter been assigned to the Gosport Navy Yard at Portsmouth, just across the Elizabeth River from the Norfolk docks. Early in his career DeBree spent some fifteen years at sea.[39] An 1831 newspaper report lists him as the purser aboard the U.S.S. *Hudson* at Rio de Janeiro.[40] Four years later DeBree was serving in the West Indies, on perhaps his last sea tour, aboard the U.S.S. *Constellation,* the 1798 frigate renowned for its battles with Barbary pirates and French warships.[41] By 1849 John DeBree's sailing days were long behind him. For at least a decade he had been a purser at the Gosport Navy Yard. (When the Civil War came, this adoptive Southerner would join the Confederate Navy as a chief paymaster. De-Bree's signature can be found on a copy of a $25,000 check for ironplate for the celebrated Confederate gunboat, the *Merrimac.*)[42]

Both professional status and wealth placed Shadrach Minkins' new master among the city's elite. In 1850 John DeBree owned properties in Norfolk worth nearly $12,000.[43] His house at 117 East Main was in one of the fashionable neighborhoods.[44] Colonel Giles Buckner Cooke, coroner, alderman, and ex-mayor, lived just two houses away. On the other side lived merchants, a livery stable owner, and another purser from the Navy Yard. Across the street farther down the block were more merchants, lawyers, ex-mayors, judges, doctors, shipbuilders, the city's "prince of druggists" T. J. Cornick, and the president of the American Insurance company.[45]

Shadrach Minkins now found himself a house servant in a considerable household. The immediate family consisted of DeBree, his wife, Mary, and their three sons: Alexander, twenty-five, then a midshipman in the navy; John, twenty-one, a college student; and William, eighteen, a surveyor. Also living in the house were the DeBrees' married daughter, Mary, her husband, John Higgins, and their infant son, Eugene. In addition to these eight whites there were six black domestic servants: a free seventeen-year-old named Rosa Stevens and five female slaves ranging in age from seven to forty-nine.[46]

We know nothing about the household routines and idiosyncrasies to which Minkins had to accustom himself. A few personal letters of John DeBree's, written during the Civil War, provide only the slightest insights into his character and personality. In a touching note to an old shipmate, enclosing a small contribution, DeBree wrote: "Am sorry to hear of your troubles. We are all suffering in a great Cause. I cannot hear from my daughter & her children & have to trust in a merciful God—that will be a father to the children and a husband to the widow." Another letter to the same correspondent ended warmly: "I remain very truly your old friend and shipmate, although I once did go through the form of cutting your throat. We were foolish youngsters in those days—do you remember our bunking it together on Ship Island!!!!"[47]

Shadrach Minkins had to adjust not only to the DeBree and Higgins families and to the other black servants but also to the requirements of domestic service and to his new status. On country estates house servants ordinarily constituted a superior social class among the slaves, although their advantages were more than offset by the disadvantages of separation from friends and family as well as constant supervision by whites. In the cities, with their sizable population of free blacks and their numerous independent hired slaves, domestic service would have conferred at best an even more ambiguous status. Whether he had the same liberties as a house servant that he had had working at the Hutchings store is not known.

The location of the DeBree household near Market Square gave Minkins ready access to Norfolk's black community. Though tightly held within invisible boundaries determined by whites, this community provided a social network of surprising range and richness. In Norfolk as nearly everywhere else in the North and South, black churches were both the religious and social centers of the community. By 1850 four black churches, three of them Baptist and one Methodist, were in operation. Although since Turner's revolt black churches had been required by law to be headed by a white minister, blacks ran their own internal affairs.[48]

Churches were not the only social organizations that drew Shadrach Minkins and other Norfolk and Portsmouth blacks together. Free blacks banded together in service organizations that included a black fire company in Portsmouth and an association for relieving destitute orphans and widows.[49] An 1852 Norfolk *Beacon* editorial complained of a black Masonic lodge and "other secret societies . . . here among the negroes" that met "regularly." "If they are benevolent, as they pretend to be," one white suggested, "there are a number of benevolent white persons in the city who would willingly superintend their affairs for them."[50]

Funerals, weddings, and revivals offered Norfolk blacks an outlet for joys and sorrows as well as extended periods of fellowship and freedom from white scrutiny.[51] Funerals could draw together nearly the entire black community. One antebellum funeral in Portsmouth was attended by nearly 2,000 blacks, at least 500 of them from Norfolk; and a Norfolk black funeral was said to have attracted 1,500 people.[52] In the early 1850s a Baptist revival drew an estimated 1,200 blacks, mostly slaves. "A more lively and exciting scene I have seldom witnessed," a white Norfolk visitor wrote of the event:

About an hour before they broke up they suspended prayer and the singing of hymns and commenced on what they term "spiritual songs." These are merely the repetition of some thrilling religious sentiment, in a lively air, rising, and keeping time with the motion of the body, not unlike the dance without a change of position. Thus, for more than half an hour, the whole audience continued standing on the seats of the pews, filling the aisles, pressing around the altar, singing in a quick movement with the shrill African voice, their song of victory. The convert was borne along in his experience, from submission of heart at the cross, to his final crown of glory. Occasionally one of the "mourners" would be *brought out,* on the announcement of which, new bursts of song would fill the house.

Although the visitor found the service "wild," he concluded that it was "more true to nature, more in sympathy with man's moral wants," and more in harmony with the "simplicity . . . of the Christian's hope than the more exact and impressive service of the cathedral."[53]

Shadrach Minkins could also meet free blacks and other slaves in innumerable informal settings—in the streets, at work, and in boardinghouses, cookshops, and taverns that catered to a black clientele. Taverns where both slave and free blacks gathered were "very common," according to one contemporary source, although these establishments were often invisible except when brought to the notice of authorities. Illicit grog shops were the source of considerable white anxiety. "Crowds of negroes congregate and spend most of their time [there] and good servants are frequently made dishonest and worthless," a *Beacon* editorial complained.[54]

Norfolk's black elite even held an occasional large party or ball such as was common in the more sophisticated black society of New Orleans, Richmond, and Savannah. One, in the fall of 1850, was an elaborate affair, with managers, tickets "on sweet scented paper," "a sumptuous board . . . groaning with the most luxurious viands," and "extravagant and costly costumes obtained to decorate and show off to best advantage the elite beaux and belles." Slaves could attend if they had permission from their masters (a requirement that was not enforced, according to angry whites who attacked the hotel at midnight and broke up the party).[55]

As the ball and its abrupt end suggest, Norfolk's blacks were constantly testing the boundaries that defined the relations between races in Norfolk. White complaints about black clothing styles, complaints that symbolized deeper anxieties about eroding social status, were common. "On Sundays and week days, chalked mulattoes and jet black 'darkies' splurge about in fine silks, satins, broadcloths and carriages," read a typical criticism in the *Argus*. "We can see no . . . objection to negroes dressing well—fine if you please," the editorial stated in good democratic fashion, but then emphatically urged that blacks "should be made to know their position."[56]

Norfolk whites appeared particularly upset that more and more blacks were ignoring the old unwritten rules of deference and subservience. In the country, refusal to adopt the scraping, grinning, self-effacing manners that signaled submission could provoke a fearful retaliation. But in the promiscuous town environment, where slaves and free blacks mixed together in large numbers, and where individual whites were faced with the task of policing hundreds of often anonymous blacks over whom they had marginal control, enforcement of social codes was problematic. A Norfolk white who signed himself "Discipline" asked: "Is there any one of our citizens, male or female, that is not, almost daily, forced to give way to bands of negro men or women, who walk the streets, three or four abreast . . . ? In the market house, in the streets, and every where else, they jostle ladies and gentlemen and push by them with the utmost impunity and violence."[57]

Signs of interracial tensions were surfacing continually in Norfolk's various courts. "Three negroes were hauled up yesterday morning charged with impudence to white persons. Two of them were ordered fifteen stripes each and the third only discharged because he was underage," read one fairly typical report. "Mrs. Van Hart complained of the impudence of a negro girl, Sarah, in the employ of Mr. Dunenburg—ordered ten stripes," ran another.[58] If the newspapers are to be believed, social disorder was threatened. During one week in 1851, "there was an unusual number of arrests of negroes for prowling through the streets—a nest of negro gamblers was discovered—a slave was arrested for cutting a free negro in a fight—assaults were committed—runaways detected." On top of this, a "serious riot" took place, during which "there were sundry fights and property [was] destroyed."[59]

Norfolk authorities and citizens struggled ineffectually with the problem of black assertiveness created by the openness and anonymity of the urban environment. There were proposals to forbid blacks from walking two abreast on the sidewalks, from wearing bonnets or silks, from carrying canes and umbrellas, and from smoking in the street. Most Southern cities had such laws on their books. In 1850 Petersburg authorities meted out a punishment of thirty-nine stripes to discourage one black from cigar smoking.[60] But in Norfolk and elsewhere generally such laws were seldom enforced, in part because commercial interests were involved. Throughout the South, attempts to close grog shops that served blacks and to forbid sales of any kind to slaves who did not have permission from their owners to make purchases typically failed because business profits would have been reduced.[61]

Shadrach Minkins grew to adulthood amid the complex and evolving black/white relations of Norfolk. By the time he came into John DeBree's possession, he would have tested the boundaries of his world many times, as young males often did. He would have learned what a life of slavery meant. And he would have learned also, and been weighing, the limited options available to him.

A remote possibility was emigration to Liberia. If John DeBree had been liberal-minded, Minkins might have earned or been given his freedom specifically for the purpose of emigrating in one of the ships sponsored by the Virginia Colonization Society. Emigrating free blacks received free passage to Liberia and support for six months after arrival. Despite the attractiveness of this support, remote Liberia held only a limited attraction for Virginia blacks. This was especially true after 1832, when in the aftermath of the Turner rebellion the motivation of the emigration society was increasingly reduced to a simple desire of whites to be rid of a troublesome "vampire population."[62] Nevertheless, although their numbers amounted to only a tiny fraction of the city's black population, Norfolk supplied a fair share of emigrants to Liberia. An 1850 letter from white minister William H. Starr sought donations to support twenty-five or more Norfolk blacks, "all respectable persons of their class, and nearly all . . . approved and pious members of the Church of God," who had expressed interest in emigrating. In 1851 Starr was again appealing for donations in anticipation of the "Liberia Packet" from Baltimore, and in 1852 eleven persons from Norfolk or Portsmouth were ready to sail.[63] Norfolk supplied a number of Liberian leaders. Black emigrant John Jenkins Roberts served as the first president of Liberia after independence in 1846, and John H. Cheesman, another Norfolk emigrant, became a judge.[64]

Shadrach Minkins may also have thought of purchasing his freedom and either trying to remain in Norfolk or emigrating to the North. Yet here again the odds lay heavily against him. For all but the best-paid hired slaves with the most generous masters, self-purchase meant saving for years or even decades for a distant and uncertain reward. If an owner died, became insolvent, or was simply unscrupulous, promises—together with hard-won savings—often evaporated. Moses Grandy, who claimed to have paid his purchase price three times before finally receiving his freedom, knew this all too well.[65] But even if Minkins could have purchased his freedom, he would have faced reenslavement if he remained in the state longer than one year—and estrangement from family and friends if he obeyed the law and removed to another state. Emancipated slaves could petition the legislature to remain in Virginia, but the chances of such a petition's being approved were slim.

Moreover, Norfolk's peculiar characteristics made it especially difficult for Shadrach Minkins and other slaves to earn their freedom. A number of trades in which blacks could ordinarily prosper—blacksmithing, for example—were dominated by whites. White barbers offered stiff competition in another area typically dominated by blacks (only one free black barber in Norfolk owned property in 1860, in contrast with many propertyholding black barbers in Petersburg and Richmond). White artisans, particularly at the Navy Yard, the area's largest employer, increasingly pressured employers to exclude free black and slave labor. Although they never succeeded in persuading major employers or the government to ban black labor, undoubtedly their hostility kept some white employers from hiring blacks and intimidated many black laborers.[66] The lack of a substantial industrial base also narrowed the avenues for advancement as skilled laborers, and hence for the accumulation of wealth. The preponderance of low-paying domestic jobs (which had created an imbalance of female free black heads of household in the city) further limited the money-earning capacity of Norfolk's black population. Free blacks and self-hired slaves alike found themselves living in poverty and squalor, jammed into ramshackle housing in a labyrinth of Norfolk back alleys. All these conditions presented Shadrach Minkins and other slaves contemplating self-purchase with powerful barriers and deterrents.[67]

By the time Minkins had taken up residence in the DeBree household in the late 1840s, his name had changed from Sherwood to Shadrach.[68] Perhaps the change was his own choice. Perhaps Martha Hutchings insisted on it. Such a change was not uncommon; owners often liked to choose new names for slaves they had purchased. But whoever made the choice, the change itself—from Sherwood, with its English sound, to Shadrach, with its rich biblical associations—has interesting potential significance. Perhaps Martha Hutchings was religious and liked "Shadrach" for its message of steadfastness and righteousness. Perhaps Minkins preferred it for the same reasons, for he was later known to be a Christian and a churchgoer, and he may have been very attracted to the image of the three fabled men from the third chapter of the book of Daniel, Shadrach, Meshach, and Abednego, who angered King Nebuchadnezzar of Babylon by refusing to renounce their God and to worship a golden image. Thrown into Nebuchadnezzar's fiery furnace, they remained miraculously untouched by the flames.

The name Shadrach thus symbolized a testing and affirmation of spirit. Perhaps Minkins relished this symbolism and took Shadrach for his name as his own quiet act of independence and rebellion. Whatever the reason for the new name, it was to prove doubly prophetic. Twice in his life, Shadrach Minkins would emerge triumphant from the furnace of slavery.

3 "The Silver Trump of Freedom"

In the spring of 1849 a ship sailed into the broad natural harbor at the southwestern corner of Chesapeake Bay and turned toward Norfolk. On board was Daniel Webster, the famous senator from Massachusetts. "Here is the celebrated riding-place, or anchorage-ground, Hampton Roads . . . the great naval station of the South," he wrote a friend.[1] From Hampton Roads Webster looked out over a vast sweep of water and a low coastal plain. To the west stood the elegant Naval Hospital and Fort Monroe. To the south lay the mouth of the Elizabeth River with the steeples of Norfolk churches on the left bank, those of Portsmouth on the right. As he drew closer, the masts of ships at the Norfolk docks and the Gosport Navy Yard pierced the skyline.

Daniel Webster's appearance in Norfolk at this time is one of the innumerable ironies of American history. The quintessential New Englander from the quintessential New England state, Webster represented much that Norfolk and the South both envied and hated. Nearly twenty years before, as a freshman senator from Massachusetts, he had begun his battle with the Southern secessionists in his famous reply to Senator Robert Y. Hayne of South Carolina. The Webster-Hayne debate was one of the most remarkable that ever filled the Senate chambers in Washington. The voice of New England high-minded conscience as well as of an almost religious devotion to the idea of Union, Webster had issued the famous challenge to the South, destined to be repeated by generations of schoolchildren: "Liberty *and* Union, now and forever, one and inseparable!"[2]

When Webster reflected on Norfolk's prospects, he inevitably measured everything by the standard of his New England. He believed that only free labor could bring New England–style prosperity to the region. He imagined a time "a century hence, when negro labor shall have been done away with, and white men become willing to work," when the swamps had been cleared, the marshes drained, and a "better general husbandry" prevailed. When all these things had come to pass, he added with understatement, "this will be a most agreeable region."[3]

But Webster was not in Norfolk to lord it over the South. While dining with relish on daily catches of bluefish, sea trout, "hog-fish," "sheepshead," and other marine delicacies he loved, he was busy building bridges, thinking ahead to the 1852 contest for the presidency, a prize he had long considered his due. At sixty-eight years of age and in indifferent health, he was running out of time. Two years before, hoping for the 1848

Daniel Webster, ca. 1850.

presidential nomination, Webster had toured the South with very limited success. Now he was again courting Southern support at a time when extremism seemed to be taking the field in Virginia and throughout the South. Beleaguered though they were, Norfolk moderates respected Webster as a Union man, and to many Norfolk businessmen and men of means the Union seemed indispensable.[4]

It is difficult to imagine what Webster was thinking as he passed through the streets of Norfolk, looking out at the black and white faces. He did not approve of slavery, and even felt repelled by it. He himself had purchased the freedom of one slave, his longtime Washington cook, and had helped in purchasing the freedom of at least one other.[5] But when he thought about the time when "negro labor shall have been done away with," the key to Webster's ideas about African-Americans may be that he saw slavery—and blacks—in economic rather than human terms. A plan was emerging in his mind, a destiny for a free nation, but where in it was the black, slave or free, to fit? Webster did not say.

Within a year Webster would take a momentous step, one fraught with contradictions, at once high-minded and transparently self-interested. And that step would entangle the life and hopes and ambitions of the great statesman with the dreams and destiny of an obscure Norfolk slave, a man named Shadrach Minkins.

A dozen years before Webster's appearance in Norfolk, a Maryland slave named Frederick Bailey—later Douglass—heard in his mind a "silver trump of freedom." Soon after Webster's visit to Norfolk, the sound of that silver trump was growing louder and louder in the mind of Shadrach Minkins. He too was soon to make a momentous decision. Legally he would still remain a slave, but once he had decided to risk all for freedom, he would no longer be a slave in his soul. Why did he decide to flee, and why did he decide at this time? Court records, newspapers, public and private documents give no clues.

A profile of the typical fugitive slave provides some broad hints that help us imagine Shadrach Minkins' circumstances and his decision. The typical fugitive (as many as 80 percent, according to some estimates) was a young adult male between the ages of sixteen and thirty-five and, by all accounts, of above average intelligence.[6] A common link among fugitives was a history of being sold and/or hired out. Slaves who had a single lifelong master, particularly those who were able to remain close to their families all their lives, were usually much more rooted. Fugitive slaves, on the other hand, typically had limited ties to their current masters and local settings. A number had been sold away from their families. Others had experienced a considerable degree of independence. Many fugitives had hired their own time, and some had even collected their own wages and arranged for their own food and housing. These circumstances loosened the bonds between owner and slave while increasing the slave's self-confidence. Minkins fits all these conditions to some degree: he was a young man, apparently unmarried; he had been sold three times; he was, by all accounts, quite intelligent; and he had a history of being hired out.

A variety of experiences played roles in slaves' determinations to flee, any of which may have affected Shadrach Minkins. Impending sale—rumored or actual—was perhaps the most powerful stimulus. Threatened punishment for some crime or misdemeanor could also impel a slave into hiding or northward, as could the loss of a friend, family member, or prospective mate through sale or death. Slaves whose family members or friends had already fled from slavery had a vital magnetic link to the North.

Strained relations between Shadrach Minkins and John DeBree and his family may have contributed to his decision, but it is just as likely that Minkins' relations with the household were entirely amicable and his work light and easily borne. Such was the case of other Norfolk and Portsmouth fugitives. George Teamoh of Portsmouth not only praised his mistress as the most "generous, virtuous and fair-minded Christian lady" but also credited her with assisting his escape to freedom.[7] Teamoh's case may have been a rare extreme, but many fugitives in common with him bore the yoke of slavery lightly. Nearly all the Norfolk fugitives interviewed in the 1850s by William Still, the black chairman of the Philadelphia Vigilance Committee, reported having been comparatively well off. Moses Armstead, a twenty-eight-year-old Norfolk fugitive, "did not make one complaint of bad treatment." Thomas Bayne had enjoyed a privileged position as a Norfolk dentist's assistant and sometime stand-in, coming and going freely. Abram Wooders, though asserting that his master had been "very severe" to his numerous slaves, reported that "he was always very kind to me." Mary Cooper "did not find fault" with her master, a Norfolk alderman.[8]

William Still and others who interviewed fugitive slaves in the North found many motivated to escape solely by a desire for a free life. "Nothing but the prevailing love of liberty . . . moved him to seek his freedom," Still wrote of Armstead.[9]

Norfolk slaves who hired their own time and contracted for their own work and living arrangements—who in many respects lived essentially as if they were free—seem to have been especially susceptible to the lure of freedom. These able, resourceful, self-supporting slaves already had the heavy economic responsibilities of a life of freedom but few, if any, of the privileges. The "freedom" they had was largely confined to making their own contracts and living arrangements—that is, to aspects that benefited their white masters. Many semi-independent slave laborers rankled under the limitations that hemmed them in. An unnamed fugitive slave from Norfolk put the matter succinctly: "It seemed hard, when I had earned my money, to have to carry it to another man, when my wife needed it herself."[10]

From the moment Shadrach Minkins decided to flee from bondage, he joined himself to the great secret northward migration. It flowed out of the South in a hundred tributaries. Thousands had gone before, thousands more were to follow. This migration is popularly known as the "Underground Railroad," but as historian Larry Gara has convincingly argued in *The Liberty Line*, the migration was not as well organized or as universal as the word "railroad" suggests. Evidence of a vast network of "Conductors," "Stations," "Employees," and "Lines"—the terms themselves often late nineteenth-century inventions or hyperbole—is sketchy. Few records were kept—the principal exceptions being black abolitionist William Still's records for the Philadelphia Vigilance Committee and Francis Jackson's financial account book for the parallel Boston organization. What is more, much of the Underground Railroad story grew up decades after the fact and was based on many second- and thirdhand accounts that cannot be verified. By the end of the nineteenth century, when Wilbur Siebert assembled the materials for his book *The Underground Railroad* (1898), fact and legend were inextricably intertwined.[11]

Many fugitive slaves apparently had no help whatever during their dangerous journey. As Larry Gara has pointed out, many fugitives who were interviewed in the North or who wrote autobiographies testified that they devised and carried out their escape entirely on their own. If they found help along the way, it was often in the form of a spontaneous gesture by local blacks.[12] Some carried forged passes—for which there seems to have been a thriving cottage industry in some places in the South.[13] Very light-skinned fugitives sometimes successfully passed as whites.

Some fugitives devised elaborate plans. Henry "Box" Brown, later an antislavery lecturer, had himself crated up in Richmond, where he worked in a tobacco factory, and shipped to Philadelphia. Fugitives hid themselves aboard ships and trains. Ed Davis, called "the salt-water fugitive," tried both. On his first attempt he hid in one of the most exposed foreparts of a sailing ship from Savannah, Georgia. For three days he was nearly drowned and frozen by the rough seas before being discovered and returned. On his second attempt he hid himself *under* a train in Macon, Georgia, strapping himself beneath a railway car in an improvised hammock. Again he was discovered and returned.[14]

A portion of the fugitive slave traffic out of the South, however, clearly was well organized, providing a degree of safety and even comfort. Some fugitives were conducted along routes as carefully planned and supervised as escorted tours. At least a few actually used the concealed trapdoors, hidden rooms, and secret passageways that populate the "Underground Railroad" legends. But direct evidence is rare, and the reputation of many a root cellar or concealed closet as a hiding place for fugitive slaves seems a product of purest imagination. Attics and cellars and trapdoors, when used at all, would have been used mainly in the South and in the hinterland between North and South. Farther North, their use would probably have reflected the self-dramatizing romantic urges of their friends more than actual necessity. In many areas in the North, despite some widespread proslavery feeling, fugitives could travel openly, without special assistance or protection unless they were hotly pursued. Often the "Underground Railroad" consisted of help with fares on the overground railroad, a few dollars in pocket money, and letters of introduction.[15] Ordinarily the purpose of these letters was to make it possible for fugitives to find beds and meals. Public accommodations were not plentiful, and those that welcomed blacks were rare.

By 1850 the movement of fugitive slaves into the free states had long since established itself in several general patterns. Slaves from the regions along the Mississippi, Ohio, and Missouri Rivers headed North into Ohio, Illinois, Michigan, and on into western Ontario. In the East, slaves crossed from Maryland and Delaware into Pennsylvania at nearly any point. The Susquehanna River and the roads leading to the small communities of Lancaster, York, and other farming towns were among the most heavily traveled routes. Relatively large communities of freeborn and fugitive blacks had grown up at Wrightsville and Columbia, thirty miles up the Susquehanna from the Maryland border and only fifty miles from Baltimore. Many fugitives from western Maryland, western Virginia (now West Virginia), and eastern Kentucky headed for the Pittsburgh area.[16] Fugitives from the Tidewater regions of Virginia, Maryland, and the Carolinas commonly escaped by water.

Estimates of the numbers of fugitives successfully fleeing from interior and Tidewater Virginia vary. Senator James Mason estimated the annual loss of slave property for all of Virginia at $100,000.[17] At an average value of $500 (a low estimate), this figure would represent only 200 slaves a year. Census figures put the loss of slave property at only one every four days.[18] Reports of Norfolk fugitive slaves suggest somewhat higher overall losses for the state, however. In 1854, apparently a particularly bad year for Norfolk-area slaveholders, the *American Beacon* complained that fugitives were escaping "almost daily." However, another *Beacon* story estimated the value of fugitives to be "over $30,000" in the preceding twelve months, which translates into only sixty slaves, roughly one a week, at an average value of $500.[19] Two months later an *Argus* editorial set the annual losses at $75,000 without providing any further evidence.[20] In 1856, when the Virginia legislature was considering new ship-inspection legislation, Norfolk was said to be losing $50,000 worth of slaves each year.[21]

Some Norfolk fugitives undoubtedly went no farther than Baltimore or Washington, where they could lose themselves among black populations of ten thousand or more. Some fled to nearby towns and cities to be close to the family and friends from whom they had been separated. Numerous advertisements for fugitives mention that they were probably "lurking" about such-and-such a place where a husband or wife or friends were known to live. Other fugitives disappeared into the Great Dismal Swamp, where they might join "maroon" camps and live undetected for years or even (according to one observer) for generations.[22] At least some remained in Norfolk for weeks, months, or even years. Six Norfolk fugitives told

William Still they had hidden for from two months to a year before making arrangements to escape to the North.[23] In 1855 three slaves assumed to have fled north months earlier were discovered and arrested in Norfolk.[24] Elizabeth Cooley, who fled to Boston, claimed to have hidden for more than two years in Norfolk before getting aboard a northbound ship.[25]

The fugitive traffic by water from Norfolk to Philadelphia appears to have been one of the best organized and most regular of the routes north, at least partly because of geography. The enormous size of Chesapeake Bay—the largest estuary in the world—and the number of its tributaries and corresponding swamps and marshes made travel by land through Tidewater Maryland and Virginia slow and circuitous. The water routes, by contrast, were direct and swift. Norfolk was ideally situated. Poised on the Elizabeth River just below the great natural harbor of Hampton Roads and only eight miles from the mouth of Chesapeake Bay, the South's northernmost major coastal port virtually invited escape by sea. Philadel-phia, up the Delaware Bay, was only a little more than 270 miles away—about a two-day trip with a good breeze. New York, on a direct line up the coast, was only 300 miles; New Bedford, Massachusetts, only about 500; and Boston, 100 miles further.

Records kept by vigilance committees in Boston and Philadelphia record the arrival of many a Norfolk or Portsmouth fugitive. In the slim records of the first Boston Vigilance Committee (1846–47), three of the twelve fugitives interviewed were connected with the Norfolk area either as a port of departure, as a residence, or both. Joshua Davis, an oysterman from Portsmouth, fled in a schooner from Norfolk to New York City, where abolitionists sent him on to Boston.[26] Another fugitive who reached Boston about the same time was Levin Walker (also known as Owen Bright), a twenty-four-year-old from Currituck County, North Carolina. Walker's case shows how family ties could be a catalyst for an escape. His father had been set free and had purchased his mother many years before. By 1847 his mother had been living in New York City for more than fifteen years. When Walker fled in a packet from Norfolk, he naturally headed straight for New York.[27]

Norfolk and Portsmouth fugitives figure prominently in William Still's extensive records of the Philadelphia Vigilance Committee in the 1850s. Although the majority of the roughly 400 fugitives mentioned by the Philadelphia Committee came from Maryland, Delaware, the District of

Columbia, and northern Virginia, more than 100 originated from the Norfolk area. The famed Wilmington Quaker Thomas Garrett, who reportedly helped hundreds of Maryland and Virginia slaves get to Philadelphia by routes that included at least one substantial leg by water, appears frequently in Still's accounts of Philadelphia activities.[28] In all probability other Northern port cities, including New Bedford, Providence, and New York, were receiving fugitives directly from the Norfolk area in the same period.[29]

If geography was one key to Norfolk's maritime fugitive traffic, another was the harbor's diverse black labor force. Like all port cities, Norfolk needed a mobile work force, and blacks supplied most of the muscle, and much of the skill, necessary for the Norfolk harbor to operate. Almost all the stevedores and dock workers were black, and so too were nearly all the truckmen and carters who swarmed upon the wharves, carrying cargoes or bringing stores for the ships' larders. Black carpenters, caulkers, and riggers were common. Boats of all kinds operated and manned by slaves and free blacks plied the waters of the harbor.[30] Slave and free black men and women worked the wharves as vendors and hucksters, fishmongers and processors, shuckers and laundresses. Black cooks, stewards, pilots, and seamen worked on ships from up and down the East Coast and beyond. The throng of black workers in the harbor created what David Cecelski has called a complex "maritime fraternity" with a vast and indispensable "collective knowledge."[31] Continued free access to the harbor and docks by this assorted collection of black laborers and watermen assured Shadrach Minkins and other slaves planning escapes of access to inside information that would enable them to evade the vigilance of Norfolk Port authorities and of unfriendly captains and crewmen.[32]

Around the time Minkins was planning his escape, three black leaders of Norfolk's "maritime fraternity" are known to have been orchestrating fugitive escapes through the harbor. Undoubtedly there were others. A Norfolk slave named Henry Lewey, Philadelphia abolitionists claimed, was "one of the most dexterous managers in the Underground Railroad agency in Norfolk."[33] Operating under the romantic code name "Bluebeard" in letters that went back and forth on the packets between Philadelphia and Norfolk, Lewey went undetected for years. He even received letters from absconded fugitives directing him where to forward their clothes and other effects.

Another Norfolk black involved in the illicit traffic was Elizabeth Baines, a slave. Reportedly she used her practically unlimited access to vessels in the harbor to help get fugitives aboard ships bound for Boston and New York. Elizabeth Cooley, a Norfolk fugitive whom Baines helped to escape, remembered in old age how she hid in Norfolk for two years before she met Baines and secured passage northward. According to Cooley, Baines knew sailing times and other critical details from working for the captains of ships in port. She hid fugitives at her home—once supposedly between the rows of corn in her garden while her house was searched—until it was safe to deliver them by boat to the waiting ships. Once the fugitives were successfully on board, Cooley claimed to remember, Baines would go about singing, "It's all right, hallelujah, glory to God!"[34]

The third Norfolk slave known to have helped numbers of fugitives was Sam Nixon, later known as Dr. Thomas Bayne. The slave and assistant of local white dentist C. F. Martin, Nixon learned the trade that in antebellum America often amounted to little more than wielding a pair of pliers skillfully. Nixon's reputation for intelligence and trustworthiness eventually led to his substituting for the doctor on many occasions. According to William Still, the slave dentist could travel about the city at all hours without being called upon to explain himself or show a pass.[35]

It is difficult to confirm most stories of black assistance. Elizabeth Baines's story, though told by a firsthand witness, was not recorded until the end of the nineteenth century and almost certainly suffers from error and embellishment. Lewey's and Nixon's stories have more credibility because they were recorded in the 1850s by William Still, who apparently knew of their activities firsthand, and Lewey is mentioned in a number of letters, including one from a fugitive in Canada.[36] Except for the little that is known about these three persons, though, there is no record of other free or enslaved Norfolk or Portsmouth blacks helping fugitives on a regular basis. The network of regular helpers was certainly larger, but perhaps not much larger, for if it had been very large there would have been more discoveries. In addition to regular helpers, other Norfolk blacks as well as whites helped a slave or two. In one instance Mary Weaver, an Irish girl, helped her sweetheart, slave John Hall, escape to Canada and later followed him there.[37]

Shadrach Minkins undoubtedly knew Elizabeth Baines, Henry Lewey, and Sam Nixon. In the streets, on the wharves, in private houses, or in any of the dozens of legal and illegal cookshops, taverns, and boardinghouses, he could have picked up information about when ships were sailing, who could be trusted, and what the safest course was. He would have known many of the black men and women in the harbor labor force. Moreover, he would have encountered many free black sailors from the North who roamed the city carrying only a pass from their captains. He may even have been recruited for flight, as slave Sarah Saunders was. Asked one day if she would like to visit her sister in Philadelphia, Saunders answered in the affirmative, and her passage was soon arranged.[38]

Fugitives and their friends in Norfolk also found willing help from some captains and crewmen of northbound ships. Four captains are known to have carried off fugitives singly or in groups of up to a dozen or even more: Captain Fountain of the *City of Richmond*, Captain William D. Bayliss of the *Kesiah*, Captain William Lambdin, and Captain Robert Lee.[39] Captain Fountain's ships, the latest of which could accommodate forty cabin and fifty steerage passengers along with a "large amount" of freight, provided a packet service to New York in the early 1850s. White Norfolk promoters placed great hopes for profits in the New York trade. Apparently their slaves looked on the direct New York connection with even greater enthusiasm.[40] According to Still's reports, Fountain almost always carried away two or more slaves. On one voyage the *City of Richmond* took twenty-one. During the voyage, to avoid detection by the authorities, one woman of enormous girth had to strip nearly naked to squeeze through a narrow opening into the hold. An engraving in Still's book shows the fugitives disembarking at League Island near Philadelphia.[41]

With the exception of Captain Fountain, the captains who carried fugitives are known to us because they were caught. Although some of these captains, and others as yet unknown, undoubtedly had altruistic motives and took little if anything in payment, others accepted the dangers because they relished the profits. Norfolk fugitives might expect to pay black or white assistants up to $25 per person for arranging passage, providing forged passes, or other services, in addition to the handsome sums required by some captains.[42] Captain Bayliss, whose fees probably represent an upper range, reportedly received $100 from John Hall for passage to Philadelphia and $240 from William Nelson for a party of four consisting of himself, his wife, his son, and a friend.[43] Although other fugitives reported paying as little as $10, Bayliss, who once took fifteen fugitives to safety, and Fountain, who at times carried as many as twenty-one or more, could have made handsome sums.[44] For a hefty fee, Captain Fountain even offered to steal family members of escaped fugitive slaves. He promised Daniel Robertson, whom he had transported from Petersburg, that he would deliver Robertson's wife to him in New York for $100. After six months Robertson was finally able to pay Fountain's price, but by then his wife had apparently been put beyond Fountain's reach.[45]

For Norfolk slaveowners, the number of escapes was alarming. A single slave could be worth $1,000 or more, an enormous investment at a time when a good wage was $2 a day and a home could be purchased for under $1,000. "A man may be wealthy today, but tomorrow his property may have vanished into empty space," intoned an *Argus* editorial.[46] Everyone in Norfolk knew that the harbor waters were the route by which fugitives escaped. By the 1850s owners tacitly acknowledged this circumstance by rarely placing runaway advertisements, which were useful primarily if the fugitives had escaped overland. Accounts of the few Norfolk fugitives captured at sea almost invariably told of schooners running aground or being forced back to port by storm, of regular shipboard searches, or of unfriendly captains discovering the fugitives en route.[47]

Alarmed by the number of escapes, Norfolk newspapers repeatedly carried calls for tougher legislation restricting the movement of local blacks. One citizen's wish list of prohibitions included church meetings after dark, debates, Sunday schools, and parades at funerals. Knowing that access to the harbor was even more critical, the citizen also called for oyster boats to be barred from sailing after dark, for black-operated boats to be required to anchor off Town Point every night, and for free black sailors from the North to be jailed until it was time for their ships to sail, as had long been the practice in Charleston, South Carolina. To guarantee the effectiveness of these measures, the author suggested organizing a secret police and an armed watch to be stationed at Town Point "to stop all vessels and boats from leaving at night." Another citizen proposed fumigating the holds of all departing ships at anchor with a noxious gas.[48]

Fortunately for Shadrach Minkins and other Norfolk slaves who yearned for freedom, the more extreme proposals were never put into effect. Whether leniency of local officials and leading citizens toward slaves, the inherently cumbersome requirements of the proposals, the complexity of port movements, or corruption among port officials was the principal reason is impossible to say. But Norfolk merchants would hardly have supported measures that further weakened trade prospects by delaying shipping and increasing costs.

Local and state efforts to plug escape routes were not the only Southern undertakings launched to thwart runaways. By 1849, when Shadrach Minkins was purchased by John DeBree, a new effort at the national level was under way to tighten the bands of slavery by making fugitives more vulnerable to capture in the North. This new development was to have a profound effect upon Shadrach Minkins and thousands of other men, women, and children who risked everything for freedom.

-For decades, strong and swift westward settlement had been straining the links between North and South. With the formation of new states, the seizure of Texas from Mexico in the 1840s, and the rush of settlers to California after gold was discovered at Sutter's Mill in 1849, the nation's political equilibrium was threatened as never before.[49] Southern ultras, wanting to guarantee their institutions forever, vociferously agitated for disunion. Many Northern abolitionists, a small but vocal minority, also favored disunion if slavery could not be abolished outright. As the arguments grew hotter, political parties, religious denominations, and the entire nation grew increasingly polarized.[50]

Into the bitter breach stepped two of the elder statesmen of American politics, Henry Clay of Kentucky and Daniel Webster of Massachusetts. Together with John C. Calhoun, the ardent South Carolina secessionist, they had been the towering figures of American politics for decades. In late January 1850 Clay put forth a comprehensive plan to settle all differences. Its eight provisions dealt with a variety of issues, the most important one being the vexing question of admitting new western states as free or slave.

For Shadrach Minkins and other American blacks, the crucial provision of Clay's compromise measures was the seventh, which called for the passage of a more effective fugitive slave law. Although the loss of fugitive slaves principally affected the border states, the issue had a powerful symbolic hold on the imaginations of Southerners. Under the old Fugitive Slave Law of 1793, enforcement provisions were vague, and Northern states could effectively nullify the federal law. Owners were usually required to capture the fugitives themselves, without the aid of state or local police—an impossible task in many Northern communities. In the case of *Prigg v. Pennsylvania* in 1842, the U.S. Supreme Court upheld a Pennsylvania law prohibiting state authorities from helping to enforce the federal fugitive slave law. In the aftermath, abolitionists forced a host of similar "liberty laws" through many other state legislatures. To ensure compliance, these laws prescribed penalties ranging from fines to prison sentences.[51]

When Clay proposed his compromise, the bill regarding fugitive slaves had already been introduced by Senator James Mason of Virginia. Mason's bill was designed to arm owners with the full power of the federal government as well as to nullify potential conflict with state laws. As initially proposed, it provided for federal warrants for arrest and empowered most federal officials to conduct hearings on whether the arrested person was a fugitive slave. It also gave federal marshals the right to make arrests in the name of owners and prescribed a penalty of $1,000 for anyone convicted of harboring or concealing fugitive slaves or assisting them to escape.[52]

Mason's bill had critics on both sides of the Mason-Dixon line. Southern radicals thought it too weak; many saw it as the only concession to Southern interests in the Compromise package. Northern critics condemned the bill for undermining the rights of accused blacks. Under Mason's initial proposal, suspected fugitive slaves were effectively denied the right to habeas corpus and trial by jury, time-honored judicial safeguards. When, after much criticism by Southerners, Mason added an amendment denying accused blacks the right to testify in their own defense, outcries from Northern critics grew even more strident. Over the next several months various attempts were made to reinsert the legal safeguards of habeas corpus or trial by jury in either Northern or Southern courts.[53] Webster himself proposed an amendment calling for jury trials in the states in which fugitives had been apprehended.[54] All these attempts failed, however; in its final form the bill denied habeas corpus, trial by jury, and the right of the accused to testify, and thus effectively treated suspected fugitive slaves as chattels—not as persons or citizens but as things—everywhere in the North.

On March 7, 1850, the Senate chamber and balconies were crammed with spectators in anticipation of a new speech on the Compromise measures. While the audience buzzed with excitement, Daniel Webster stepped to the fore. Known for his imposing appearance and great rolling rhetoric, he rose to his full height, his deep eyes flashing beneath dark, heavy brows. "I wish to speak today, not as a Massachusetts man, nor as a Northern man, but as an American," he began. His speech poured forth, filling the breathless hall with Webster's familiar theme of the sacredness of the Union, a theme that no one but he could make so spellbinding. Webster criticized both North and South, abolitionist as well as Southern secessionist. But it finally became clear that he was standing firmly with Clay and the Compromisers—although he did express a desire to alter some of the most severe provisions of the proposed fugitive law.[55]

Webster had barely finished his speech before Northern abolitionists began to denounce him. For many Northerners—not only abolitionists, but also Free-Soilers and many Northern Democrats—it was beyond imagining that Daniel Webster, the grandiloquent voice of Northern values, the kind of hero that made people strain for adjectives, would support such a measure. They accused him of selling his principles for another chance at the presidency—or in order to line his pockets.[56] They called him a Southern toady and a traitor to freedom. In his poem "Ichabod," abolitionist poet/editor John Greenleaf Whittier, echoing Dante, pictured Webster as so corrupted that his demon-tormented soul had been plunged into the depths of hell even while his living body still walked the earth.[57] Ralph Waldo Emerson wrote bitterly in his journal, "The word *liberty* in the mouth of Mr. Webster sounds like the word *love* in the mouth of a courtezan."[58]

Webster's motives in supporting the Compromise and its new fugitive slave provisions were complex, but his support was not inconsistent with his previous views. Webster had always been opposed to the extension of slavery into new territories, and the Compromise measures, which Clay had discussed privately with Webster before presenting them, technically satisfied this requirement (although they left open whether slavery could be introduced into New Mexico and Utah). Moreover, Webster apparently tried sincerely to see that fugitives were accorded a jury trial, and he apparently genuinely believed that the nation was in peril. "I am tired of standing up here, almost alone from Massachusetts, contending for practical measures, absolutely essential to the good of the country," he wrote wearily to his friend Peter Harvey from Washington in August.[59]

Webster's biographers still debate his motives for accepting the Fugitive Slave Law. But for the thousands of fugitive slaves who lived in the North, and for the innumerable slaves like Shadrach Minkins who yearned to find sanctuary there, questions of character and motive were beside the point. Daniel Webster's idea of "American" did not include them. His "practical" view of the Compromise measures had added the weight of his substantial influence to the forces arrayed against them. In favoring the slaveowner who came north—to Philadelphia, to New York, to Boston—in search of his runaway slaves, Webster supported a measure that stripped people accused of being fugitive slaves of all rights enjoyed by citizens. He had helped to make it much more likely that slaves like Shadrach Minkins who were willing to risk their lives for freedom would be returned to bondage.[60]

On the day when Shadrach Minkins decided that the moment had come to seize his own freedom, he may have known little of Daniel Webster and the grand movements in Washington. What he did know was that if he traveled a few hundred miles northward, he would be free. At nine o'clock on the night of May 3, 1850, the curfew bell sounded as usual. "Slaves without a pass, get off the streets and back to your homes," it said. "The jail and the lash await," it warned malingerers.[61] But that night the curfew bell no longer tolled for Shadrach Minkins, and it never would again.

In all likelihood Shadrach Minkins escaped by sea. Numerous ships bound for New York, Philadelphia, Baltimore, Portland, and other Northern ports arrived and departed through the first two weeks of May. Minkins may have hidden aboard the *Alvaro Lamphir,* a schooner bound for Boston that arrived in Norfolk on May 4, or else aboard the schooner *Vesper,* bound for New Bedford, which reached the city the same day. Or he may have fled aboard one of the Baltimore or New York packets.[62]

If his escape had been arranged with the captain and crew, Minkins might have had a fairly easy time of it. Once out at sea, dangers diminished. When the captain and crew were involved, the fugitive could appear on deck, dine in the open, breathe in the sea air, and rest, having to hide only in port and when other vessels were in sight. The main worries were the worries of all seafarers—storms and shipwreck. More than a few fugitives were discovered when bad weather delayed a voyage or forced a ship back to port. A ship bearing one fugitive turned back to Norfolk after encountering ice near Philadelphia.[63] The coasts were littered with shipwreck debris. Reports of ships lost in the coastal trade were as common as reports of automobile accidents are today.

On the other hand, if Minkins was hidden away on board by crewmen, or stowed away without their knowledge or with the aid only of loading crews, the entire voyage would have remained very dangerous. A captain who found a stowaway fugitive aboard would do almost anything in his power to see the slave returned, so great was the fear of Southern wrath. A captain who was rumored to have landed a fugitive slave in the North dared not drop anchor again in a Southern harbor unless he could prove that he had no complicity in the affair and, usually, unless he also paid the owner the slave's full value. Persons suspected of assisting escapes could find their lives threatened. When Captain Willett Mott, a Norfolk ship chandler, was accused of aiding slaves, he had to flee with his family. When he later attempted to return to the city to prove his innocence, a hostile mob made him run for his life.[64]

Out of fear of Southern retribution, many Northern captains felt compelled to return fugitives discovered aboard their ships. Sometimes captains simply hailed passing southbound vessels and unceremoniously transferred their unwanted charges.[65] Other captains turned back to Norfolk or some other Southern port even though doing so might involve days of delay.[66] One Boston ship heading home from Wilmington, North Carolina, turned around to return a fugitive although it was already three or four days into its homeward voyage. Some captains eager to save time tried to keep fugitive slaves imprisoned below deck throughout their sojourns in the North, although they risked the wrath of abolitionists if they were found out. When a slave named Columbus Jones escaped ashore at Hyannis, Massachusetts, from a ship in which he had been confined, Edward B. Bacon, a Southern sympathizer and master of the schooner *Elizabeth B,* went out of his way to entice Jones aboard his own ship by convincing him that "the people of Hyannis were much excited and it would not be safe for him to go among them."[67] (Bacon was afterward arrested by Massachusetts authorities.)

Stowaways often had to endure not only the agonizing fear of being discovered but also great physical discomfort. Fifty-two years after escaping aboard a Norfolk schooner, the celebrated fugitive George Latimer still vividly recalled the long hours he and his wife spent "under the fore-peak . . . lying on the stone ballast in the darkness."[68] Anthony Blow, crammed into a tiny hiding place, had to endure a storm-tossed voyage that took eight days instead of the expected two, all the while suffering from the heat of the nearby boiler.[69] If the winds were unfavorable and the voyage perforce extended, fugitives risked running out of food or water. The air was often rank and stifling below decks, exacerbating the seasickness that many of the fugitives undoubtedly suffered. There were other terrors. Once, the hold of a Norfolk schooner opened at a New York dock was found to contain the body of a male slave, apparently asphyxiated by thick, pungent turpentine fumes.[70]

Soon after he left the DeBree household, perhaps within hours, Shadrach Minkins began his perilous journey to freedom. Whatever the physical accommodations, the journey would have been a dark voyage of the mind, filled with sadness and terrors. If anything went wrong, the consequences might well be life-threatening. Or Minkins might find himself on the auction block, facing a life in slavery in the Deep South from which the only hope of escape would be death. Minkins also had to endure the fearful losses and nagging anguish and guilt that flight inevitably brought. As historian Herbert Gutman has noted, William Still's *Underground Railroad* is "filled with letters [from escaped fugitives] showing the psychological costs of flight."[71] The ties of kinship and friendship were severed at a stroke. Would he ever again see the faces or share the embrace of parents or friends left behind? What would happen to those he had abandoned, those who might have needed his help or protection? These fears and worries haunted fugitives for years after their flight.

Shadrach Minkins survived all the dangers and made his way safely to Boston. A later report in William Still's Philadelphia Vigilance Committee accounts contains a single tantalizing piece of information about his escape. The report notes the arrival in March 1856 of a schooner from Norfolk captained by the renowned Captain Fountain. Fourteen fugitives were aboard, including twenty-eight-year-old Rebecca Jones and her three children, Sarah Frances, Mary, and Rebecca, all slaves of W. W. Davidson of Norfolk. Rebecca Jones had been promised freedom, but soon after her owner died she grew increasingly convinced that she and her children were to be sold instead. With ten others, she and her three girls fled aboard Fountain's schooner to Wilmington, Delaware, where Quaker abolitionist Thomas Garrett "had men waiting til 12 o'clock till the Captain arrived at his berth." From Wilmington the entire group was sent on to Still in Philadelphia. Before going on to Boston, Rebecca Jones told Still that six years earlier, her husband had escaped from Norfolk "in company with the noted fugitive, 'Shadrach.' "[72]

BOSTON

4 "Cradle of Liberty"?

The Boston that Shadrach Minkins entered in May 1850 was a thriving city of more than 130,000, surpassed in population only by New York, Philadelphia, and Baltimore. Like them, and indeed like Norfolk, Boston had a long history as a commercial seaport, a center for its region. But Boston was in many ways the antithesis of the Southern city Minkins had left. Whereas Norfolk was a slow-paced throwback to the commercial era of the early republic, Boston was the financial, political, social, and cultural hub of the surging new industrial economy. The city shoreline bristled with docks, and hundreds of masts rose from Boston Harbor. A colossal spider's web of railroad tracks reached out from the center of the city toward the west, north, and south, connecting Boston to the manufacturing centers of Lowell, Worcester, and Lynn and to markets all through New England, the mid-Atlantic states, and the Midwest.

Commerce was not the only force transforming Boston. Waves of immigrants from Scotland, Wales, Germany, and, by the late 1840s, especially from Ireland were inundating Boston, revolutionizing the city and its culture. In 1850 foreign-born persons and their children accounted for roughly 45 percent of all Bostonians; by 1855 they would account for over 50 percent.[1] This influx literally altered the face—or faces—of the city. An "Old Resident" of Boston remembered wistfully in 1851 that the people on the street had once been "all familiar." All that had changed:

> The population has no longer a homogeneous aspect . . . you no longer see exclusively the pale, sharp, serious faces, and the quick

gait and uniform costume which belongs to Yankees. Odd hats and caps, shoes, coats, and other garments of peculiar fashion; moustaches and beards; lazy and slouching movements, animated vehement gesticulations . . . all convince you that the people who find home and occupation in Boston are not of one but many nations. If you cast your eyes up to the signs over the shop doors, you will see German names . . . French . . . Irish and Scotch.[2]

The influx of people with strange names and speech and clothing provided the hands and arms and backs and muscles that carted the materials, manned the shovels, and tended the machines in hundreds of shops and factories of the early Industrial Revolution. It also created the familiar problems of modern urban life—poverty, overcrowding, disease, crime. Hundreds of vagrant children walked the streets begging, selling apples, picking up chips or junk, or stealing.[3]

For Shadrach Minkins and the 2,500 other blacks in Boston and its suburbs, the changes that were transforming the city yielded opportunities but at the same time threatened their tenuous place. From the early years of settlement, blacks had been part of Boston, brought from Africa and the West Indies primarily to fill positions as household servants.[4] By 1752 more than 1,500 free blacks and slaves lived in the city, accounting for slightly more than 10 percent of the population. However, by the first national census in 1790, Boston's 766 African-Americans—most of them free—made up only 4 percent of the population. By 1820 the black population had rebounded to pre-Revolutionary totals but continued to fall sharply as a percentage of the total population. Between 1820 and 1850 barely 300 blacks were added to the population, while the white population, augmented by immigration from across the Atlantic, sometimes grew by 300 persons a week. In 1850 blacks made up less than 2 percent of Boston's population.[5]

Where Shadrach Minkins lived during his first months in Boston is not known, but residential patterns for the city make some reasonable guesses possible. Boston's peninsular geography, which necessitated "sinuous windings" of streets "set at defiance by their abrupt terminations," combined with its rapid nineteenth-century growth, resulted in makeshift, primitive conditions in the inner city, particularly for the lower classes.[6] The compiler of the first atlas of the city found such a jumble of shanties

Boston's West End (Sixth Ward) neighborhood, showing the all-black Smith School, 1849.

and sheds in the lanes and yards and alleys that he simply gave up trying to map them.[7] Cellars were jammed with humanity, mostly Irish. A coroner's inquest into the death of an Irish immigrant named Cornelius Sullivan revealed that he and twelve others, including his wife and four children, had been packed into a cellar barely eighteen feet square and five and a half feet high. The report called Sullivan's home a "fair sample" of the dwellings on Ann and Broad Streets.[8]

Boston's blacks were not as crowded or poorly housed as the most destitute immigrants. Nevertheless, for blacks, Boston's reputation as the center of the American Revolution—its Faneuil Hall called the "Cradle of Liberty" for the number of radical meetings it sheltered—and of the abolition movement had never been translated into social and economic reality. According to urban historian Leonard Curry, Boston in 1850 was "the most thoroughly segregated city in the nation in its residential patterns."[9] Many neighborhoods were virtually closed to blacks.[10] As late as 1860 a local black claimed that it was "five times as hard to get a house in a good location in Boston as it is in Philadelphia."[11] The vast majority of black Bostonians lived on a few blocks in the Sixth Ward, known as the West End, on the back side of Beacon Hill.[12] Southac and Belknap Streets were populated almost exclusively by blacks. Many addresses were for such-and-such a "court" or "place"—terms which today suggest the privacy or luxury of exclusive development but which in the nineteenth century usually indicated tiny substandard dwellings, often closely packed, in narrow alleyways. Blacks also seem to have lived more frequently than native-born whites in small buildings built at the rear of lots.[13] In Boston as elsewhere in the North, a few blacks were even reduced to occupying cellars, the common residence of the most destitute of the Irish. The cellar of the African Meeting House in Smith Court regularly served as a residence for one or more blacks.[14]

Steep rents and extremely limited housing choices compelled many black families to take in boarders to make ends meet. Tax and census records for 1850 show that shared housing was common. Some dwellings originally intended for single families had become virtual hotels. The 1850 census recorded six unrelated blacks (including William and Ellen Craft, a fugitive slave couple from Georgia) and one white domestic servant living with black leader Lewis Hayden, his wife, and their two children at 66 Southac Street.[15]

Young single males like Shadrach Minkins typically became boarders in black households or found lodging in one of several roominghouses catering to blacks, principally seamen.[16] When the 1850 census was taken, two roominghouses in the Second Ward (East Boston, adjoining the harbor) contained twenty and twenty-two persons respectively. Roominghouses and private homes gave black newcomers a buffer against the strangeness and impersonality of city life, introducing them to what social historian Carol Stapp describes as an intricate "crisscrossing pattern of interaction" among business associates, friends, families, fellow church members, and neighbors.[17]

Minkins may have found shelter among the many Virginia blacks who had come to the city before him. Several dozen slaves from the Randolph plantation near Norfolk County had been freed and brought to Boston in

1847. Free Norfolk blacks, including Moses Grandy, as well as numerous Norfolk fugitives had found their way to the city. When Norfolk slave Mary Milburn escaped to Boston in the mid-1850s, she reported finding so many Norfolk acquaintances that she could almost imagine herself "back in the old country."[18]

Ironically, it was a connection with a white Southerner that helped Shadrach Minkins get his footing in Boston. Shortly after Minkins arrived in the city, he ran into William H. Parks, a commission merchant who had formerly lived in Norfolk. Minkins and Parks were well acquainted. When Minkins had been working for Martha Hutchings at her store in Norfolk, Parks had worked there for a time in the counting room. What Minkins felt when the two men first met can only be imagined. Meeting any white Southerner who could identify you as a fugitive slave was a situation fraught with anxieties. Parks could easily have notified authorities in Norfolk. Many in Parks's position would have begun calculating the reward they could earn by this lucky discovery. But Parks seems instead to have taken a friendly interest in Minkins, giving him his first work in the city.[19] Probably the work was no more than a simple chore, but for a fugitive slave the chance to earn money—and to keep it rather than have to turn it over to the master—was a memorable opportunity. Frederick Douglass has written vividly of cherishing the first two half-dollars he earned in the North shoveling a load of coal.[20]

Soon after meeting William Parks, Minkins found more steady work as a waiter at the Cornhill Coffee House in Cornhill Court. Less than a block from the Court House, the restaurant-hotel stood in the heart of Boston's business and government district. Immediately in front of the coffeehouse rose the four-story Joy Building, nicknamed "the elephant of Boston" soon after it was built in 1808. An 1830 engraving of the Joy Building shows the coffeehouse peeking out from behind. The sign above the door reads "W. Fenno," for "Bill Fenno," a Court Street confectioner who opened the restaurant about 1812 and soon made it famous for steaks and chops. Sometime after 1826 Fenno had sold the remodeled building and business to the Taft brothers. Around the time Minkins went to work there, the Cornhill was one of the city's finest restaurants. Elaborately printed menus preserved from the same period list an array of soups, game, fish, eels, shellfish, and other delicacies in addition to the standard

The Joy Building, Boston, 1830. The sign "W. Fenno" (left) marks the location of the Cornhill Coffee House, where Minkins worked briefly as a waiter.

fare of boiled, roasted, and broiled meats. "Dinners in private rooms if requested," one menu announced, and there is also a printed menu for a special "Dinner for Twelve Gentlemen."[21]

The Cornhill Coffee House gave work to Minkins and other blacks when they may not have had a lot of choices. As was true for every black in the North, Shadrach Minkins found his economic opportunity restricted by long-established patterns of custom and prejudice. In immigrant-swollen Boston at midcentury, competition for even the most menial jobs could be fierce, even in the few occupations in which blacks had enjoyed a seeming preference—domestic service, for example, and barbering, a related occupation. Boston's 575 black workers identified in the 1850 census were found in forty-six different occupations.[22] Only a handful were professionals or skilled laborers. There were 2 black doctors, 4 clergymen, 1 lawyer, and several builders, carpenters, painters, blacksmiths, shoe- or bootmakers, and tailors.[23] Five Boston blacks were restaurateurs, 5 ran hotels or boardinghouses, and almost a dozen operated clothing stores.[24] The 48 black barbers and hairdressers, accounting for nearly 10 percent of all black workers, represented the major small-scale entrepreneurial occupation to which antebellum blacks had access nationwide.[25]

Figures for low-status employment tell the story of Boston racial prejudice more directly. Boston's 142 black seamen accounted for almost one-quarter of all working black males.[26] They were part of what historian Samuel Eliot Morison called "the international proletariat of the sea"—immemorially represented in the polyglot whaling crew of Herman Melville's 1851 novel, *Moby Dick*.[27] Another 115, or one-fifth of Boston's working blacks, identified themselves as common laborers, the lowest and least descriptive of all categories of labor. Of other racial and national groups, only the Irish constituted a greater percentage of common laborers.[28] There were also 48 black servants, 24 black waiters, and 36 black shop assistants. Blacks also accounted for many of Boston's wood sawyers, bootblacks, and secondhand clothes dealers.[29] But of Boston's 4,000 clerks, only 3 were black.[30]

Although the income of a waiter could be meager, the thriving Cornhill Coffee House trade probably provided Shadrach Minkins with a better than average income. Minkins also appears to have lived at the hotel. William H. Parks later testified that Minkins "went . . . to live at Taft's." The federal census taker who visited the hotel in October 1850 listed two blacks among the residents. One of them, who gave his name as "Frederick Johnson" and listed his place of birth as Virginia, was very possibly Shadrach Minkins.[31]

The main disadvantage of Minkins' job was that Cornhill Court was near the hub of Boston's commerce and government, an area frequented by Southern businessmen visiting the city. Surrounding streets and lanes were crowded with shops and offices. As a waiter at the Cornhill Coffee House in 1850 and 1851, Minkins was always in danger of encountering someone from Norfolk who would report him to DeBree or the Boston authorities.[32] William Parks had in fact already pointed Minkins out to an itinerant circus worker from the South.[33]

In addition to the risk of capture and the economic barriers, Shadrach Minkins and other fugitives in Boston daily faced small and great humiliations proceeding from racism. Again and again contemporary writers commented on the deep and widespread racial prejudices they found in Boston even in the middle decades of the century. The number and sharpness of the remarks stand in vivid contrast to the city's much-vaunted love of freedom. Commenting in 1850 on the situation of the North in general and of Boston in particular, Boston's Roman Catholic *Pilot* noted that "the mass of free blacks form here a degraded caste."[34] Some years later the Boston *Congregationalist* concluded that although Boston and Massachusetts whites were less subject to racial prejudices than whites elsewhere in the North, they were still thoroughly infected with racism.[35] British traveler William Chambers found in Boston the same "rigorous separation of races" he encountered elsewhere in the North.[36]

Most of the daily indignities were suffered quietly, and Boston black leaders liked to point to instances of progress rather than to negative examples. Fearing real or imagined reprisals, many blacks kept silent. But Frederick Douglass, never one to hold his tongue, delivered a stinging indictment of his experience of racism when he had first come to Boston in the early 1840s. A two-year sojourn in England, where he was not only accepted but welcomed by aristocrats and commoners alike, made him recall his early experiences in Boston with acute bitterness. "I remember, about two years ago," he wrote in 1846 shortly before returning to the United States,

> there was in Boston, near the south-west corner of Boston Common, a menagerie. I had long desired to see such a collection as I understood was being exhibited there. Never having had an opportunity while a slave, I resolved to seize this, my first, since my escape. I went, and as I approached the entrance to gain admission, I was met and told by the door-keeper, in a harsh and contemptuous tone, "—We don't allow niggers in here!" . . . While passing from New York to Boston, on the steamer "Massachusetts," on the night of the 9th of December, 1843, when chilled almost through with the cold, I went into the cabin to get a little warm. I was soon touched upon the shoulder, and told, *"We don't allow niggers in here!"* On arriving in Boston, from an anti-slavery tour, hungry and tired, I went into an eating-house, near my friend, Mr. Campbell's, to get some refreshments. I was met by a lad in a white apron, *"We don't allow niggers in here!"* A week or two before leaving the United States, I had a meeting appointed at Weymouth . . . On attempting to take a seat in the omnibus to that place, I was told by the driver (and I never shall forget his fiendish hate), *"I don't allow niggers in here!"*[37]

Douglass' experience, with its relentless hateful refrain, was undoubtedly familiar to Shadrach Minkins and to all Boston blacks.

When Shadrach Minkins arrived in Boston in 1850, the racial climate had been improving ever so slowly. Three years later, Boston black leader William Nell would be able to note that "to a very great extent, the enlightened public sentiment . . . has rendered obsolete the exclusion of colored persons from places of public resort."[38] Later in the decade Walt Whitman, visiting Boston to supervise the printing of the third edition of *Leaves of Grass*, noted with surprise that "at the eating houses, a black, when he wants his dinner, comes in and takes a vacant seat wherever he finds one—and nobody minds it."[39]

Nell's and Whitman's comments suggest considerable progress, though by no means complete success, in eradicating racial prejudice from Boston. Nell admitted this himself when he looked "forward" to the time when Boston would finally "conquer her prejudices against an injured and patient race."[40] Restaurants, theaters, and hotels would continue to exclude black customers through the 1850s—and beyond.[41] Boston's segregated school system would not be abolished until 1855, after more than a decade of complaints and petitions. A single black school, the Smith School on Joy Street, served black primary students from the whole city, forcing some children to travel great distances (or forcing their parents to find housing in the crowded Sixth Ward).[42] A few Boston churches continued to relegate blacks to a rear gallery. At the wealthy West Church on Cambridge Street, in sight of the State House dome, long-standing custom confined the few blacks who attended to a degrading "pigeon house" situated in the most remote section of the gallery. Even in the abolitionist 1850s, pleas by the West Church's venerated senior minister, the Reverend Charles Lowell, could not persuade his congregation to end the decades-old practice.[43]

The evidence of segregation and racial prejudice indicates that Boston continued to impose daily humiliations on Shadrach Minkins and other blacks. He almost certainly heard the refrain that persisted so painfully in Frederick Douglass' consciousness: "We don't allow niggers in here."

Despite these shortcomings, Boston offered Shadrach Minkins and other blacks some compensations. A vigorous black community life was nourished by deep roots going back to before the Revolution. With the founding of the First African Baptist Church (later the First Independent Baptist Church) in 1805, the modern community life began to take shape. The church building in Smith Court was completed in 1806 and still stands today under the name of the African Meeting House. Reportedly the oldest extant black church building in America, it is the site at which the New England Antislavery Society was formed in 1832 under the leadership of William Lloyd Garrison.[44]

By 1850 Boston's five black congregations (two Baptist and three Methodist) totaling nearly 600 members formed the center of a thriving black community. Independent black churches served as focal points of social and political as well as religious activities. They were the networks through which Boston's blacks created a common identity and achieved common goals and where individuals gained a sense of dignity, strength, and control over their lives.[45] As historians James and Lois Horton have observed, each black church served as "a training ground for leaders, a place where common laborers could gain positions of status as deacons and officers of church groups, a place for education and training of the young, a place for entertainment and social life, and a meetinghouse for the exchange of thought, both political and social, free from the pressures of white society."[46] They were also important as centers of abolitionist activity within the larger black community and as relief organizations for impoverished fugitives and free blacks.

For fugitive slaves like Shadrach Minkins, the most important black church in 1850 was the Twelfth Baptist Church on Southac (Phillips) Street. Sometimes known as the "Church of the Fugitive Slaves" because of the large number of fugitives among its members, the Twelfth Baptist was the most recently founded of the five churches. Its minister, Leonard A. Grimes, had come to Boston from Washington, D.C., in 1848. A dynamic man who had been arrested for assisting fugitive slaves in the South, he soon became the most active and visible of Boston's black ministers. His flock of fugitive slaves and friends rapidly outgrew the upstairs room in which they had been meeting, and construction of a new church building on Southac Street was soon begun.[47]

In addition to churches, Boston's blacks were served by a variety of black social organizations, some dating from the early decades of the century. The African Lodge No. 459, founded in 1787 and later renamed the Prince Hall Lodge, was the first black Masonic lodge in the nation.

By the late 1840s three other black lodges had been formed. Two women's organizations, the United Daughters of Zion and the Female Benevolent Firm, came into existence at roughly the same time and were still operating in the early years of the twentieth century. There had been a dramatics club and a predominantly black organization that sponsored debates and lectures. Although some black social and cultural organizations were short-lived, they indicate the existence of a developed and relatively complex, multilayered community at the top of which was a small educated black elite. Apparently Boston's black society was minimally delineated by lightness or darkness of skin tone, a factor that commonly determined social caste among urban blacks in the South.[48]

Another strength of black Boston was its long tradition of vigorous community leadership and protest against discrimination and injustice. In 1773 Boston blacks had petitioned the Massachusetts legislature to abolish slavery, citing the desecration of their family ties. By the late 1840s and early 1850s, Boston blacks had led or been part of many campaigns for equal rights, including an attempt to repeal the Massachusetts law against miscegenation and a successful movement to pass laws against discrimination on railroads and other public transportation.[49]

A militant revolutionary thread also ran through Boston's black community. Perhaps its most overt manifestation appeared in 1829, when black Bostonian David Walker issued his angry pamphlet, *Walker's Appeal . . . to the Colored Citizens of the World.* Walker's incendiary purpose was not only to awaken his "afflicted, degraded and slumbering brethren" in slavery to a true sense of their miseries but also to rouse them to action—violent action if necessary—to gain their freedom.[50] In 1842, after George Latimer was arrested as a fugitive slave, Boston blacks had led in forming the New England Freedom Association to "succor those who claim property in themselves, and thereby acknowledge an independence of slavery."[51] Although it is not known how long this organization functioned, many of its leaders remained part of the black community and so were ready to execute its aims, even without the sanction of the formal organization.

Although none of Boston's black leaders attained the renown of Frederick Douglass or Charles Lenox Remond of Salem, many were notable. The acknowledged head of black Boston and its general in the

Lewis Hayden, clothing merchant and community leader.

war to defend fugitive slaves was clothing dealer Lewis Hayden. Hayden was a fugitive slave himself, having fled with his family from Kentucky to Canada. After six months he returned to the United States and settled in Detroit, where he led efforts to establish a school and participated in other black community activities.[52] In 1846, hoping to join forces with leaders of the abolition movement, he moved to Boston, first residing at 8 Southac Street, and shortly thereafter moving up the steep, narrow street to number 66. This house soon became a center of black abolitionist activities and is today a chief site of pilgrimage on Boston's Black Heritage Trail. Often the Hayden house was home for half a dozen or more fugitives in addition to other boarders and the numerous members of the Hayden family.

Harriet Beecher Stowe once reportedly found thirteen fugitive slaves crammed into the house.[53] A portrait of Hayden shows him standing erect, dignified, and unsmiling. The overall impression is of a man of great seriousness and fierce determination. He was the one to whom everyone would look when Boston blacks were threatened.

Another of Boston's black leaders was William Cooper Nell, William Lloyd Garrison's protégé and friend. Unlike Hayden and most of Boston's other black leaders, Nell was a native-born Bostonian. He was also a second-generation activist, his father having been one of the founders of the first black antislavery society in the nation. In the 1850s the younger Nell was to play a leading role in petitioning the Massachusetts legislature to erect a statue commemorating Crispus Attucks, the black who had fallen at the Boston Massacre in 1775. Nell also helped lead the Garrisonian campaign to integrate Boston schools. Nell's *Colored Patriots of the American Revolution* (1855) was the first important historical work by an American black.[54]

Some other leading black Bostonians were John T. Hilton, Joshua B. Smith, and William J. Watkins. Hilton, a hairdresser from Pennsylvania, was the most active black member of the Massachusetts Antislavery Society. An articulate speaker and a tireless organizer, he was behind many of black Boston's public meetings and celebrations. Smith, known as "the prince of caterers," was almost as active as Hilton and Nell. Like Hilton a native of Pennsylvania, Smith participated in many black community activities. His work as a caterer brought him into contact with many influential Bostonians and made him an especially valuable link between Boston's black and white societies. Watkins, a second-generation activist from Baltimore, was in the forefront of the black community during his four-year residence in Boston beginning in 1849.[55]

Shadrach Minkins would not remain in Boston long enough to become very involved in the city's black community. He attended a black church, although it is not absolutely certain which one it was. One later report claimed that Minkins had been a member of the Zion Methodist Episcopal Church on West Center Street. The case is stronger, however, for Minkins' membership in the Twelfth Baptist Church. A reporter for the New York *Independent* was later told that Minkins had been a member of the church, and the Reverend Leonard Grimes, minister of the Twelfth Baptist, identified himself as Minkins' pastor and stated that Minkins attended his church.[56]

Although Shadrach Minkins' connections with the black community network were the tenuous ties of a newcomer, that network was there behind him and all the other blacks of the city. The Boston tradition of black militancy that had produced David Walker's famous *Appeal* was there, too. When Minkins' time of trial arrived, Boston's black network and black militant tradition would prove to be the most vital of resources.

5 "A New Reign of Terror"

Shadrach Minkins had been in Boston hardly four months when national politics and national ambitions suddenly changed the world around him. On September 18, 1850, when Millard Fillmore penned his signature on the Fugitive Slave Law, the final piece of the Compromise of 1850 was in place. The nation had been saved, its wounds healed—or so Compromise supporters believed. "I think the country has had a providential escape from very considerable dangers," wrote Daniel Webster with relief.[1] Spontaneous celebrations, complete with "bonfires, processions, serenades, speeches, suppers, drinking, and cannon-salutes," had already broken out in Washington with the news that the Compromise had passed. When one procession stopped at Webster's Washington doorstep for a speech, Webster began by quoting the triumphant opening words from the (darkly Machiavellian) speech of Shakespeare's *Richard III:* "Now is the winter of our discontent made glorious summer by this sun of York."[2]

For Shadrach Minkins and for fugitive slaves and black communities from Boston to San Francisco, President Fillmore's simple gesture had an entirely different meaning. Before the new bill became law, many fugitive slaves and their families had enjoyed the considerable protection of Northern indifference or hostility to Southern "rights." In many areas, state laws and local sympathy made action by masters and agents against fugitive slaves an unlikely, if not dangerous, enterprise. Many fugitives had lived for years—some for a decade or more—with little fear. True, not every Northerner welcomed them, and there had always been successful recoveries as well as kidnappings in which Northerners cooperated. But now whatever peace and security the fugitives had found had been traded by the federal government for domestic harmony between North and South. Having been in touch with their friends and families or even their masters back in the slave states, many fugitives were easy to locate. The new law immediately disturbed their waking and sleeping moments. Would agents of their owners shortly be prowling the streets? Would local authorities conspire with owners in remanding slaves? Who was most in danger? Who could be trusted? Were free blacks safe? Who should flee, and to where?

The new Fugitive Slave Law had seismic repercussions in many black communities. In New York City, fugitive slave Harriet Jacobs vividly recalled, the law precipitated "a new reign of terror." Residents of twenty years or more fled from the city to safety in Canada. Although Jacobs and her family remained, they found themselves virtual prisoners in their home, particularly in summer, "when snakes and slaveholders make their appearance." Jacobs wrote that she "seldom ventured into the streets . . . [and] went as much as possible through back streets and by-ways." Finally, though, a rumor circulated that her owner knew of her presence in New York, and she fled to Boston. Some time later she returned to New York City, but while scanning the lists of city hotel guests she came across the name of a daughter of her deceased owner. "Reader," she wrote in her autobiography, "if you have never been a slave, you cannot imagine the acute sensation of suffering at my heart." Hidden in a carriage, Jacobs fled again to New England.[3]

By October many Northern fugitives who had thought themselves secure had either fled their homes or were on the verge of doing so. Reports from Pittsburgh at the end of September suggested that an enormous migration to Canada West (Ontario) was under way there. One report claimed that more than 300 had fled, including almost all the waiters in the hotels. Another report gave convincing figures of daily departures of large groups: "Sunday thirty fled; on Monday, forty; Tuesday, fifty; on Wednesday, thirty." The groups were reported to be well armed with pistols and bowie knives.[4]

In the first month after the law took effect an estimated 2,000 blacks left the North for Canada. A dispatch from Toronto reported that "almost

every steamer" was arriving with fugitive slaves aboard.[5] When Southerners reportedly applied to Chicago authorities to recover several fugitives,
the Chicago *Western Citizen,* an antislavery paper, wrote that "the rush of
the fugitives for the protection of the British Dominions" became "immense." The *Western Citizen* noted that the fugitives included many long-
established citizens "who have acquired a comfortable homestead in our
midst by honest industry." To pay for their escape, the fugitives often had
to sell their possessions for a pittance. Hundreds upon hundreds were
arriving in Canada poorly prepared for a new beginning in a new country.
Jobs were scarce in Canada, and relief programs, where they existed,
could not possibly cope with the numbers. "We are informed," the *Western
Citizen* wrote, "that there are many thousands . . . in a state of want
bordering upon starvation, utterly unable to procure employment, or
means of sustenance."[6]

In Boston the new law produced some immediate panic, although it is
hard to know exactly how many fugitives actually fled. One exaggerated
report claimed that 40 percent had left the city within twenty-four hours
of enactment of the new law,[7] but Theodore Parker, a well-placed Boston
abolitionist, asserted that only forty (fewer than 10 percent) were known
to have left in the first few days.[8] Nevertheless, the number of fugitives on
the verge of flight was undoubtedly high.

At the end of September a case in New York City shattered any notion
that Boston's blacks were protected by their abolitionist friends and by
distance from the Mason-Dixon line. On September 28 a fugitive named
James Hamlet was seized by officers, given the speedy "summary" hearing called for by the new law, and sent back to his owner in Baltimore, all
within a few hours.

The Hamlet case shocked blacks far from slave-state borders. New
York was more than 100 miles from the nearest slave state, had a black
population of more than 10,000, and was an abolitionist center. If blacks
were not safe there, could they be protected in Providence, New Bedford,
or Boston? Moreover, Hamlet's owner appeared to have been aided by
New York City's Union Safety Committee, an organization formed to assist
slaveowners in recovering fugitive slaves from New York (and for promot-
ing Union-Whig politics).[9] Would Boston fugitives face such organized
and powerful enemies?

If the Hamlet case intensified fears among blacks far from slave-state borders, it gave confidence to the Union-Compromise forces. A few days after Hamlet was delivered to his owner, Compromise architect Henry Clay predicted confidently that "reason and law will finally achieve a noble triumph." In only two instances, Clay pointed out, had the law not been properly enforced. Attempts to oppose enforcement had been "invariably repressed," and "a great and salutary change" toward public acceptance of the law promised success for the forces of Union and Compromise.[10] Numerous editorials and sermons, especially in Boston, supported the operation of the new law. "To me it is incredible, amazing, mournful!!" lamented Harriet Beecher Stowe. "I wish father [Lyman Beecher] would come on to Boston and preach on the Fugitive Slave Law, as he once preached on the slave-trade, when I was a little girl in Litchfield [Connecticut]."[11] (In less than two years, Stowe herself would preach the sermon she called for, to millions of readers, in the form of a novel called *Uncle Tom's Cabin*.)

News of James Hamlet's rendition was still echoing in their ears when Boston's fugitive slaves and free blacks met at the end of September at the black Baptist church on Belknap Street to discuss their prospects. Most of Boston's fugitives who had not yet fled from the city would have been in attendance at this momentous meeting. Lewis Hayden, perhaps the most trusted and most militant community leader, was elected president. William Craft, a fugitive slave from Georgia, was chosen as one of the vice-presidents. For secretary the assembly picked William C. Nell. The meeting denounced the Fugitive Slave Law and its supporters in thundering tones. Hayden called on the assembled crowd to exert a "united and persevering resistance to this ungodly anti-republican law." One of the resolutions declared, "They who would be free, themselves must strike the blow."[12]

At the meeting, black lawyer Robert Morris was named head of a special committee to prepare a plan to meet the new emergency. A week later, on the evening of Friday, October 5, people crowded into the African Meeting House in Smith Court to debate the Morris committee's report and resolutions. The audience was predominantly black, but many of Boston's white abolitionists, including William Lloyd Garrison, were present to lend their support. The preamble to the resolutions was a stirring recital of Boston's

historic place in the quest for liberty. The name of Crispus Attucks, the
black martyr of the Boston Massacre, was invoked, as were the Bill of
Rights and Patrick Henry's "Give me liberty or give me death" speech. In a
chorus of defiant voices, speaker after speaker rose to echo Henry's sentiments. Charles Lenox Remond of Salem called on the audience to make
Massachusetts a battlefield in defense of liberty. Joshua B. Smith declared
that he "had lived long enough" if he could no longer live a free man in
Boston. According to one report of the meeting, Smith then "showed a long
knife to the audience, and advised them to buy Colt's revolvers."[13]

The militant resolutions, unanimously adopted, all proclaimed eternal
resistance to the Fugitive Slave Law. Boston's fugitives were warned to be
on guard. Several resolutions called on Boston authorities to refuse to

Caterer Joshua B. Smith, who advised Boston's fugitive
slaves to buy Colt's revolvers.

participate in prosecutions. Still others called on white Bostonians for help. One resolution asked Boston ministers to dedicate a day or part of a day to preaching and praying against the law. "Denounce the law!" a separate "Address to the Clergy of Massachusetts" demanded. Another called for a grand meeting of all Boston citizens at Faneuil Hall to organize resistance to the Fugitive Slave Law.

For Shadrach Minkins, the most important resolution approved at the African Meeting House that night was one that called for establishing a League of Freedom to "rescue and protect the slave, at every hazard." According to one speaker, its members were to be "actors, and not speakers merely . . . men of over-alls—men of the wharf—who could do heavy work in the hour of difficulty." Soon these black "actors" would play supporting roles in a drama in which Shadrach Minkins would, unwittingly, be assigned the leading part.

The meetings of Boston's black citizens called attention to the plight of the city's fugitives and may also have dissuaded some from flight. By the middle of October Theodore Parker, the fiery renegade Unitarian minister, was reporting that in the previous ten days only "ten or twenty have gone from here to foreign lands."[14] Elsewhere in Massachusetts the initial panic also subsided when the predicted rash of arrests failed to materialize. A few fugitives who had left returned. In the first week in October a meeting of citizens in Lowell, Massachusetts, even passed a resolution recalling three fugitives who had fled, assuring them that they would be protected and had no cause to be afraid.[15]

Some comfort had also come from the convention of the Massachusetts Free-Soil Party on October 3. Charles Sumner, his political star rising in the continuing disintegration of the Massachusetts Whigs, made a memorable, fiery speech at the convention. The opinion of the people, he proclaimed, "like the flaming sword of the cherubim at the gates of Paradise . . . shall prevent any Slave Hunter from ever setting foot in the Commonwealth."[16] There is no doubt that Sumner's words and the "vast enthusiasm" they were accorded were sincere. But were they a statement of commitment or merely the hyperinflated rhetoric of a politician seizing the high ground?

The verdict about whether Boston was safe was still out and would remain so for some time. But Boston seemed a better haven than Philadelphia, Pittsburgh, or New York. On October 2 regional papers announced that 30 fugitives had arrived in Boston from New York City in the aftermath of the Hamlet case. They were reportedly determined to "go no further, but remain here, arm themselves, and abide the result." The *Liberator* solicited clothing and employment for them. By the end of the month, when the number of arrivals from New York had swelled to 100, the *Liberator* announced that an agent had been appointed and an employment office established for the refugees.[17]

Boston fugitive slaves and their friends may have gained confidence from the fact that the first cases had been confined almost exclusively to border states. However, their fears were aroused again by a widely reprinted story that "propositions have already been made to men holding office in this city, to make arrests of sundry fugitives."[18] Now the mere appearance of the U.S. marshal on the streets could create enormous excitement.[19] At the end of the first week of October the *Boston Daily Evening Traveller* was reporting that "quite a number of families, where either the father or mother are fugitives, have been broken up, and the furniture sold off, with a view of leaving for safer quarters in Nova Scotia or Canada."[20]

In the midst of so much uncertainty, spirits were roused and courage fortified when the meeting of Boston citizens called for by Boston's blacks came off on October 14, at Faneuil Hall. In attendance were Boston's black leaders, leading white abolitionists, and a large group of middle- and upper-middle-class white sympathizers—Boston's solid citizenry. Frederick Douglass was there, invited from Rochester, New York, to lend his fire to the occasion. "It was a grand meeting," wrote abolitionist Caroline Dall afterward. "There was but one feeling among the 6,000 persons assembled there, and that was to trample this law under foot."[21]

Even the opening prayer, delivered by revered West Church minister Charles Lowell (the only respectable Boston minister willing to be associated with the fugitives' cause, according to Wendell Phillips), was suitably adamant. It called on God to "hasten the time when, without violence and bloodshed, every yoke shall be broken, and the oppressed go free."[22] Wendell Phillips, Richard Henry Dana, Jr., and others gave stirring speeches, but none was more incendiary than that by Frederick Douglass. His words were full of knives and thunder. He advised Boston's blacks that they had every right to defend themselves against kidnappers who tried to steal their liberty. He undoubtedly gave the crowd some version of his usual succinct recipe for nullifying the Fugitive Slave Law: "a half dozen or more dead kidnappers."[23]

The meeting called for a new "Committee of Vigilance and Safety" modeled after the old, defunct group of 1846. According to the minutes, the purpose of this new committee was to "endeavor by all just means to secure the fugitives and colored inhabitants of Boston and vicinity from any invasion of their right by persons acting under the law."[24] Leaders of the meeting boasted that they had "not the smallest fear" that a fugitive slave could be carried off from Boston into bondage.[25]

Across the country other meetings of black and white citizens had been echoing these defiant words. In Chicago a citizens' meeting heatedly demanded a law forbidding city officers from aiding in fugitive slave cases. "I have never witnessed such excitement in my life . . . if any arrests are ever made here, terrible scenes will ensue, and much bloodshed," wrote one Chicagoan.[26] In Springfield and Lowell, in New York City, Rochester, Pittsburgh, and many other cities and towns, similar words challenged the new law.[27]

The Boston meeting made a lot of noise, and that was an important—if ultimately not very persuasive—first step toward reassuring the city's nervous fugitives. They needed to hear the voices of Boston's whites raised in their defense. A follow-up meeting on October 17 began the business of organizing resistance to any attempt to arrest Boston's fugitive slaves. A Committee of Vigilance, composed of members from every ward, was to act as a sort of civil defense league. Initially only 80 members were named, but within the next year membership would reach 200. For president the meeting chose Timothy Gilbert, a Washington Street manufacturer of pianos who had earlier proclaimed his home a refuge for fugitives even if "every other door in Boston is shut."[28] Recognizing that the committee was unwieldy, an executive committee of 8 was named to run day-to-day activities in defense of fugitives. At its head was Theodore Parker. Also appointed were two prominent black leaders, Lewis Hayden and Joshua B. Smith.[29] A legal committee, made up of as many as 30 lawyers, was also asked to serve temporarily as an "alarm" committee.

To pay for resistance to the law and to provide for destitute fugitives, the Vigilance Committee appointed a finance committee of eight members, including future governor John A. Andrew and black lawyer Robert Morris, to raise $1,000 immediately. In the next ten years the committee would raise over $8,000 from such contributors as Ralph Waldo Emerson, Samuel Gridley Howe, Charles Lowell, the "ladies of Lancaster," and 100 other donors. Many contributions would come in as a result of an appeal sent to 1,600 Massachusetts churches (only a tiny percentage responded). Of the funds raised through various appeals, about half would eventually be used for legal expenses in the defense of fugitives. The Vigilance Committee treasury was also to be a ready source of money for food, fuel, clothing and shelter, medical care, and transportation expenses. In ten years, more than 430 fugitive slaves would be mentioned by name in the records as having received aid. The committee paid all or part of the fares to Canadian sanctuaries for more than 100 fugitives.[30]

Over the next ten years, the Vigilance Committee not only provided money for defending and caring for Boston's fugitives but also built a loose defensive network. The committee prodded other communities to form vigilance committees. Its network of spies—mostly chambermaids and hotel porters—passed along warnings to fugitives. Its legal committee became a constant source of irritation to Boston's federal officials and to Southerners attempting to recover their slaves. In times of crisis, the committee posted hundreds of warnings all over the city, assembled crowds to intimidate and threaten, and generally created havoc. Led by sometime doorkeeper and agent Captain Austin Bearse, the Vigilance Committee attempted several daring rescues of captured fugitives with his sleek thirty-six-foot sloop, the *Moby Dick*.[31] But dramatic rescues and hairbreadth escapes were rare. Mostly the Vigilance Committee provided money, railway tickets, supplies, and legal help to Boston's fugitive slaves and their families.

The white majority of the Vigilance Committee members (at no time were more than 8 of the 200 members black) were important for legitimizing the committee's work. A Whitmanesque catalogue of Boston's occupations, the members represented Boston's solid citizenry. Nearly half were professionals. In addition to the large contingent of lawyers, there were nearly a dozen doctors and a dozen ministers as well as several editors, publishers, and superintendents of various institutions. There were a ship captain, a hotel owner, and manufacturers of paper hangings and pianos. Skilled trades were represented by housewrights, carpenters, printers, a cigarmaker, a daguerreotypist, a mason, a blacksmith, a chair-painter, a maker of marble castings, and a "japanner" (lacquer applier). By far the largest group consisted of merchants and storekeepers—sellers of seeds, furniture, thread, confections, dry goods, clothing, books, shoes, woolens, hats, soap, candles, leather, paper, medicines, groceries, and "East India" goods. These members were wealthy enough to underwrite the committee's operations themselves, if need be. Their names—published by the committee in a circular—helped ensure other contributions and gave an aura of middle-class respectability to the otherwise radical-sounding organization.[32]

In actuality the white members of the Vigilance Committee were hardly radicals or revolutionaries. "Half of them were non-resistants," the hot-blooded Unitarian minister of Worcester, Thomas Wentworth Higginson, was to complain in his journal during a later case. According to Higginson, most members of the committee, though "full of indignation," were "extremely anxious not to be placed for one moment outside the pale of good citizenship."[33] They believed in working within the political and judicial systems, no matter how corrupted or unfair those institutions had become. Only a small percentage of members—Parker, Bearse, and Higginson among them—advocated force to achieve their ends, and not even all of these few were willing to carry arms. During later crises Higginson would be driven to distraction by the committee's propensity to inaction and indecision, to words rather than deeds. When he wanted ball and powder, the committee was content to play the Greek chorus and point "the finger of scorn" at the slaveowners and their agents when they passed in the street. Abolitionist Deborah Weston, referring to a later case in which the Vigilance Committee was immobilized by nice scruples, echoed Higginson's complaint: "People are not much for a rescue who are to[o] conscientious to bribe a man."[34]

Black members of the Vigilance Committee and a network of blacks in the community, however, were in no position to be as indecisive or as passive as the white members. They were armed and ready. The black community, too, was actively carrying out other expressed goals of the Vigilance Committee. Black Bostonians took on most of the actual relief work, with the few black members of the committee contributing much more than their small numbers suggest. Black members were the link between the committee and the black community and oversaw most of the relief work. Initially a relief committee of four members, three of them black (Lewis Hayden, Joshua B. Smith, and William C. Nell), saw to the needs of fugitive slaves in the city, especially those newly arrived. Later, when a single agent for relief work was named, the committee chose Nell. Fugitive slave George Teamoh remembered seeing Nell "during the most inclement weather and in the mid night hours . . . plodding his weary way through slush and mire" to assist endangered fugitives.[35]

Of all blacks involved in efforts to support and protect fugitive slaves, Lewis Hayden was the most active. His name echoes through the Vigilance Committee financial records. "Lewis Hayden boarding Fugitives John Simmons, Wm Miller, James Jackson, Solomon Banks, George Reason, Isaac Mason & Wife," reads the first major entry in the records, typical of many that were to follow over the next ten years. A sampling of other entries reveals that Hayden was on hand to aid Boston's fugitives in every way possible: "Lewis Hayden carriage hire to send John Armisted and other fugitives out of the city," "Lewis Hayden clothes for S. Ward fugitive," "Lewis Hayden boarding Pews & Hall Fugitives two weeks," "Lewis Hayden posting 500 Bills," "Lewis Hayden for Julia Smith funeral of her child $20," "Lewis Hayden furniture for Jane Wilson & children."[36]

Other blacks whose names appeared frequently in the financial records were William C. Nell, Joshua B. Smith, and Reverend Leonard Grimes. The financial records also name dozens of less well-known black residents who boarded fugitives in their homes—persons such as Isabella Holmes, daughter of Father Snowden, Boston's senior black minister; Peter Randolph, a member of a family of slaves who had been freed and brought to Boston to settle in 1847; and Mrs. Charles Williams, wife of a fugitive who had fled to Canada. Undoubtedly, too, there were other blacks who helped fugitives but did not seek reimbursement, or received it second hand, from the Vigilance Committee treasury.

To a writer for the *Boston Daily Bee*, the whole Faneuil Hall meeting for Boston's fugitive slaves had been " 'Much Ado About Nothing' ": "OF-FICE—PLACE—POWER—MONEY . . . are the only objects of the white men who took part in the meeting last night."[37] The *Boston Daily Courier*, eager to have another reason to denounce abolitionist hysterics, agreed. "Slave-catchers are among us, forsooth!" scoffed the paper. "Nobody . . . has seen any such animal."[38] But the *Bee* and *Courier* writers grossly underestimated the intensity of Southern feelings toward Boston. Boston held a uniquely symbolic place in the Southern imagination. That Boston should thrive by trading with the South was galling; that Boston provided a base of operations for rabid abolitionists like William Lloyd Garrison (Virginia Governor John Lloyd typically had referred to him as "that fiend") was maddening.[39]

Given the Southern obsession with Boston, an attempt on Shadrach Minkins or another Boston fugitive was practically inevitable. Moderate Southerners wanted a successful prosecution to prove that the North would cooperate with the South. "It is with them [the Bostonians] to decide the question," the *Baltimore Sun* pronounced. Whatever happened in Boston would "give tone to public sentiment in all the northern states on this subject."[40] Southern extremists eager for more evidence that secession was the only alternative hoped for a failure in Boston. The law, they claimed, was a subterfuge, a mere magician's trick, with no substance to it. The Compromise was one more Northern "aggression," one more nail in the coffin of slavery willingly hammered in by Southerners themselves.

The self-interest of New York and Boston merchants and their allies also made a Boston case practically inevitable. Stung as much by Southern talk about boycotting Northern goods as by threats of disunion, they seemed eager to send a conciliatory message—in the form of a remanded slave—to the South. No Compromise supporter yearned more for a successful outcome in Boston or believed he stood to gain more personally from the new Fugitive Slave Law than Daniel Webster. His final chance to gain the presidency and to be the nation's savior rested on it. Over the next seven months the aging secretary of state and his supporters would labor hard to grease the gears of the new national machinery for reclaiming fugitive slaves.

The *Boston Bee* and *Courier* writers who dismissed the fears of the city's black community also ignored history. Even under the old, weak Fugitive Slave Law of 1793, which often allowed state courts and officers to block rendition, fugitive slaves had been seized in Boston, although none had been returned through official action. In 1793 a fugitive was arrested but managed to escape from confinement in a Boston courtroom, and in 1823 another avoided rendition, though by what means is unknown. In 1836 two black women, Eliza Small and Polly Ann Bates, were seized as fugitive slaves aboard a vessel lying at anchor in Boston Harbor and kept in confinement on the ship. Judge Lemuel Shaw, ruling that the captain had no right to convert his ship into a prison, released the two from custody. Before the owner could attempt to arrest the pair under the 1793 law, a black crowd surrounded the two women, carried them into the street, and put them in a carriage that whisked them off to safety. The pro-South press sputtered and fumed, but the fugitives and their rescuers were never caught.[41]

Two other early Boston fugitive slave cases, one in 1842 and the other in 1846, created much turmoil. The 1842 case of George Latimer, like Shadrach Minkins a fugitive from Norfolk, Virginia, was the most famous of Boston's pre-1850 cases. Hidden with his wife in the hold of a ship, Latimer had fled to Boston via Baltimore and Philadelphia. Within days of arriving in Boston he had the great misfortune of encountering a white employee of his master's and, in consequence, was soon arrested.[42] Latimer's case was attended by an extraordinary outpouring of sympathy and anger. A committee organized his legal defense, a "monster" petition was passed about, and even a newspaper, the *Latimer Journal and North Star*, was published to support his cause. A guard of black citizens watched over the place where Latimer was confined to prevent his being removed by the owner. Finally, fearing (apparently rightly) that Boston blacks would stop at nothing to keep him from removing his slave from the state, the Norfolk owner sold Latimer his freedom for the bargain-basement price of $400, barely one-quarter of what he had originally demanded. It was a triumph of sorts for Boston's antislavery forces, and a meeting of Norfolk citizens raised an outraged cry of protest.[43]

Four years after the Latimer case, abolitionists learned that another fugitive, name unknown, was confined aboard a ship in Boston Harbor but were unable to prevent the ship from sailing. In anger and anguish, they formed the first Boston Vigilance Committee. A record book kept by the committee agent contains the stories of nineteen blacks who applied to the committee for legal and financial aid over a five-month period. Most of the nineteen—one of whom was strongly suspected of being an imposter—were newly arrived from the South, principally Virginia. The agent's records break off in 1847, an indication that in the absence of new attempts to arrest fugitive slaves, the Vigilance Committee lost its momentum and dissolved.[44]

For Shadrach Minkins and Boston's other blacks, the lesson of this history of fugitive cases was that Southerners had come to Boston before, and would undoubtedly come again, to recover their slaves. George Latimer had been "rescued" from reenslavement only through purchase, and it was not hard to imagine that under slightly different circumstances— the new Fugitive Slave Law, for instance—he would have found himself returned to his master in Norfolk. Boston's blacks knew that the abolitionists were not in power—were not even a majority. They knew that the city was the center of Unionist sentiment in the state. They knew that most of Boston's federal officials were Webster men. And they knew that passing resolutions against the Fugitive Slave Law was one thing, but preventing the law from operating successfully was another.

On October 14, the same day that the Boston Vigilance Committee was formed, Daniel Webster, now secretary of state, passed through Boston. He had meant to "meet the People," as he liked to say, but ill health forced him to proceed directly to his estate at Marshfield. Undoubtedly, too, he knew his presence in Boston at this time would only incite his opponents. "The Abolitionists, & the quasi-Abolitionists are furious," he wrote to President Fillmore. "Their only topic at present is the Fugitive Slave Law; & their conduct in this respect is wicked & abominable in the extreme. Their press only recommends resistance, by force, & to the death, in the case of any arrest."[45]

Webster had never been able to understand the violent attacks on him for his support of the Compromise and the Fugitive Slave Law. Now he was especially exasperated because it seemed that the great opportunities presented by the Compromise were being wrenched from his grasp by the very Massachusetts Whigs who should have been looking to him for direction and guidance. In the letter to Fillmore he poured out his resentment. The Massachusetts Whig Party, he wrote bitterly, "is at this moment sorely afflicted by *three* priests, yea *four,* who have gradually run, or are now running into extravagant abolitionism." This had happened, he reasoned, because the men who had come into politics were not practical men, not political men. "For practical, useful, conservative measures of government, they care not," lamented Webster. Their "higher law" politics were "merely politics of opinion; their controversies, controversies of sentiment." They worried over such questions as "Is slavery scriptural, or antiscriptural?" or "Does the color of the skin affect the rights of the individual enveloped in it?" Webster dismissed all such "philosophizing" contemptuously. To him and to his conservative Whig friends such as Rufus Choate, such talk was womanish, even immoral, in its refusal to face the responsibility of preserving the peace and safety of the Union through compromise.[46]

Although he still enjoyed the devotion of many supporters in his home state and throughout the nation, Webster now seemed besieged and afflicted at every turn by stings and slights and betrayals. "The Postmaster at Lowell is represented to be a brawling abolitionist," Webster wrote the president irritably from his Franklin, New Hampshire, farm. "I shall inquire into this, when I return to Boston."[47] Even arranging a dinner at his Marshfield home could lead to an insult that would be trumpeted across the nation. According to a story that appeared in newspapers as far away as New Orleans, when Webster requested the Revere House in Boston to send six cooks to prepare a feast at his home for the Turkish sultan, the cooks—all blacks—refused. The cooks were reported to have said they would "see him in hell first."[48]

What made all of this even more frustrating to Webster was that he believed the abolitionist fear of the Fugitive Slave Law to be mere histrionics. "No case of arrest had happened, & few, if any are likely to happen," he wrote Fillmore. Despite this disclaimer, however, Webster and his friends in Boston, and Fillmore and others in and out of the administration in Washington, were busy trying to clarify the vagaries of the new law in anticipation of new cases. Attorney General John Crittenden had already concluded that habeas corpus, the ancient and venerable protection against illegal confinement, could legally be denied in fugitive slave cases.[49] On October 15 Charles Pelham Curtis, a prominent Boston lawyer and a close Webster associate whose brother, George T. Curtis, was a new Fugitive Slave Law commissioner, wrote Webster asking him to clarify the extent of the commissioner's authority ("Is the Commissioner's court an inferior Court?" he asked). Curtis also wanted to know what legal standing a commissioner's judgment had.[50] Clearly, supporters of the law in Boston, in consultation with Webster, were attempting to prepare for *something*.

Meanwhile fugitive slaves from farther south kept pouring in—reportedly 100 or more in the month since the Hamlet case in New York at the end of September. The Vigilance Committee busied itself trying to find employment for the many who had "no present means of subsistence."[51] The stage was set for the first Boston test of the new Fugitive Slave Law. It would prove to be a drama the likes of which had not been seen since the campaign to free George Latimer in 1842. The result would not turn out to be quite what Daniel Webster had hoped for.

6 "Much Excitement Prevails"

On Saturday, October 19, three men—Willis Hughes, John Knight, and Alfred Beal—arrived in Boston from Macon, Georgia, and took rooms at the United States Hotel on Beach Street opposite the Worcester Railway terminal. Hughes, a Macon jailer, was seeking to recover the fugitive slave couple William and Ellen Craft for prosperous Macon businessman Robert Collins. Beal was apparently on the trail of a fugitive slave named Jones and possibly other fugitives.

The third man, John Knight, had accompanied Hughes from Macon but later claimed to be merely a businessman who had come to Boston to buy machinery "for the establishment of a bucket factory." Knight said he had learned of Hughes's mission only after they had arrived in New York. Given that Knight's partner in the proposed "Bucket Factory and Variety Works" was Willis Hughes, this claim is unlikely. In addition, Knight knew both Crafts well, having once worked with William Craft in a cabinet shop in Macon. Hughes, who knew neither of the Crafts personally, obviously needed Knight to point out the two to officers and to verify the identity of the fugitive couple in court— if matters ever got that far.[1]

The man behind this effort to test the Fugitive Slave Law, Robert Collins, was a staunch Whig-Unionist leader, and by many measures a progressive.[2] He had holdings of thousands of acres in and around Macon and had been a major force in developing both Macon's railroad and telegraph systems. As a slave-owner he prided himself on his advanced views on slave management. His 1852 prize essay on the management of slaves would recommend, among other things, that intermarriage between slaves of different estates ought not to be forbidden but should be discouraged, not only because it could lead to difficulties but also because the couple "cannot live together as they ought, and are constantly liable to separation, in the changing of property."[3] At his death in 1861 Collins would leave an estate with 102 slaves valued at nearly half a million dollars.[4]

Even before Willis Hughes attempted to seize William and Ellen Craft in Boston as Collins' property, they were famous for their legendary escape in 1848. The light-skinned Ellen, daughter of a liaison between a wealthy planter and a slave, had dressed herself up as a white male plantation owner, ostensibly on his way to the North for medical treatment. To conceal her smooth cheeks, she tied a scarf around her mouth, feigning a toothache. Knowing that she would be asked to sign papers to obtain tickets (she was illiterate and could not even sign her name), the couple pretended that Ellen suffered from acute arthritis and tied a poultice around her hand. Her husband, William, much darker-complected, played the role of the devoted slave. He answered inquiries, purchased

William and Ellen Craft, the first fugitive slaves pursued in Boston under the 1850 Fugitive Slave Law.

railway tickets, made excuses, and generally fussed and fawned over "Massa" in an approved and thoroughly convincing fashion.[5]

Despite a few heart-stopping moments when disclosure appeared imminent, the Crafts' scheme worked beautifully, and they traveled on the trains from Georgia to Philadelphia virtually unmolested. There they revealed themselves, to the delight and adulation of Philadelphia abolitionists. For a time they were the darlings of the antislavery lecture circuit in the United States and England, where they were sent for several months. Their remarkable story guaranteed audiences as well as sympathy and revenues for abolitionist coffers. Their notoriety, however, also made them vulnerable. Back in the United States, it was no longer considered safe for them to travel on lecture tours. For security, they went north to Boston and moved into Lewis Hayden's house on Southac Street as boarders. A skilled carpenter, Craft soon was operating his own furnituremaking and repair business in a shop on Cambridge Street. In the 1850 census he estimated his gross income at $700, his tools and inventory at $130. He had even been able to take on an assistant.[6] Ellen worked as a seamstress.

From a Webster-Union point of view, the attempt to return the Crafts to slavery was a poor choice for testing the new Fugitive Slave Law. The Crafts were intelligent, self-reliant, and independent—hardly the simple, benighted, dependent slaves of Southern mythology. In Boston William had rapidly risen to a position of leadership in the black community. When Boston blacks assembled at the end of September to organize against the Fugitive Slave Law, he was chosen one of the vice-presidents of the meeting. Ellen's almost-white complexion, ladylike appearance, and skill hardly matched Southern depictions of their slaves. For a Southerner to attempt to lay claim to these resourceful, hard-working, intelligent residents of Boston and to force them back into slavery seemed an outrage against the fundamental republican ideology on which the United States rested.

Willis Hughes remained in his hotel room on Saturday and Sunday. On Monday morning he approached federal officers with his request for assistance, and from that moment Hughes would begin to suspect that the abolitionist boast that no fugitive could be returned from Boston was true.[7] To be successful, Hughes needed secrecy and speed. The events of the last week of October were to prove that neither of these would be possible. From

Boston's federal officials he would get little more than excuses, denials, and delays. His requests would make them squirm—many knew that it was political suicide to have their names associated with the prosecution of a fugitive slave. They supported the Fugitive Slave Law and Daniel Webster in principle, but no one wanted the certain notoriety of being the first to put the machinery of the new law into operation against a Boston fugitive.

Applying first to Judge Levi Woodbury, of the U.S. Circuit Court, Hughes was summarily rebuffed. Woodbury sent Hughes to see George Lunt, the U.S. district attorney, who gave him the lame excuse of being too involved in another case and too wary of fugitive slave cases. "A disgrace to his country, his profession, and his office," Hughes later declared of Lunt. Hughes was then sent to see Benjamin Hallett, one of the U.S. commissioners in Boston, but Hallett bluntly refused to sign his name to an arrest warrant. According to Hughes, Hallett advised him to arrest the Crafts without a warrant and bring them before him—a recommendation Hughes knew to be ludicrous. No Southerner could simply seize a fugitive slave on the streets of Boston without drawing a crowd and perhaps risking his life.

After being stymied by Boston's indecisive and evasive federal officialdom and wasting precious days, Hughes finally secured the legal services of Seth J. Thomas, "Colonel" Thomas as he was known after his brief service in the Massachusetts infantry in the 1830s. A friend of Webster, whose office was near his own, Thomas was regarded as "an eminently safe lawyer, conscientious in the preparation . . . and fair in the presentation."[8] Accompanied by Thomas, Hughes went before Judge Peleg Sprague, of the U.S. District Court for Massachusetts, but found nothing more than "the same tortuous, twisting, shuffling, contemptible evasion." Finally, after many hours of fruitless efforts, Hughes and Thomas went before George T. Curtis, another U.S. commissioner. Curtis also "desired time to conquer this abstruse and difficult subject," as Hughes noted with contempt, but finally agreed to call a meeting of the commissioners and judges that night to discuss what course to pursue. At the meeting, Curtis and the others decided to issue the warrant, but with the stipulation that it be issued in open court on complaint of the claimant.

On Friday morning, October 25, after a full week of running from office to office, Hughes appeared in the federal courtroom to obtain the warrant.[9] The opportunity to have the Crafts arrested quietly and their case heard quickly had long since passed. Hughes's mission had already been published in a Macon newspaper by the time he arrived in Boston, and on Tuesday Knight visited Craft in his shop. It is also possible that information about Hughes's attempts to secure warrants was leaked early in the week by an abolitionist in District Attorney Lunt's office. But when the warrant was issued on Friday in open court, naming both claimant and fugitive, all of Boston and all of the nation were in on the secret. By Saturday newspapers were carrying the electric news that the Fugitive Slave Law was about to have its first test in Boston. One version, published in the Norfolk *American Beacon*, read:

> Boston, Oct. 25.—The U.S. Marshal in this city has now in his possession warrants for the arrest of a large number of fugitive slaves.
>
> Much excitement prevails among the negro population. The court-house has been surrounded by them all the morning. According to accounts they are determined to resist, even to the shedding of blood, any attempt at carrying back to slavery their colored brethren. A negro named Latimer, who has resided here three or four years, has been pointed out by his master. The impression is that serious consequences will follow if an attempt be made to arrest him. It is said that several arrests have been already made secretly, and that one or more are in prison in Leveritt street. The Judge [Sprague] was interrogated this morning in reference to the subject by negroes and their abettors, but he would not answer pro or con.[10]

Whether or not warrants were in fact issued against "a large number" of fugitives, only three persons were ever named. One was William Jones, a waiter at the Parker House who had apparently already left for Canada.[11] The other two were William and Ellen Craft.[12]

With news that the warrants were in the U.S. marshal's hands, Boston's blacks reportedly were "mustering strongly" in readiness to effect a rescue in the event of an arrest.[13] Because the Crafts were so well known, frustrating the attempt on their freedom was crucial. If Southern owners could seize the Crafts, then the ordinary anonymous fugitive was doubly endangered. So the black community rallied. Even before the warrant could be delivered to the marshal, Hughes complained later, a man was standing on a dry-goods box outside the Court House urging fugitives and their friends to arm themselves with pistols and daggers and talking of murdering all slavecatchers. The crowd grew to a thousand or more.

Members of the crowd constantly passed in and out of the marshal's office, and the marshal's every move was watched.[14]

On the evening after the warrants were issued for the Crafts, Boston's blacks and some friends, including Charles Lenox Remond of Salem's black community, met at the Belknap Street Church to prepare for united resistance. Their first two resolutions, unanimously adopted, left no doubt about their intentions:

> *Resolved,* That God willed us free; Man willed us Slaves. We will as God wills; God's will be done.
>
> *Resolved,* That our oft repeated determination to resist oppression is the same now as ever—and we pledge ourselves at all hazards, to resist unto death, any attempt upon our liberties.[15]

The Boston Vigilance Committee was busy campaigning in support of the Crafts. Its members posted 300 handbills describing Hughes and Knight throughout the city. Vigilance Committee escorts dogged the Georgians' steps everywhere. Lawyers on the legal committee harassed them by filing complaint after complaint. Hughes and Knight found themselves arrested so often for offenses ranging from the serious to the ridiculous that one newspaper joked about the arrests as a twice-daily dosage. They were arrested for slandering William Craft and injuring his business (Hughes had said that William Craft had stolen the clothes he escaped in), for carrying concealed weapons, for smoking in the street, even for swearing in the street.[16]

Emerging from the court one day after being arrested for attempted kidnapping, Hughes and Knight found themselves surrounded by an angry crowd of 2,000 (in Knight's estimate), the majority of them black. When Hughes tried to escape in a carriage, the crowd made a rush, precipitating a mad chase through the streets. The Georgian escaped, only to be arrested again—for driving too fast and for "running the toll when chased over Cambridge bridge." Once more they had to be bailed out by pro-South sympathizers—for another $10,000 each.[17] On the afternoon of the same day, while a great crowd had gathered around the Boston Court House, a warrant for slandering Ellen Craft and injuring her business was served on the two men. They escaped being mobbed only through the help of the arresting officer, who allowed them to remain at their hotel while their bail was arranged.[18]

The whole affair had the slapstick air of a folk morality play, with Hughes and Knight unwillingly playing the part of the black-hatted villains. Spirits were high among the Vigilance Committee members and Boston's blacks. The Southerners were being made fools of while Boston's federal and local authorities stood by, apparently doing the least they could, under the law, to help the slave hunt.

The legal committee of the Boston Vigilance Committee further complicated matters for the claimants on other fronts. First, they threatened to raise thorny technical legal questions. According to reports published in several newspapers, they threatened to contest the authority of any commissioner or marshal's officer who participated in an actual arrest and to try to wrest the case from federal jurisdiction. One strategy was to serve the marshal with a writ *de homine replegiando,* which required a hearing in a state court, the moment that an arrest was made. The legal committee also planned to charge William Craft with nonpayment of debt or, if he resisted arrest by the federal officers, to have him arrested under state law for violent assault. All these strategies were designed to get him out of the federal marshal's hands and into the hands of sympathetic Massachusetts officials after an arrest had been made.[19] As Massachusetts law did not recognize slavery, state officials would release the Crafts, and they could escape.

The legal committee's most effective strategy may have been what prevented William and Ellen Craft from ever getting into the marshal's hands in the first place. This strategy exploited the fact that fugitive slave cases were civil rather than criminal cases. Committee lawyers planned to argue that because it was a civil case, the marshal had no authority to break through the "outer door" of a house to arrest the Crafts. Committee lawyers warned the marshal, Charles Devens, that they would bring suit against him if he exceeded his authority one iota.[20] Devens, himself a lawyer, was reportedly told by Judge Peleg Sprague that the Vigilance Committee lawyers were essentially correct as to the law.[21] Devens had no liking for the duties imposed on him by the law and no desire to do more than the law actually required of him. He was an intelligent man, later a distinguished lawyer, Civil War general, and statesman. He had to know that becoming a tool for Daniel Webster and the faltering pro-South Whigs of Massachusetts would haunt him later. Devens also had to worry about risking his life and the lives of his men in a violent assault on William Craft's stronghold.

Under the threat of prosecution at the slightest misstep, Devens proceeded cautiously—incompetently, the owner of the Crafts would charge, although Webster later described him as "very well disposed, but . . . not entirely efficient," and the U.S. attorney general would conclude only that "a more commendable activity might probably have been exerted."[22] At first Devens resisted serving the warrant, citing conflicting reports about the Crafts' whereabouts. Later, when William Craft was known to be barricaded inside his carpentry shop, the marshal apparently went to serve the warrants, but when Craft refused to admit the officers, Devens returned quietly to his office with his mission uncompleted.

While the Georgians had been trying to wrest a warrant from Boston's reluctant federal officials, William Craft and his friends were organizing for violent resistance. Throughout the ordeal, Craft remained "cool and resolute," one friend reported.[23] When a Boston sympathizer suggested that the couple should submit to arrest and then allow Bostonians to purchase their freedom, Craft flatly refused the idea.[24] He armed himself with an arsenal of weapons—a revolver, pistols large and small, and knives—and insisted on going about his daily routine as usual. Only with difficulty had friends finally persuaded him to send his wife to a safe location and to keep out of sight himself. He would not hide, however. He merely moved his clothing and his bed into his carpenter's shop and waited, ready to resist the officers to the death.[25]

Visitors to Craft's carpentry shop on Cambridge Street reported that it was as heavily guarded as any fortress. No one could approach within a hundred yards of the shop "without being seen by a hundred eyes," wrote the *New York Daily Tribune* correspondent. According to the *Pennsylvania Freeman*'s Boston correspondent, the entire West End in the Sixth Ward had been turned into a fortified arsenal: "Many of the houses in Belknap and Cambridge streets are provided with ammunition . . . Swords and dirks, &c, are plenty, and bayonets 'right up.' "[26]

For a time, the parties remained at a standoff. The marshal's men reconnoitered but found that Craft was heavily guarded behind his locked door. Ellen, who had at first been hidden at the house of Unitarian minister Theodore Parker, was moved to a safer location outside the city. At the most perilous moment, Craft reportedly moved to Lewis Hayden's house, where "a band of brave colored men [were] armed to the teeth" and gunpowder kegs in the basement threatened the marshal's forces with immediate annihilation; Craft was also moved at least briefly to "the South End of Boston" for safety.[27] Meanwhile excited crowds continued their vigil around the Court House and the Georgians' hotel, eager to partici- pate in the sport of slavecatcher-baiting. "Slave-hunters, slave-hunters! there goes the slave-hunters!" rang out the cry whenever Hughes or Knight appeared on the street.[28]

Finally, on Wednesday, October 30, a delegation of Vigilance Commit- tee members led by Theodore Parker, the chairman of the executive board, visited the two Georgians at their rooms in the United States Hotel. Parker told them that "they were not safe in Boston another night."[29] Hughes and Knight knew when they had had enough. Between the foot- dragging of federal and local officials and the harassment by the Vigilance Committee, the Georgians had had their fill of frustration and humiliation and were glad for an excuse to make their exit. They promised to leave immediately but delayed a day. Perhaps Hughes hoped for reinforce- ments, but it is more likely that the scrappy Georgian merely wanted to avoid the impression that he had been frightened into retreat. Neverthe- less, on November 1 he and Knight left Boston on the New York train. Hughes vowed that he had not given up, but after spending a few days in New York, he learned that the Crafts had left Boston for an unknown destination.

For Boston abolitionists, the effort to save William and Ellen Craft was an unqualified triumph. The Crafts were safe; no blood had been shed; the Fugitive Slave Law had been evaded without serious incident; Boston's federal officials, short of resigning their offices outright, could hardly have acted more favorably toward the fugitives. "Everybody satisfied—and yet the law not executed, while nobody is 'to blame,' " wrote Charles Sumner's abolitionist friend Gamaliel Bailey, slyly professing himself "mystified" at this result. Of the political outcome, however, Bailey had no doubts: "You have whipped Webster, and turned Massachusetts right side up," he exulted. "You are a glorious set of fellows."[30]

But Webster was not willing to concede himself whipped. By November 15 he had been in the city many days trying "to put this business of the attempt to arrest Crafts into a better shape," as he wrote to Fillmore from Boston in a letter marked "private & confidential."[31] Webster did not know that he was too late. A week before, the Vigilance Committee had sent the Crafts secretly to Portland, Maine, and from there to Nova Scotia and St. John, New Brunswick, where they boarded a steamer for Liverpool. For many years thereafter the Crafts enjoyed the protection of the British crown. They made many successful speaking tours, received an education, and were feted by nobility. Their lives in Britain, chronicled in stories and letters printed in the abolitionist press, became a standing rebuke to the United States.[32]

What Webster did know was that he was struggling for his national program of reconciliation and for his political life. And in his view, both were being piddled away by irresolution and incompetence. After arriving in Boston, he could scarcely keep his temper at the messy state of affairs he met with. "The general weight of U.S. officers in this district is *against* the execution of the Fugitive Slave Law," Webster complained bitterly to the president. He had called on Charles Devens to execute the law or make his reasons public. District Attorney Lunt, whom Webster detested, had made him boil. Not only had Lunt acted "cowardly" by refusing to advise the claimant, but he had "no talent, no fitness for his place, and no very good disposition." Nor did the claimants escape Webster's censure. Hughes the agent "has used no very great discretion, and has acted clumsily," Webster reported.[33]

The whole state of affairs was a great defeat for Webster's hopes, the greater still because his Boston friends had let him down. One of Webster's greatest boosters, George T. Curtis, as well as other Whig officials, had acted timidly when decisiveness was required. If only his friends had seized the opportunity, the law might have been executed according to his conception, and Webster might have found himself lionized as the savior of the Union. Now, amid the accusations and recriminations, the excuses and criticism, he seemed like a bumbler. About the best he could do on the legal front was to try to see that prosecutions were begun against those responsible for the Crafts' escape. In this, too, he would fail.

An antiabolitionist outburst on the same day Webster wrote of putting things "into a better shape" seemed to confirm his hopes. On the evening of November 15 an abolitionist crowd had gathered at Faneuil Hall. The occasion was to be a grand celebration, full of speeches and tributes, welcoming British abolitionist George Thompson back to Boston. It was

Thompson's first visit since an ill-fated appearance in 1835, when a mob of "gentlemen of property and standing" had broken up an abolitionist meeting and, failing to find the British interloper, nearly lynched William Lloyd Garrison in Thompson's stead.

This time Thompson's reception was less violent but not much different in other respects. The Faneuil Hall crowd was soon infiltrated by a band of rowdies intent upon disrupting the proceedings. The meeting opened calmly enough, with election of officers and a welcoming address by Garrison. Boston in 1850 was not the Boston of 1835, Garrison told the crowd, and they responded with cheers. But before Garrison had finished, "a stream of men 5 or 6 abreast," according to one observer, had begun to pour in at the door. The noise of this advancing phalanx made it impossible for many in the audience to hear. At first Garrison appeared not to have noticed the invasion, although Caroline Dall, sitting in the balcony, reported that their entry occupied a full ten minutes.[34]

After Garrison sat down, Wendell Phillips stepped forward and tried to make himself heard above the din made by the intruders. From her seat in the balcony Caroline Dall could see men advancing toward the platform in a wedge, then two wedges, only to be stopped by the crowd occupying the front. Fights broke out, accompanied by "riotous yells and confusion." Dall remembered afterward that a "familiar whistle" seemed to be the signal for successive rushes toward the stage. As the intruders regrouped after each new assault was repulsed, they gave three cheers for Daniel Webster—and, according to another account, for the Union, Governor Briggs, and the Continental Congress. On the platform, Phillips, growing hoarse trying to outdo the boisterous hecklers, was compelled to retire to his seat. One after another the scheduled speakers stepped forward, opened their mouths, and were met with such a din that each was forced to follow Phillips into retreat. Thompson, Frederick Douglass, William F. Channing, Theodore Parker—none could make themselves heard above the clamor. Douglass, who "was hissed and hooted in a very uproarious manner," had to retire "amid a shower of little missiles." Finally, the lights were turned down. Someone, perhaps the Boston police chief, stepped forward, declared the meeting dissolved, and ordered the people to disperse.[35] Thompson was once again forced to make his escape amid tumultuous noise and chaos.[36] Afterward the abolitionists charged that the police had colluded in disrupting the meeting.

There is no evidence to connect Webster and his friends directly to the Faneuil Hall incident. It is unlikely that Webster personally had a hand in planning or approving the disruption or even knew of the plan. But if Caroline Dall is correct, the rowdies were following someone's orders, and it is reasonable to suspect someone in the Webster camp.

Following the Thompson meeting, Webster and his friends took steps to rally support and to rechannel public opinion. A meeting of Boston's wealthy and powerful friends of the Union had been in the works for some weeks. The meeting, one of many such scheduled in major cities, was designed to create a groundswell of popular sentiment for the Union-Whigs and, possibly, a Union party. In Boston, Fugitive Slave Law Commissioner George T. Curtis had taken the lead in arranging for speakers, circulating a petition, and otherwise superintending the details.[37] It was to be a grand demonstration to the nation of Boston's fidelity to the Compromise—or servility to the South, as the abolitionists insisted.

All was in readiness for the November 26 show. For the Webster camp, the timing could not have been more opportune. To many law-and-order men in Boston and throughout the nation, the hounding of the Crafts' pursuers made Boston abolitionists look like villains—arrogant, abusive, reckless of the law.

The Union meeting took place at Faneuil Hall, Boston's "Cradle of Liberty," an irony gleefully seized on by the abolitionist papers. All the Webster Union-Whigs turned out, the same prominent Boston businessmen, lawyers, and even ministers who had signed the petition supporting Webster and Compromise the previous spring.[38] They filled Faneuil Hall with talk of saving the failing Union with Compromise medicine. Most of the speakers lashed out against abolitionist fanaticism.

The most chilling words spoken at the Union meeting were uttered not in anger but in mild tones. They were the words of Benjamin Robbins Curtis, an eminent Boston lawyer who was to be appointed to the U.S. Supreme Court within a year. Fugitive slaves, proclaimed Curtis, were "strangers." They had invaded the sovereign soil of Massachusetts without invitation. "With the rights of those persons I firmly believe Massachusetts has nothing to do . . . they have no right to be *here*. Our peace and safety they have no right to invade."[39] Though admitting that fugitive slaves had natural rights, Curtis reduced them to the status of foreign intruders. This was a horrendous departure from Massachusetts and U.S. legal traditions, an assault on the most basic liberties upon which the nation had been built. It was, nevertheless, the view of human rights called for in the Fugitive Slave Law, a view that would be echoed a few years later in the Supreme Court's Dred Scott decision (from which Curtis, in an about-face, strongly dissented and which led to his resignation from the Court).[40]

Webster himself was not on hand at the Union meeting to hear Curtis' ominous words. The secretary of state had retired from the scene to Washington so that new voices could be heard on the subject ("my opinions are well known," he wrote). Webster also apparently wanted the Boston meeting to have the appearance of a "spontaneous" upwelling of pro-Union, pro–Fugitive Slave Law sentiment.[41] "The world is filled with the fame of your great meeting," he wrote excitedly on December 8 to one of its organizers.[42] By then he had been seeking to exploit the meeting for over a week. "The resolutions, & the speeches are admirable," he wrote enthusiastically to his friend and backer Peter Harvey on November 29, three days after the meeting. "Print 50,000 copies of the whole proceedings, speeches & all, & send 20,000 here for distribution in the South. Nothing can do half so much good."[43]

From Webster's point of view, there were many reasons for optimism. "There is an evident, & a vast change of public opinion in this quarter," he had written sanguinely to Fillmore upon reaching Boston on November 5. The Union meeting had flashed the Boston-Unionist message to the nation and at least temporarily laid to rest the city's exclusive association with "mad abolitionism." Mention of Webster's name had been "greeted with loud and long continued cheering," according to the papers.[44] Hundreds of men, Webster reported, had volunteered to assist the marshal in enforcing the Fugitive Slave Law.[45] Georgian John Knight had already testified that Boston public opinion was turning in favor of enforcing the law. Although "businessmen, and men of property generally took little interest in the matter, but said that the law ought to be executed," Knight was convinced that "if it came to a trial of strength, the negroes and abolitionists would be put down."[46] In his annual message President Fillmore expressed his confidence that "the great majority of our fellow-citizens . . . in the main approve, and are prepared, in all respects, to sustain" the Fugitive Slave Law.[47]

Others knew better. "It is out of the question to awaken any *feeling* in favor of such a law. It is a great folly on the part of the South to ask for it;

for the moment it is stringently enforced, it becomes inoperative . . . unless the South has the sense & the grace to yield to the general conscience of mankind on this subject, the union is gone."[48] So wrote Webster's friend Edward Everett to him on December 9 before thinking better and canceling the passage. Its milder substitute merely expressed sorrow at the South's conduct and so saved his beleaguered friend's feelings. There was no sense in wasting ink on a point Daniel Webster had become unable to accept, let alone comprehend. His mind was made up; his course was set. The law would be made to work.

For Shadrach Minkins and Boston's other blacks, the Crafts case and the Union meeting gave increasing urgency to their fears. It was no longer a matter of whether the Fugitive Slave Law would reach to Boston. The issue now was, *when* would the next attempt on a Boston fugitive be made? In an apologetic letter to the Crafts' owner, President Fillmore seemed to promise the trial of strength to which Knight had referred. Although Fillmore had not ordered additional troops to Boston immediately, he promised to use all the federal force that was necessary to execute the law in the city.[49]

Boston's fugitive slaves, mere "strangers" according to Benjamin R. Curtis, were justified in feeling themselves increasingly estranged and frightened. A rumor circulated that as many as 600 federal troops were being sent to Boston to aid the marshal.[50] Another claimed that the pro-Union forces were raising a fund to assist agents to reclaim slaves and to compensate owners for their risks.[51] If these rumors were true, the fugitives' defense was entering a new phase. Resisting individual owners, operating independently, was one thing; resisting a conspiracy of owners and Northerners, aided by a standing army, was another.

Shadrach Minkins and the other Boston fugitives waited uneasily for affairs to settle down. Some of them even chose to do their waiting at a safe distance from the city. According to a later account, Minkins himself fled from the city about this time, although he almost certainly returned shortly afterward.[52]

In a matter of weeks, new attempts would prove that the fears of fugitives and their friends were more than justified. The first, which occurred at the end of November, was an unusual case involving Cornelius

Sparrow, a free black from Norfolk who had fled North, and a female slave who had fled with him. Instead of trying to arrest the fugitive woman, the owner, merchant Aaron Milhado, attempted to use the threat of arrest—applied by letter from Norfolk—to force Sparrow and the fugitive to pay for her freedom. It was a long shot on Milhado's part, and amounted to nothing less than blackmail.

Milhado's plan might have worked. It involved using—in fact bribing—the U.S. marshal to play the part of the heavy. To "avoid a confrontation," Milhado adopted a simple expedient of writing to Charles Devens to ask him to recover $650, the supposed value of the woman. The Norfolk merchant probably hoped that Devens' delicate position would work to his advantage. Because Devens was still under suspicion for alleged dereliction of duty in the Crafts case, he might willingly seize the opportunity to assist in this one and restore himself to the good graces of his federal employers. As an additional inducement to cooperation, Milhado promised Devens that if he were successful, he could keep $200 for himself.[53]

Milhado calculated wrong. A lawyer by training, Devens knew that the procedure outlined in the Fugitive Slave Act was for the recovery of the *body* of a fugitive slave; nothing was said about the recovery of the *value* of a fugitive. In addition, Milhado had not sent any legal documents or obtained a warrant. The marshal knew, therefore, that he had no obligation under the law whatever, and, as in the Crafts case, he was very careful not to exceed his authority. He (or Deputy Marshal Riley) did contact Cornelius Sparrow, with whom the woman was living (some reports said she and Sparrow were married) to inform him of the request that had been made by the woman's alleged owner. Later Sparrow called at the marshal's office and was advised to consult with Robert Morris, the black attorney, who told him to ignore the owner's request. Afterward, according to reports, Devens wrote Milhado a note explaining that acting as the slave-owner's agent was incompatible with his official duties. "A glaring instance where a gentleman was surreptitiously deprived of his property," fumed the Norfolk *Southern Argus*.[54]

Notification by the marshal's office alerted Cornelius Sparrow and the woman and gave her time to go into hiding. Vigilance Committee records show that within three months Sparrow "& wife" were sent to Halifax, Nova Scotia, for their safety.[55] But Milhado's attempt gave renewed warning to all Boston's fugitives. As long as there was an active case of any sort involving a fugitive slave in Boston, all fugitives seemed more vulnerable.

For Shadrach Minkins, the Sparrow case, involving as it did a Norfolk fugitive like himself, undoubtedly raised new fears. The case would have been the subject of much debate in Boston's black community, and almost certainly Minkins knew the Norfolk woman sought by Milhado. And although it was reassuring that the woman had not been arrested, Minkins had no guarantee that she would not be—or that he was not the next target. By about this time three Norfolk merchants, William Parks, William Marcus, and William Robertson, had already seen Minkins in Boston. Parks, the commission merchant from Norfolk who gave Minkins his first job in Boston, may have informed DeBree of Minkins' whereabouts long before the Crafts case. William Robertson, a clerk from Gordon's Banking House in Norfolk, and William Marcus, a commission merchant, had also seen Minkins, perhaps at the Cornhill Coffee House or possibly on the streets, and they also could have informed DeBree.[56] We know that at least once Minkins tried to send a message to his family through William Marcus.[57] Perhaps Minkins figured that having been seen, he might as well make the best of the encounter. Perhaps he was already known to be in Boston. Or perhaps, believing himself entirely safe in Boston, he heard that Marcus was in town and, desperate to communicate with home, called on him to ask him to carry a letter to Norfolk.

Antislavery papers had warned fugitive slaves about the dangers of attempting to communicate with friends or family in the South, particularly through white Southerners. Innumerable fugitives had been located and some of them returned to slavery because, out of loneliness or worry or overconfidence or any of a dozen other motives, they had sent messages to friends and family left behind.

In January at least two more slaveowners, both from North Carolina, came to Boston attempting to recover their fugitive slaves. At least one of the slaves, a man, was known to have come north concealed in a Northern ship. According to a report from Boston, the man had found work with a sympathetic manufacturer in the city. A warrant reportedly had been issued and given to Marshal Devens.[58] The other fugitive sought in early January may have been a North Carolina woman named Elizabeth Blakeley, whose history Wendell Phillips described in an antislavery speech in 1852. According to Phillips, Blakeley had managed to get aboard a Boston-bound vessel in North Carolina, concealing herself in a narrow space barely two and a half feet wide. After surviving a thorough search of the vessel and being nearly suffocated when the vessel was "smoked," she suffered grievously from freezing temperatures during the journey, before arriving safely in Boston, probably in January 1850.[59]

The North Carolina owners met with no more success in prodding Boston's federal bureaucrats to their duty than Hughes had when pursuing the Crafts. Before Marshal Devens had a chance to arrest the fugitives, news of the owners' mission was leaked out. The story given out by Devens to one of the owners was that the slaves had fled. The owner, however, thought Devens was lying and that the slaves were hidden in the city waiting until he was gone. Several other fugitives, according to another account, had barricaded themselves inside a house. Three deputy marshals ("ruffians, cast off constables," sneered the *Commonwealth*) appeared at the house with warrants but returned empty-handed.[60] One of the Carolinians concluded that trying to recover fugitive slaves in Boston was "useless." "That part of the population not active in resisting the law, were perfectly *passive*," he charged. He was certain, however, that "a large majority of the people were in favor of executing the law."[61]

The failure of these attempts provided Shadrach Minkins and Boston's other fugitives with a glimmer of hope and not much more. The news from other Northern states was decidedly discouraging. By the second week of February there had been reports of more than 60 separate legal or extralegal attempts to recapture fugitives on Northern soil. These attempts involved more than 105 blacks, many of whose names will never be known.[62] While many of these fugitives managed to elude arrest, a number of them were captured and returned to slavery, sometimes without attracting any attention. In the first five months of the Fugitive Slave Law, slaves were returned to the South from Cincinnati, Ohio; from Quincy, Shawneetown, and Marion, Illinois; from Danville, Harrisburg, Philadelphia, and Uniontown, Pennsylvania; and from New York City. Seven were reportedly returned from an unknown location in Michigan. In Bedford, Pennsylvania, a band of as many as 10 fugitives were tracked and ambushed. Seven were returned to slavery, several were reported missing, and at least one was killed.[63]

Of the fugitives who appeared before federal judges or commissioners, only a small percentage had been released—Henry Garnet in Philadelphia; two women in Steubenville, Ohio; and a few others. A few more avoided being returned to slavery when sympathetic friends and neighbors raised money to purchase them from their owners. (In some cases, however, owners were determined to prove their rights, or were afraid of being condemned at home, and so refused to sell without first returning home with their remanded slaves.) Occasionally the hearing before the commissioner amounted to nearly a full-blown trial—though of course without a jury, without the right of the accused to testify, and without a right to habeas corpus. In the most widely reported of the cases, Henry Long was returned to Alexandria, Virginia, from New York City after a hearing lasting more than two weeks. A waiter at the Pacific Hotel, Long was seized the day before Christmas while at work. Despite an array of distinguished counsels, including John Jay, Long was taken south by federal marshals and delivered to his owner, who, insisting on making a show of his rights, not only refused Northern offers to purchase Long but sent him to the auction block in Richmond later in the month.[64]

Other fugitives were remanded to their owners by federal authorities at lightning speed with little regard for legal niceties. In December one Philadelphia black man, Adam Gibson, found himself arrested, remanded (despite testimony by persons who swore they had known Gibson in Philadelphia years before the alleged escape had taken place), and taken south only to have the alleged owner dumbfounded to see a total stranger delivered to him as his slave.[65] Gibson was still in the custody of a federal marshal when this discovery was made (marshals were responsible for delivering fugitives if a rescue was threatened and the owner requested assistance), and the two returned to Philadelphia. The outcome might have been very different if he had been in the custody of a professional slavecatcher.

Many fugitives who lived near the borders of Pennsylvania, Ohio, Indiana, and other states never saw a courtroom or a warrant but were silently kidnapped and spirited back to the South. Along the border free blacks were nearly as vulnerable as fugitive slaves. Kidnapping of free blacks had been a lucrative business for decades; the Fugitive Slave Law, together with rising slave prices, intensified it.[66] At least two gangs reportedly were kidnapping blacks along the Pennsylvania border, one near Gap (Lancaster County) and another near Chambersburg. In Harrisburg a Fugitive Slave Law commissioner named Richard McAllister and several police officers had turned part-time bounty-hunters. They spent their time searching for and rounding up every fugitive they could find, collecting their regular salaries while quietly pocketing substantial rewards offered by owners.[67] Several of the officers were later tried for kidnapping free blacks. There is strong reason to suspect that Commissioner McAllister was a party to these kidnappings, although he was never charged.

Shadrach Minkins and Boston's other fugitive slaves were lucky at least to be so far from the Mason-Dixon line. But they had learned that Boston was far from an ideal haven. The Crafts case and subsequent events had revealed the city to be a microcosm of the nation's conflicting ideologies and contradictory impulses regarding slavery and the race issue. Moreover, many Southerners longed more than ever to see a fugitive slave returned from Boston.

7 "A Thing … or a Man?"

On the occasion of his first antislavery address in August 1841, Frederick Douglass had electrified his Nantucket audience. While the cheering for Douglass echoed through the hall, William Lloyd Garrison stepped to the podium. Garrison asked only "a few simple, direct questions," of which a friend and biographer remembered the first and the last. The questions framed the issues in the most basic terms possible. "Have we been listening to a thing, a piece of property, or a man?" Garrison asked the crowd dramatically.

> "A man! A man!" shouted fully five hundred voices of men and women . . .
> "Shall such a man ever be sent back to slavery from the soil of Massachusetts?"—this time uttered with all the power of his voice . . . Almost the whole assembly sprang with one accord to their feet, and the wall and roof of the Athenaeum seemed to shudder with the "No! no!" loud and long-continued in the wild enthusiasm of the scene.[1]

In 1841 Garrison had no way of knowing then how often his boast or the resolve of the crowd was to be tested. But after the Crafts escaped in 1850, a new test in Boston was certain.

That new test was not long in coming. On the night of Wednesday, February 12, 1851, John Caphart (sometimes spelled Capehart), a constable from Norfolk, Virginia, arrived bearing owner John DeBree's legal papers and power of attorney. He quietly set about seeking a warrant to arrest Shadrach Minkins.[2]

If anyone could get a fugitive slave out of Boston, it was fifty-year-old John Caphart, a tough veteran of a rough-and-tumble seaport. In 1849, charged with brutally beating a mate on the brig *Royal,* Caphart had readily confessed to the deed, adding that he felt himself "perfectly justified" by the mate's "rudest and most insulting manner."[3] When nearing sixty, he would still be rugged enough to capture singlehanded a band of armed and extremely dangerous mutineers.[4] Caphart used his contacts and fearsome reputation as constable and nightwatchman to attract customers to his other enterprises: a private slave jail, a debt collection service (*"by warrant or otherwise"* his advertisement stated), and a slave-trading business ("highest prices given").[5] He specialized in slavecatching. "I am often employed by private persons to pursue fugitive slaves . . . I never refuse a good job of that kind," he later testified.[6] At the request of courts or owners, he had flogged many wayward slaves while they "hugged the widow" (that is, whipping post), earning fifty cents for each slave flogged.[7] The price "used to be 62 cents," Caphart noted matter-of-factly.[8]

Bostonians studied John Caphart's appearance and read much into it. Richard Henry Dana remembered that Caphart had a strong frame, "a restless dark eye, and an anxious careworn look."[9] An abolitionist poster warning citizens to beware of Caphart both captures and caricatures his rugged, uncouth appearance:

> He is a *thin, tall* fellow, rather *lean* and *lanky,* and about *six feet long.* His hair is *reddish* or *dirty brown,* like *weather-beaten tan* in color; is *long, straight,* and *lank, thin* on the top of the head, and *parted on one side.* His face is *rather short* for a man so long, rather *square shaped;* an uncommonly *hard, bad face,* and *ugly,* not only in form and feature, but expression,—*a face which seems made for a slave hunter,* or by his business.
>
> When last seen, said *JOHN* had on a *dark blue piratical looking long cloak,* a *light brown* body coat, and a pair of *dirt-colored* pantaloons.[10]

He was, in other words, hardly a man Bostonians would wish to invite into their parlors. The emphasis on ugliness and disharmony of features was clearly intended to create a portrait of a soul out of joint. An earlier *Commonwealth* notice had played on the same theme more explicitly, describing Caphart as "a man with a scarred nose, a twist in his mouth, and a pair of mismatched eyes, with [a] peculiarly fiendish expression."[11] Harriet Beecher Stowe, who was to open her story of *Uncle Tom's Cabin* with a portrait of crass slave dealer Haley, wrote later that Caphart's shocking words and uncouth appearance helped her create her book by giving her "an insight into the character of a negro catcher."[12]

Boston's federal authorities, however, were in no position to concern themselves with the real or imagined character traits of the person with whom they had to deal. They knew that this time they had to act decisively, and apparently they readily gave Caphart their full cooperation. The warrant to arrest Minkins was issued quietly, out of public sight, by Commissioner George T. Curtis. On Friday evening it was quietly handed to special U.S. Assistant Deputy Marshal Charles Sawin for execution. The federal marshal, Charles Devens, was in Washington, where he had been summoned to answer questions about his conduct in the Crafts affair. An Irishman named Patrick Riley, Devens' assistant deputy marshal, had been left in charge. The summons of the scrupulous Devens to Washington may have been a ploy to get him out of the way, leaving Riley to direct the arrest. If so, the arrest was a fairly elaborate plan involving Washington authorities and, possibly, lawyers for the New York Union Safety Committee. President Fillmore, no less than Daniel Webster, was intensely interested in a positive outcome in Boston.

The morning of Saturday, February 15, was sullen. Rain pelted the city almost continuously. "A grand time for the water cure operators," joked student William Hoyt in his diary, "for all they would be obliged to do would be simply to hold their patients out of a window, & they would get sufficiently moist."[13] The marshal's men were in the sodden streets early, hoping to surprise Minkins before the city was fully awake. This time, unlike the corresponding stage of the Crafts' episode, their operations went unobserved. This time, the Vigilance Committee had no advance knowledge of the deputy marshal's intentions. There would be no crowds of hecklers dogging their heels. The slaveowner's agent would not be harassed by endless suits and arrests concocted by Vigilance Committee lawyers.

In fact, because of the secrecy surrounding the proceedings, the main source of information about the actual arrest would be U.S. Deputy Marshal Patrick Riley himself.[14] Before eight in the morning, one of his deputies called at Riley's house. Minkins was already at work at Taft's

Cornhill Coffee House, Riley was told. Arrangements were in order to make the arrest there at eight o'clock. Riley left for the Court House, giving orders that Minkins be taken there as soon as the arrest was made.

The morning dragged on without any word from the men surrounding the Cornhill Coffee House. At ten a deputy finally reported to Riley that "it had been arranged not to make the arrest until eleven." Riley urged greater haste, but it was not until ten minutes before eleven that the deputy returned to report that all was in readiness. Riley went "immediately with Mr. Warren, Mr. John H. Riley, and other Deputies, and there found all our men, nine in number, stationed in and about the house." But Charles G. Forbes, the circus traveler who had been engaged to make the identification of Minkins, still had not arrived. Riley and one of his men went into the dining hall and, "to avoid suspicion," ordered coffee. They were waited on by a stout, copper-colored man, one of several black waiters at the restaurant. Their waiter, unknown to them, was the very man they sought, Shadrach Minkins.

The two marshals drank their coffee and waited for the man who had promised to identify Minkins. The minutes ticked away, but still he did not come. Riley must have been growing increasingly apprehensive. If Minkins somehow were not arrested, and the story got out, another outcry would arise against the officers in Boston, and he would find himself following Devens to Washington to explain his failure. "Not hearing any thing from our assistants," Riley later related, "we took our coffee, and rose to go out and learn why we had not heard from them." By then it was nearly eleven-thirty. Minkins preceded them into the hallway toward the barroom carrying their money to make change.

In the passageway, two of Riley's men who had been stationed outside, Assistant Deputy Marshals Charles Sawin and Frederick D. Byrnes, suddenly appeared, and "each took the negro by an arm, and walked him out of the back passage way." It is not altogether clear from this account whether Riley knew immediately that the right man had been seized. Nor does his account say that Forbes was in the hallway with Byrnes and Sawin, but it seems likely that he was.[15] Fortunately for Riley, the man proved to be Shadrach Minkins. Fortunately for Riley, Minkins did not resist. Fortunately, there were no cries for aid, no interference from bystanders. It all happened quickly and quietly. In a matter of minutes, the officers walked Minkins out the back passageway, through a building

Excitement in Court Square during the Thomas Sims case in April, 1851. Chains and guards had been added to protect the Court House.

at the rear, out across Court Square, and up the stairs of the Court House to the U.S. Court Room on the second floor.

What Shadrach Minkins' state of mind was at the moment of arrest can only be guessed, but the later testimony of Simpson Clark, one of the assistant deputy marshals, provides some clues. According to Clark, upon being brought into the courtroom, Minkins began pouring forth "wild remonstrances, questions, and explanations to the men who had captured him and to the bystanders" alike.[16] The officers may not have told him, at least until they had reached the security of the Court House, just what he was being arrested for. But even if Minkins was not told exactly why the officers had seized him, he had to have a good idea. All fugitive slaves imagined this nightmare moment. In his autobiography Frederick Douglass wrote sympathetically of those who, having reached the free states, were driven by this fear to turn around and go back to the bondage of their masters. "A freeman cannot understand why the slave-master's shadow is bigger, to the slave, than the might and majesty of a free state," Douglass explained. "The master is to him a stern and flinty reality, but the state is little more than a dream. He has been accustomed to regard every white man as the friend of his master, and every colored man as more or less under the control of his master's friends—the white people."[17] Douglass himself, through the aid of English friends, had his free papers purchased—papers that freed him from real and imagined demons.[18]

On reaching the Boston Court House, Deputy Marshal Riley began preparing for trouble. He knew before the crowds began to assemble that news of the arrest would spread quickly among Boston's blacks and their friends. He knew enough from the Crafts case four months earlier to expect continual harassment. His band of about a dozen deputies could easily be overpowered. So Riley's first thoughts were of obtaining assistance from the city officers and officials. He went straight to City Marshal Francis Tukey's office to inform him of the arrest and warn of probable trouble. From Tukey's office he hurried to see Mayor John P. Bigelow to alert him of the need to prepare for the crowds that would surely assemble.[19] Returning to the U.S. Court Room, Riley ordered all doors except the main entrance closed, and he placed guards at that door. Only then did he officially inform Minkins of the charge against him and ask if he desired legal counsel. Minkins answered that he did.

While Riley was making his preparations, the electric news that a fugitive slave had been arrested was spreading from Court Square through the surrounding streets and into the black neighborhoods on Beacon Hill and throughout the city. From their nearby offices and homes, Vigilance Committee lawyers hastened to the defense of yet another Boston fugitive. Charles List, secretary of the committee, was one of the first to arrive. He found Minkins talking too freely as he struggled to comprehend his situation amid the sudden shattering of his world. Deputy Simpson Clark later recalled that after Minkins had been brought in,

> he asked who it was that claimed him; I referred him to Mr. Sawin. Mr. Sawin named one person to him, and he [Minkins] said he did not know him. Mr. Sawin then named another person, and he said he did not know him. He then said he was named Shadrach and commenced to tell me the circum-

stances of his running away, but I advised him not to speak to me about it as I might be made a witness against him. I told him not to tell any one but his counsel; and Mr. List, his counsel, told him the same, and he stopped talking to the officers and others.[20]

News of the arrest spread rapidly, "and in the space of thirty minutes from one hundred to one hundred and fifty of them had crowded into the courtroom, together with some fifty white persons, chiefly reporters, lawyers, free soil agitators and others." To one reporter in the courtroom, some of the blacks appeared "exceedingly excited" and looked "as if they were about to spring over the rail and tear the prisoner away."[21]

By the time the hearing began, something like an hour later, half a dozen lawyers from the Vigilance Committee had assembled to plot Shadrach Minkins' defense. In addition to Charles List there were Samuel E. Sewall, the experienced defender of many slaves; Ellis Gray Loring, scion of the prominent Loring family; Robert Morris, the first black admitted to the Massachusetts bar; Charles G. Davis of Plymouth, later active in defending another Boston fugitive slave, Thomas Sims; and the adventurous young Richard Henry Dana, Jr., early in his law career after having spent two years before the mast. John G. King, a lawyer from New Hampshire, also came, bringing his partner to help with the defense. Marcus Morton, a prominent member of the Boston bar and the one lawyer Minkins asked for, was assigned to negotiate purchasing Minkins' freedom in the event he was remanded to DeBree.[22] However, Morton apparently never worked on the defense. Charles Sumner, who might have assisted, begged off—he was still deadlocked in the battle for senatorial nomination that was to drag on for several months more—but may have offered informal advice to the counsels.[23]

The lawyers divided into two groups. The main group was assigned to orchestrate the formal defense before the U.S. commissioner against the claim of DeBree. The other group, which included Robert Morris and Dana, was assigned to make a kind of flank attack before the Massachusetts state judiciary with a petition of habeas corpus. While this group organized, John G. King filled out a power of attorney, read it to Minkins, and obtained his mark. Minkins was "a good deal excited," King remembered, "and I had to guide his hand."[24]

Samuel Sewall and Ellis Gray Loring took charge of Minkins' defense before the commissioner, assisted by King and others. With Minkins in the prisoners' bar, an officer on each side, and Commissioner George T. Curtis on the judge's bench, the proceedings began. The Fugitive Slave Law called for a "summary" hearing, not a trial. Curtis asked the counsels for Minkins if they desired more time, which of course they did. They had known of the case only fifteen minutes before, Sewall argued. Caphart's lawyer, Colonel Seth Thomas, Webster's friend and the Boston lawyer who had represented the Crafts' claimant and other Southerners, pressed for a speedy outcome. "There is nothing in the case but a question of identity," Thomas argued.

In truth Thomas was nearly right. Under the Fugitive Slave Law, Minkins was allowed none of the ordinary civil liberties accorded to citizens. In federal eyes, he was not a citizen. (The U.S. Supreme Court would later confirm this in the Dred Scott case). He could not testify. He could not have his case heard before a jury. He was not entitled to the protections afforded to citizens under habeas corpus. He was hardly guaranteed any positive rights at all. The sole purpose of a hearing before the commissioner or judge was to establish the authenticity of DeBree's documents— little more than a mere formality—and Minkins' identity. There would be no appeal. Once Commissioner Curtis was satisfied that Minkins was the fugitive described in DeBree's certified documents, the hearing would be at an end. The whole might of the federal government could then be turned to the task of transferring him to the custody of his master.

Commissioners and lawyers for alleged fugitives—when fugitives managed to obtain legal counsel at all—could insist that the owner's documents be complete and fully authenticated and that reliable witnesses corroborate the identification of the accused. Still, the law did not demand anything complicated. In some "summary" hearings under the new law, fugitives were on their way back to slavery in less than half an hour. A few fugitives were lucky if their hearings lasted five minutes. Some hearings were held secretly, with none but the alleged fugitive, the claimant, the arresting officers, and the federal commissioner present. Fortunately for Shadrach Minkins, Commissioner Curtis was eager to show that the summary hearing called for by the law did not deny all due process. Under the circumstances, Curtis concluded, "a postponement to Tuesday" did not constitute an "unreasonable delay."[25]

Getting a three-day postponement was a small victory for Minkins' side, as it gave his attorneys time to plot the most effective defense. Their options, however, were extremely limited. The best chance for securing Minkins' release, if he was actually the fugitive sought by DeBree, lay in questioning the authenticity of the documents and accuracy of the identifications presented in evidence against him. Minkins' attorneys asked to examine the claimant's documents, to which Seth Thomas finally agreed, insisting first on reading them aloud to the courtroom. Most pertained to John DeBree's hearing before Judge Richard H. Baker, of the U.S. Circuit Court of Norfolk, when DeBree had offered evidence to certify Minkins' purchase, identity, and escape. The papers included an authenticated copy of the proceedings before Judge Baker and depositions tracing the successive sale and ownership of the fugitive up through the time of his purchase by DeBree from one John Higgins. Additional papers certified John Caphart's power of attorney for the "apprehension, prosecution, transportation, and restoration to the present claimant" of the fugitive.[26]

When the reading was completed, the papers were turned over to the defense lawyers for study, and court was adjourned until the following Tuesday. Curtis permitted the defendant and his lawyers to remain in the courtroom to plan the defense. DeBree's documentation proved to be extraordinarily thorough. Although the paper record did not contain a complete history of Minkins' enslavement, and in particular provided no evidence that his original enslavement had been legal, the fact of successive ownership over a period of years was well documented. Ordinarily this would be all the proof necessary for the commissioner to remand a fugitive slave to his owner.

One glimmer of hope for the defense was the vague description of Shadrach Minkins in DeBree's documents: "Said person appeared to be about twenty-five or twenty-six years of age . . . about five feet seven inches in height, of a complexion between that of a black and a mulatto, which is sometimes called a bacon color, stout, square built, and of pleasing address." This description, said a *Commonwealth* writer, was "applicable to a hundred men in Boston."[27] If Curtis were lenient with the defense, he might rule that the vague description of the fugitive was enough to dismiss the charges against Minkins. Perhaps other technical objections could be found.

But a sympathetic ruling from George T. Curtis was improbable, to say the least. The commissioner was a Webster Whig through and through.

His whole family were mainstays of what remained of Webster's Whig party base. George T. Curtis had led the efforts to organize the pro–Fugitive Slave Law Union rally at Faneuil Hall in November, at which his brother, Benjamin R. Curtis, had presided. If the Compromise of 1850 and the Fugitive Slave Law could carry Webster and the Whigs into power, George T. Curtis, a lowly federal commissioner, could ride the Webster coattails to power and fortune. So as commissioner, Curtis could be expected to be scrupulous—but only to a point. He could be expected to strive for the appearance of impartiality. But in all likelihood he would give DeBree and Caphart, not Minkins, the benefit of the doubt.

While the hearing before Commissioner Curtis was going on, Dana and Morris, assisted by others, worked on the petition of habeas corpus. What the abolitionist lawyers were trying to do was a classic states'-rights move, neatly stealing a page from the favorite Southern defense of their "peculiar institution." The legal instrument to accomplish this end was also classic—the petition of habeas corpus, meaning "have the body." The strategy was to present a petition of habeas corpus before state officers, who, if they accepted it, could force the U.S. marshal to bring Minkins before a Massachusetts judge in a Massachusetts court.[28] And because Massachusetts laws did not recognize slavery, the state court could declare that Minkins was unlawfully restrained and order that he be released. Many sympathetic state judges throughout the North were ready to issue just such orders whenever a fugitive slave was brought before them. Sometimes this resulted in the fugitive's release and rapid disappearance. At other times a state judge's order began a judicial circus, with the state court releasing the alleged fugitive and the U.S. marshal immediately rearresting him or her under the same or a new complaint. Potentially, the cycle of arrest-release-arrest-release could be repeated almost endlessly.

Dana was assigned the task of preparing the actual petition. Working from the office of Deputy Marshal Riley, which had been lent to the defense, he shuttled to and from the courtroom. Finally the documents were in readiness, and Dana hurried to find Lemuel Shaw, chief justice of the Supreme Judicial Court of Massachusetts, the highest judicial office in the state. One of the most venerable jurists in the nation, Shaw was nearing the end of a distinguished law career spanning nearly fifty years.

In 1836 in the case of the slave child "Med," Shaw had been instrumental in extending the principle of law that a slave brought voluntarily into a free state, even temporarily, was by that action freed from slavery forevermore. So it was not without some hope of a favorable interpretation that Dana approached Shaw.[29]

Yet Shaw's earlier decisions hailed by abolitionists had involved slaves brought into the state by their masters, not fugitive slaves. Dana's chances of a sympathetic ruling from the chief justice were sharply limited by the fact that this was a fugitive case and by Shaw's "robust" Whig principles. A longtime friend and admirer of Webster, Shaw never wavered even when other Whigs were deserting Webster for his support of the Compromise measures. "A glorious thing to have so distinguished a man as Mr. Webster elected Pres[iden]t of the U.S.," Shaw maintained as late as 1852, just four months before Webster's death. Although Shaw never said that he approved of the Fugitive Slave Law, his modern biographer, legal historian Leonard Levy, has concluded that "there is nothing in the cast of the man's mind, temperament, or associations" to indicate he opposed it.[30] In 1842 in the fugitive slave case of George Latimer, Shaw had ruled against a petition similar to the one brought to him by Dana.[31]

Thus it was not entirely surprising when the habeas corpus petition in Minkins' behalf met with a cold rebuff from Shaw. According to Dana, who caught up with the chief justice in the lobby of the Supreme Court Room, Shaw dismissed the petition out of hand, declaring irritably, "This won't do. I can't do anything with this." Pressed for an explanation, Shaw pointed out that the petition was not signed by Minkins—an omission that Dana knew was clearly allowed for. Habeas corpus protected the rights of persons illegally restrained, and persons illegally restrained were often, for that very reason, unable to sign petitions. Shaw's objections were "frivolous and invalid," Dana noted angrily, knowing that the real objection was Shaw's unwillingness to interfere. Perhaps Shaw saw himself as helping Webster to the presidency. Dana left, smarting under Shaw's disdain.[32]

By the time Dana returned to the courtroom after his unsuccessful meeting with Chief Justice Shaw, Commissioner George T. Curtis had already adjourned the hearing, which was set to resume the following Tuesday morning at ten. Immediately Riley and his officers began clearing the courtroom, "making the most absurd exhibition of pomposity, in ordering people about," according to Dana.[33] As one of Minkins' counsels, Dana was hardly one to sympathize with the nervous Riley, who had much cause for anxiety. He and his small band of officers were vastly outnumbered by the crowd outside, which continued to grow. So far as he could tell, none of the city officers he had requested to control the crowds had appeared in the hall or the square in front of the Court House. Two of Riley's men discussed what they would do if the courtroom were attacked. "Kill the negro," one reportedly said, and Charles G. Davis, overhearing, exploded, "You ought to have your throats cut."[34]

Clearing the courtroom was no easy task. It was crowded with whites and blacks. The blacks, said the *Boston Daily Times*, were "looking daggers."[35] An assault on the officers was almost palpable until suddenly Riley received reinforcements from six or eight city constables. Their arrival, which gave the deputy marshal a force of a dozen or more, may well have prevented a rescue attempt at that moment.[36] As the room slowly emptied, one tall black who seemed particularly reluctant to leave went up to Minkins, addressing him as "Fred" (or "Minkins" according to another source), and, in words loud enough for Curtis, Riley, and others nearby to hear, told him, "Don't be afraid; we'll stand by you." Constable Edward Jones remembered also hearing the words "till death," but this alarming message may have been mostly a projection of his fears. Riley saw to it that this man was immediately escorted out. Minkins' "pluck was aroused by this apparent sympathy, and . . . he stripped off his coat, loosened his kerchief, and with a quick shake of his head and a determined look, remarked, 'If I die, I die like a man.' "[37]

Eventually Riley and his men, with the assistance of the city constables, managed to clear the courtroom, where it appeared Minkins was to be kept confined. The Massachusetts "liberty law" of 1843 forbade the use of state jails in fugitive slave cases, and the federal government had no jail of its own nearby.[38] (Anticipating the difficulty, Riley had requested permission to hold Minkins at the federal navy yard in Charlestown, but that permission had been denied by the commandant.)[39] Minkins' attorneys were allowed to remain in the courtroom to confer with him about his case.

After the courtroom had been cleared of spectators, Deputy Marshal Riley tried to persuade the city officers to remain to help repel any attempt to rescue Minkins, but by then they were getting nervous about their participation. Constable Edward Jones tried a variety of excuses: his family was sick, he said, and he had other business to attend to. The real reason for Jones's nervousness was that he knew that Massachusetts' "liberty law" forbade state officers from helping to enforce the federal Fugitive Slave Law. Finally at one o'clock Jones was given permission to leave and went home briefly, but he soon returned to the Court House and went straight to the Municipal Court Room, also on the second floor. There he found municipal court crier Henry Homer and other city officers huddled in earnest session. The topic was whether they could lawfully assist the deputy marshal to detain a fugitive slave or even to maintain order outside the courtroom where a fugitive slave case was being heard. As Jones entered, the assembled officers were listening attentively to Homer, who was reading aloud to them from the *Revised Statutes of Massachusetts*.[40] With the city officers in conference in another part of the Court House, Riley was left with only a handful of men.

The defense lawyers who remained were still discussing a new habeas corpus strategy when Elizur Wright, the feisty editor of the Conscience-Whig *Commonwealth*, arrived about one-thirty and insisted on being admitted as a member of the press. The deputy marshal soon had reason to regret letting him in, for the sharp-tongued Wright began arguing heatedly with him over Riley's remarks about contributing to purchasing Minkins' freedom from DeBree. Claiming later to have mistaken Riley for the owner's agent, Wright replied angrily that he would rather "give the money for pistols."[41] A shouting match ensued between the two men, with Riley demanding that Wright leave, and Wright insisting on his right to remain. When Wright learned the identity of his adversary, he calmed down. "I did not know I had the honor of talking to the Deputy Marshal," he remarked with hardly veiled sarcasm, and Riley, for his part, grudgingly permitted the editor to remain.[42]

About ten minutes later Riley turned to Minkins and told him that he would soon have his dinner. Minkins stood up and put on his coat. Then Riley directed his men to clear the room of the remaining defense lawyers and friends. By this time Dana had retired to his office across the street. A few minutes after Riley's order, Robert Morris and Ellis Gray Loring also left. At ten minutes to two, only Charles G. Davis, Elizur Wright, and the Reverend Leonard Grimes, who had arrived just before Wright, remained in the courtroom with Minkins. Davis and Wright were making their way toward the door slowly, to the annoyance of the officers.

Out in the hallway, tensions were high. When the courtroom had first been cleared, spectators had joined the growing throng in the corridor, on the stairs, and outside in Court Square. As two o'clock approached, an estimated 200 people had gathered. Some were undoubtedly spectators attending to other business at the Court House. That Saturday, four other courts in the building were in session, hearing cases mostly of petty theft and drunkenness, and the corridors and stairs would have been busy even without the sensational case being heard in the federal courtroom on the second floor.[43]

Most of the people in the hallway and around the courthouse were black men, and they were growing increasingly anxious and bold as the minutes passed. Whenever Robert Morris emerged from the courtroom, they pressed around him, eager for information.[44] The crowd also plied others for news about what was going on inside. Each time the courtroom door was opened from within, the officer guarding it had to wrench it back from the grasp of the men in the hall to get it closed. One white man, who was later identified as Joseph K. Hayes, a Vigilance Committee member, stopped in the hall as he was leaving and told the crowd to "stand by" Minkins and to follow the officers wherever he was taken.[45] "I'm ready, I'm prepared," a black man with a knife was reported to have answered.[46] The boldest among the crowd were uttering similar words. One man was heard to say, "I'll lose or spill the last drop of blood I have before he shall be carried out of the courthouse."[47] Someone else reportedly said that if they all rushed into the courtroom, they could "easily get him out."[48] Still another boasted that he would throw cayenne pepper in Deputy Byrnes's eyes and would hold onto the courtroom door until his arms came off.[49]

8 "Plucked as a Brand from the Burning"

From the time that the hearing had adjourned, Officer Calvin Hutchins had been nervously guarding the outer main door of the courtroom, which opened outward into the hall.[1] All the other doors were locked. As the last of the lawyers and visitors were leaving, he would open the door just enough for them to squeeze through into the crowded hallway and then pull it shut again by the handle. At a few minutes before two, he opened the door to allow attorney Charles G. Davis and *Commonwealth* editor Elizur Wright to leave. Once again, many black and brown fingers gripped the edge of the door from the outside. While Hutchins struggled to keep the door from being pulled open into the hall-way, Davis managed to slip through the opening into the crowd. This time, however, Hutchins could not pull it back. The words "Tear him away" and "Come in" echoed in the air.[2]

What finally precipitated the decision to attack the door is uncertain. Perhaps the men outside it were spurred by the rumor that Minkins might be taken to the Charlestown Navy Yard and from there be sent directly back to slavery.[3] Some witnesses later claimed that a leader or leaders suddenly appeared at the Court House. One witness testified that a black man had come up the stairs with a stick (a cane, according to another witness) and said, "Boys, are you ready? Now is the time or never."[4] A story later circulated that the man who led the rescue had known Minkins as a boy in Norfolk.[5] Still others thought they saw Charles Davis or Elizur Wright give a prearranged signal as he emerged from the courtroom. Some people standing in Court Square claimed to have seen a man suddenly appear in the Court House doorway and motion to the crowd with a stick. This "signal," however, may have been merely the spontaneous gesture of a man caught up in the excitement of an assault already begun. Another witness remembered that the appearance of a large black man dressed in a sou'wester cap with its sides turned up prompted the remark, "You are just the man we want," and with the large man leading, the assault began.[6] Charles Davis described "some men ascending [the stairs] who had a very determined look, with their faces somewhat disguised by having their hair brushed down over the face, and coats buttoned up around their cheeks."[7]

Davis' description of the men on the stairs carries much weight. It is supported in general outline by a number of other witnesses. It also roughly matches an account given many years later by black leader Lewis Hayden, who confided to a friend that he had led the assault. His men had been armed, he said, and were ready to use their weapons if attacked.[8] It is not known whether Hayden and his band, whose sou'wester and oilskin garb suggested that many were sailors, were part of the crowd all along or, after planning the assault, perhaps at Hayden's house, had rushed to the Court House. Later it was reported that at about the time of the assault "a band of negroes," some wearing sou'westers and some carrying them, were seen walking "two by two, with a marching step," in a nearby street. This report, however, sounds fanciful and was never corroborated.[9]

At the moment that the assault on the outer courtroom door began, Officer Simpson Clark rushed to Hutchins' aid, and together the two men struggled with all their might to prevent it from swinging open into the hallway. For perhaps a minute the two officers kept the door from opening farther, but finally the crowd "twitched it round." Clark appears to have lost his hold first. With half the counterweight gone, Hutchins, still gripping the door handle, was carried out into the hallway as the door swung wide open.[10] In an instant, fifteen or twenty black men surged into the opening. "Blows were passed at me, and some kicks," Hutchins recalled later, but he was unhurt. "Knife him," Hutchins heard one of the men say, but that man was immediately rebuked by an older man, who urged, "No, hurt no one."[11]

Inside the courtroom, the battle at the door had sent officers scurrying.[12] When the assault began, Minkins was with Reverend Leonard

Grimes, flanked by two officers. "I stayed with Shadrach, and had hold of his hand," Grimes recalled.[13] Deputy Marshal Patrick Riley was standing nearby. Several of the marshal's men were near the door, and others scattered around the courtroom. Altogether, Riley had fewer than a dozen officers to repel the attack. The noise at the door sent nearly all rushing to Hutchins' aid. Riley, according to his later statement, ran toward the door with Minkins' guards, turning back just long enough to warn the fugitive, who had started to move toward a side door, that he would be shot if he tried to escape.[14] Minkins ducked down behind a table. Later, a witness who saw Minkins run from one side of the courtroom to the other said he looked frightened and confused.[15]

Riley and his men managed to reach the green baize inner door, which opened into the courtroom, just as the outer door was pulled open. Planting his feet against the judge's bench, Riley strained to push the door closed, assisted by one or two others. From outside the green door, Simpson Clark struggled to pull the inner door closed toward him.[16] For a moment the effort was successful. Although the crowd had pushed the inner door open slightly, the officers had just as quickly closed it, pinning one of the attackers momentarily between the door and the frame. In a minute or two, however, the attackers pushing against the door with superior numbers forced it open again, and the marshal and his men had to give way.[17] In streamed Minkins' rescuers, all of them black. In came Elizur Wright, swept along on the tide (Officer Byrnes later insinuated that Wright came in voluntarily at the head of the crowd, but under cross-examination conceded that Wright had had no choice). "Shoot the big nigger," Byrnes was reported to have shouted from behind the door, where he and Riley had been pinned—and appeared content to remain. "Not in this courtroom you don't," Elizur Wright supposedly answered.[18]

The events of the next few moments happened so fast, according to some observers, that Minkins was frightened and hardly knew whether he was among friends or foes. The crowd, numbering about twenty men in all, raced to where he stood, seized him "by the collar and feet," and fled toward the courtroom door. Constable Edward Jones and Calvin Hutchins tried to hold the rescuers inside the courtroom but were quickly overcome. The rescuers, four or five half-carrying Minkins, stampeded through the doorway, crossed the hall, and raced pell-mell down the stairs to the first floor.[19]

Standing in the rain out in Court Square, Benjamin T. Cheney, an Adams Express delivery man, saw a person "with a small round stick, like an officer's staff, coming down the steps of the second west door, beckoning with it." Then Cheney saw the crowd in the square rush toward the west Court House door. Some of them went in, but "almost instantly" were thrust back out again. "After quite a number had come out," Cheney continued, "a person holden by ten men on each side, appeared without a coat or a hat, with his breast bare."[20] Isaac Snowden, a young black medical student returning home from lectures at the hospital, also saw the rush in Court Square and the rescuers bursting from the door. He remembered that the man borne along was "in his shirt sleeves, of ragged and rough appearance."[21]

At the same moment, attracted by the commotion, Richard Henry Dana, Jr., looked toward the Court House from his law office window across the street and saw "two huge negroes bearing the prisoner between them with his clothes half torn off."[22] Another witness recalled that one of the men who held Minkins was a short man, the other tall and wearing a sou'wester cap.[23] To Dana, Minkins appeared "so stupefied by the sudden rescue and the violence of his dragging off that he sat almost dumb, and I thought had fainted." The rescuers were carrying him "as they would a child, in their arms."[24] Other witnesses agreed that Minkins was treated pretty roughly in the precipitous scramble. Assistant court clerk-crier Henry Homer claimed he saw Minkins' hat and coat being torn off and thrown in the mud as the rescuers struggled with their prize through the crowded square. The rescue party was "followed by a crowd of negroes, and joined instantly by the whole concourse of the street & Square." Several people reported seeing a black woman put her hand on the fugitive's hair and shout, "God bless you." "Such Cheers, & shoutings!" wrote Dana.[25]

With Minkins still in their rough grip, the rescue party crossed the square. Minkins, who had by then partially "recovered his legs," was being pushed along at a rapid gait "which his limbs seemed unwilling to achieve."[26] The rescuers headed north along Court Street, 200 or more following like the tail of a comet. After reaching the Revere House in Bowdoin Square, they slowed their pace a little and turned west into Cambridge Street. At that point some of the curious followers like lawyer Joseph Willard lost sight of them.[27]

In a few minutes the rescue party and its sizable escort of onlookers reached the corner of Cambridge and Garden Streets on the back side of Beacon Hill, almost a quarter of a mile from the Court House. They were then at the edge of Boston's Sixth Ward, the home of many of Boston's blacks. Suddenly the rescue, which had gone like clockwork, dissolved into chaos. Accounts vary about exactly what happened in the next few minutes, but all agree that the fugitive and several men got into a cab standing on Garden Street opposite Daly's stables, perhaps planning to speed out of the city. By most accounts, the cab never moved, perhaps because the driver, fearful of the crowd, never budged from the spot where he stood twenty feet away, or because the remaining crowd, surging around the cab, blocked the way. Some of the people in the crowd began shouting for Minkins to get out. One man climbed on a wheel and, according to one observer, broke a window with his fist. At this point the occupants of the cab got out and started out again on foot up the steep hill to Southac Street.[28]

Reverend Leonard Grimes, who had followed the crowd at a distance, caught up with them at the corner of Garden Street during the cab incident and followed them up the hill. On Southac Street the crowd paused for a moment in front of Grimes's Twelfth Baptist Church but did not go in.[29] One of the leaders, who two witnesses later claimed was Lewis Hayden, turned to face the crowd. "Gentlemen, if you want the man to get clear, stay back," he pleaded.[30] But when the rescuers headed down sharply pitched Southac Street in the direction of the Charles River, the procession still resembled a parade far more than a carefully planned escape. If the deputy marshal's men had been in pursuit, they could have located the fugitive and his friends with their eyes closed. (Although Riley later claimed that he had sent men in pursuit, no officer seems to have followed the crowd for more than a few blocks. Assistant Deputy Marshal Frederick Byrnes remained back at the courtroom "guarding the furniture" against an attack.)[31]

John Randolph, an unemployed waiter who boarded at Lewis Hayden's house, 66 Southac Street, was at home "learning to read" when the noise of the passing crowd interrupted his studies.[32] When he stepped outside he saw Minkins, still coatless, hatless, and (some later claimed) shoeless—the very picture of the forlorn, hunted fugitive—pass in the narrow

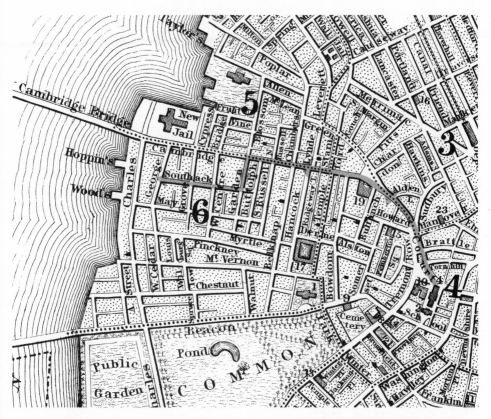

Detail of 1851 map of Boston showing the route of Shadrach Minkins' rescue party from the Court House to the West End (Sixth Ward).

street accompanied by the exuberant crowd. Randolph admitted that he recognized Minkins, whom he knew rather well ("he has called upon me"). Under cross-examination in a later case arising out of the rescue, Randolph stated that he could not identify any of the others, although he remembered that "two or three . . . had on oil cloth jackets and tar-paulin hats." Then came the following exchange between Randolph and Assistant District Attorney Nathaniel P. Lord:

Lord: Did you speak to Shadrach when you saw him in the hands of the crowd?
Randolph: I did not.
Lord: Did you not think he required some assistance?
Randolph: I don't know that I thought anything about it at the time.
Lord: Didn't you suppose something was the matter with him?

Randolph: I had my suspicions that something was going on.

Lord: Then why did you not speak to him?

Randolph: Because he appeared to be in a *great hurry*, and it is against my principles to stop a man when he is in a hurry!

"Great laughter" filled the courtroom, the *Commonwealth* reported.[33]

At the foot of Southac Street, where it ended at West Cedar, part of the remaining escort turned right while the larger number turned left toward the Boston Common.[34] After Minkins and his escort had passed, all up and down the back streets of Beacon Hill knots of black residents talked excitedly about what they had seen and what it meant. The street gradually quieted down. Minkins and his noisy rescuers had evaporated as silently as raindrops after a summer shower.

What happened next remained shrouded in mystery for many years. Some said that Minkins was put into a cab immediately and driven out of the city over the Charles River into Cambridge. Others believed that Minkins was hidden in one of the houses on Beacon Hill. Only two days after the rescue the *Courier* reported that Minkins temporarily "took refuge in the house of some of his friends." For a time suspicions centered on Hayden's house.[35] Prosecuting attorneys were later to try, unsuccessfully, to get witnesses to name Hayden's residence as the place where Minkins was concealed. Hayden's house was so well known as a center of black resistance, however, that rescuers would have endangered both their own and their friend's safety by taking him there. Moreover, this time the marshal had ample reason for a search: a criminal law had been broken. The rescuers desired no confrontation of this type; they needed concealment and alibis.

Not until after Lewis Hayden's death in 1889 was the place of Shadrach Minkins' concealment finally revealed. According to a friend, Hayden had privately disclosed that on Southac Street he and Robert Morris "escorted Shadrach away from the crowd" and "safely lodged him in the attic of a widow, Mrs. Elizabeth Riley, one of our race, whose fidelity and humanity we all fully confided in." Her house, according to contemporary records, was in Southac Place, one of many narrow lanes that led into the interior of the block.[36] The entry was only a few doors from Lewis Hayden's house at 66 Southac Street. Although the proximity to Hayden's house made the location dangerous, it also made it convenient to conduct arrangements.

With Minkins safely tucked out of sight in the attic, Hayden and the other rescuers finally had breathing room to consider their problems. The rescue had been carried out in broad daylight. Dozens, perhaps hundreds, of persons had had close but fleeting glimpses of the rescuers. To establish alibis, the leaders of the rescue apparently determined to disperse into the community and make themselves as visible as possible. A dozen people would later swear that during the approximate time of the rescue, Hayden was calmly going about his business. The boarders at Hayden's house swore that he had arrived for midday dinner at the usual time, around two-thirty. They were certain, too, that he had not brought a dinner guest. Many black and white storekeepers and clerks along Cambridge Street also remembered seeing Hayden in his store within about fifteen minutes after the rescue.[37]

It is, of course, possible that all the witnesses who helped establish alibis for Hayden were lying. Certainly the boarders at Hayden's house could have made up the story that Hayden was there at two-thirty for dinner, and the shopkeepers along Cambridge Street could have been lying as well. But it seems equally plausible that Hayden was the beneficiary of everyone's slightly blurred sense of time that afternoon. Within fifteen minutes he could have been accompanying Minkins to a hiding place, making an appearance at his store on Cambridge Street, and eating dinner at home. His appearances on the street and in his store should have been enough to raise a reasonable doubt in any impartial juror's mind.

For the next stage, the rescuers chose a young Irish cabman named Thomas Murray to play an unwitting role. To be certain that they were not being followed, they directed Murray about from corner to corner in a manner that must have been exceedingly perplexing to the driver. First Murray was instructed to drive to a corner where he was to meet two men. The two men appeared as promised, but instead of getting in they told him to drive to the corner of Southac and West Cedar Streets and wait for further instructions. Murray drove his cab there and sat for five minutes before one of the men reappeared and directed him to the next corner, the intersection of May and West Cedar. He drove to the corner and pulled up. After a moment, Murray later testified, "two colored men came along and got in."[38] He recognized one of the men but did not know his name. Later he learned that the man was Lewis Hayden. The other man proved to be Shadrach Minkins.

Despite the elaborate precautions of the rescuers, prosecutors were later able to find two witnesses to the scene. West Cedar Street resident William C. Reed, looking back on the day four months later, recalled that at about three-thirty a carriage had pulled up at his door, number 51. In a few moments, according to Reed, a man he was sure was Lewis Hayden, wearing dark clothes, came along with a man he did not recognize, dressed in a "light jacket and souwester hat."[39] Reverend Grimes also admitted that he saw "the person said to be Shadrach afterwards at the corner of Cedar and May streets . . . going towards Charles street."[40]

With the two men aboard, Murray turned the cab toward the Cambridge bridge a few blocks away.[41] When he stopped to pay the toll, Murray caught a glimpse of what he thought were pistols lying on the seat between the men inside. He drove across the bridge and continued about a mile on the road leading to Harvard College before one of his passengers commanded him to stop. Lewis Hayden pressed three dollars into Murray's hand, twice the usual fare. Perhaps Murray earned the bonus when later testifying in court that he could not remember which way his passengers had gone.

According to Hayden's own account, he next secured a horse and chaise and drove with Minkins "to Watertown, where we spent the afternoon, returning to the home of Rev. Joseph C. Lovejoy in Cambridge."[42] Lovejoy was a member of the Vigilance Committee. His brother, antislavery editor Elijah Lovejoy, was the famous antislavery martyr murdered in 1837 in Alton, Illinois, when an infuriated mob attacked his printing office.

After putting Minkins into the safe custody of Lovejoy, Hayden returned to Boston and "secured a light wagon and two horses."[43] In the meantime, "feeling the need of aid," Hayden called on his friend John J. Smith, a barber and another of the leading black activists of Boston. A free black from Richmond, Virginia, Smith had arrived in Boston in 1848. Reportedly his barbershop soon became a rendezvous of "secret councils" that "devised ways and means of protection and general assistance" for fugitives.[44] Smith joined Hayden in his enterprise, and the two men drove the wagon to Lovejoy's house in Cambridge, where the fugitive Minkins climbed aboard. With Smith at the reins, the wagon rolled out of Cambridge.

From Cambridge, Minkins' path grows fainter and fainter. Several people, unable to resist the temptation for instant heroism, claimed credit for having driven Minkins on this leg of his escape. Implausible stories tell of other drivers and other destinations. One story reports that the wagon with Minkins traveled by indirect route to Concord.[45] Given the sodden condition of the roads that night and the consequent slowness of travel, any but a direct route to Concord seems unlikely. Hayden's account mentions only two stops, one at Lovejoy's house in Cambridge and the other in Concord.[46]

9   "Never Was a Darker Day"

$\mathbf{A}$s Saturday ended, reports of Shadrach Minkins' rescue, many of them considerably exaggerated, began to circulate. The *Boston Daily Evening Traveller* hastily reported that "a hundred or more" had poured into the courtroom to rescue Minkins. A last-minute insertion in the *Boston Daily Journal* claimed that "some three or five hundred persons, together with a few whites, made a stampede." The *Journal*'s exaggerated figures were soon being repeated in other newspapers in Boston and around the nation. By Monday the *Boston Daily Times* was reporting to its readers that the rescue had been perpetrated by "a band of two hundred negroes . . . supplied with arms and . . . determined to use them against all who obstructed them." Many reports cited 300 "rioters," roughly fifteen times the actual number of rescuers.[1] "Overwhelming force suffered to accumulate by . . . the city authorities," wrote U.S. Commissioner George T. Curtis to Daniel Webster.[2]

Regardless of the number of rescuers, Boston abolitionists were jubilant. "Today will ever be a holy day in my calendar, for another slave has been rescued from the fangs of the slave hunter," Dr. Henry Bowditch, a prominent member of the Vigilance Committee, gleefully pronounced. "I think it is the most noble deed done in Boston since the destruction of the tea in 1773," Theodore Parker wrote in his journal. Wendell Phillips also played on parallels with the American Revolution: "We hope the same spirit is alive, as laughed to scorn the mother country shutting up our harbor to starve us into compliance."[3] Many ordinary citizens were roused by news of the rescue. Young Bostonian William Hoyt, who only a few days before had been "skulking about Boston in disguise of Father's hat & great coat delivering Valentines," interrupted his standard descriptions of his social life to note in his journal what he had learned of the rescue. "I never heard of anything being done so beautifully and quickly, and in order," he commented, adding that "at the dinner table Father & Henry had quite a spat on the subject."[4] The same evening apprentice printer John Watterston Smith, inspired by news of the rescue, composed a poem opening with the lines

It makes me truly glad to see
A deed done of this kind,
For it tells me, there yet exists
A Conscience and a Mind.[5]

Wasting no time in seizing what amounted to a unique opportunity to propagandize for the abolitionist cause, Elizur Wright cannily rushed out a *Commonwealth* Sunday extra. As few newspapers then published a Sunday edition, Wright practically had the field to himself. Bostonians arose on the morning after the rescue to posters hawking the special edition under the boldface heading "KIDNAPPERS DISAPPOINTED." Punning on the language of the judicial system that had just been circumvented, the poster declared that Shadrach had been freed "by a writ of Deliverance issued under the Higher Law" and added defiantly, "TAKE CARE OF KIDNAPPERS!!"[6] Theodore Parker reportedly created a sensation during his Sunday morning services at the Melodeon theater. After reading a notice that "Shadrach, a fugitive slave, desires prayers of this church, and of all Christian people, to aid him in his efforts to escape from the hands of the slavehunters now seeking for his life," Parker pointed dramatically back over his shoulder and announced that the fugitive was already far away.[7] "The vast audience immediately . . . burst out with a thunder of applause," wrote a young worshipper in the audience.[8]

Over the next few weeks, jubilation would echo and re-echo in the abolitionist press across the nation. Writing from Ohio, Henry C. Wright, confessing himself "wild with joy," proclaimed: "SHADRACH, the betrayed, abused, outraged slave, is free—is rescued from the Hyena fangs of this Slave-hunting, kidnapping government . . . 'TE DEUM LAUDA-MUS! Bless the Lord, Oh my soul.' "9 Wright filled a column with this giddy euphoria.

Both Southern extremists and pro-Compromise/pro-Union papers responded predictably. The Boston Union-Whig papers were furious. "Mob Law Triumphant," proclaimed the *Boston Daily Courier* headline. "Such a disgrace never fell on Boston before."10 "One of the most lawless and atrocious acts that ever blackened the character of any community," sputtered the *Boston Daily Times.*11 "Nothing has occurred in the State so dishonoring to its people, since the adoption of the Federal Constitution, as this mob and its results," stated a letter in the *Boston Daily Advertiser.* The *Boston Herald* warned that the incident threatened all the "dearest rights, when our courts of justice are not safe from the fierce invasion of an insane mob." Even the *Boston Investigator,* the much-despised organ of freethinker Abner Kneeland, found the rescue "altogether wrong, and no excuse can justify it."12

Among Boston's pro-Compromise newspapers there was much criticism of local blacks, but only one, the *Boston Daily Times,* was flagrantly racist in its response. An editorial railed against "the predominancy of Negro-dom in the Athens of America" and warned readers to expect "the edicts of these black masters as if our city had suddenly transferred to the dominions of His Sooty Majesty Emperor Soulanque of Haiti."13 The next day the *Times* made good on its promise by supplying several columns of "news" supposedly taken from a paper called the *Ebony Illuminator.* The "news" consisted of a communication from "His Highness, Pompey Squash I, Emperor of Massachusetts," a report on the reorganized black city government ("Board of Aldermen—Bone Squash, Dandy Jim . . ."), on the new government's ordinances ("5—Ordered, that it shall be lawful to kill a white man whenever a black desires the pastime"). Also included was a report of social events at the supposed emperor's court ("Empress Dinah will receive an illustrious company this evening in the palace Snowball . . ."). This ridiculing of blacks and playing on racial fears was the familiar stuff of the racist imagination. Years before, similar pieces had been published as broadsides.14 Black Bostonians knew this kind of racist reaction well, but it would have been especially unnerving at a time when, more than ever, local blacks needed the support of the white community.

THE LAST AND GREATEST REVOLUTION!

OVERTHROW OF THE WHITE POWER AND THE ESTABLISHMENT OF THE

BLACK EMPIRE

OF MASSACHUSETTS!

ANNO DOMINI—1851.

The Messages—Edicts—Manifestos—Rules—Regulations—and General System of Government under the New Order of Things!

—GREAT SEAL—

"THE DEVIL TO PAY AND NO PITCH HOT."

The feat is accomplished! The power of the whites is overthrown, and we, the people of Massachusetts, can now luxuriate under the Empire of the Blacks, *a la mode de St. Domingo.* In order to fully understand the new organization that has so magically taken place, and to appreciate the blessings which will accrue to the poor whites who have so long been suffering under oppressors of their own complexion, we append a few extracts from the new official government organ, *The Ebony Illuminator,* of yesterday morning :—

[From the Ebony Illuminator, Feb. 17.]
IO TRIUMPHE!
AN ADDRESS FROM HIS HIGHNESS, POMPEY SQUASH I., EMPEROR OF MASSACHUSETTS.
COURT HOUSE,
CITY OF BOSTON, Feb. 15, 1851. }
MY PEOPLE:
The palace of the white rascals is now in possession of our noble soldiery. The mealy-faced cowards could not withstand the terrible onslaught of our glorious veterans, and flew like cotton bolls in tornado, to a place of temporary safety. They will, however, be instantly pursued, captured, and hung like dogs to the nearest tree.

Part of a racist response to Shadrach Minkins' rescue, *Boston Daily Times,* February 18, 1851.

*   *   *

In newspapers across the nation, the Boston rescue of Shadrach Minkins was the leading story for a week and more. Many papers mirrored the Boston Whig denunciation of Minkins' rescue. "An outrage upon the country and a deep stain upon the city of Boston," cried the *New York Express* on Monday. "If we are not mistaken, this is the greatest outrage that ever occurred in the United States," proclaimed the rabidly antiabolitionist *New York Herald*.[15] "If it be necessary to shed blood and take life, in vindicating the law, let it be done, even if a thousand be sacrificed," another *Herald* piece declared.[16] "The city of Boston is a black speck on the map, disgraced by the lowest, the meanest, the BLACKEST kind of NULLIFICATION(!!)," shrieked the *Savannah Republican*.[17]

But other newspapers in Boston and around the nation tried to put the events in perspective. The stridently antiabolitionist *Boston Daily Advertiser* declared it would withhold judgment for the present, "[as] we are not sufficiently acquainted with the facts of the case, to be able to judge where the greatest blame ought to rest." "The outrages and aggressions of the North are familiar to our readers," stated the *Richmond Examiner* calmly, adding, "we have not yet, however, abandoned all hope that the recent lawless acts at the North will burn into the hearts of the masses there a sentiment of the necessity of prompt and decided action." The *Louisville Daily Journal* lashed out at extremists of both camps in an editorial entitled "Northern and Southern Professors of Treason." In place of the infamous South Carolina toast, "a rope to every Northern Abolitionist," the paper proposed a toast recommending using both ends of the rope, one end for the Southern disunionists and the other for the Northern ones. "Kentucky would gladly furnish all the necessary hemp," the paper added. The *New York Commercial Advertiser* claimed that "a day or two's reflection will show that this Boston affair has been immensely overrated."[18]

In Washington Shadrach Minkins' rescue set off a week of urgent questioning, hasty consultations, long speeches, and hard words. On Monday a round of telegrams from Secretary of State Daniel Webster to his Boston friends and federal officials solicited information about the rescue. "The President is surprised that no information has been received from you respecting this occurrence," Webster telegraphed Marshal Devens, apparently not realizing that Devens had been in Washington to be questioned about his conduct in the Crafts case.[19] To a friend Webster anxiously queried, "Was it by connivance or absolute force? did the Marshal do his duty? Answer."[20] He commanded George T. Curtis, the commissioner, to send by telegraph "the precise facts attending the rescue of the alleged fugitive." The next morning Curtis telegraphed back, "gross negligence of the city; marshal's department not fully prepared." The rescue, Curtis added, was a case of "levying war" against the United States—that is, of treason.[21] Webster was soon echoing Curtis' words.[22]

On Tuesday, three days after Shadrach Minkins' rescue, the Senate chamber and galleries were packed to hear the response of aging elder statesman Henry Clay, architect of the Compromise measures. "I will never forget the anger that shrivelled up the already wrinkled face of Henry Clay, nor his sharp voice," wrote Moncure Conway, a young divinity student who witnessed the scene from the balcony. The "outrage" was worse, Clay shouted, because it was committed "by negroes; by African descendants; by people who possess no part, as I contend, in our political system."[23]

Senator John Davis of Massachusetts attempted to defend his state against Clay's charges, but Clay got the better of the exchange. Watching from the gallery, William Wetmore Story, the Boston lawyer turned sculptor, felt "ashamed for my state." Davis "had no pluck in him . . . [and] trembled under Clay," Story wrote. "Our people cower—the South domineers."[24]

After additional speeches, including one by Jefferson Davis of Mississippi arguing that if the people of Massachusetts uniformly resisted, then "the law is dead" and there was no point in using federal force, Clay's motion demanding a formal explanation from the president regarding the Boston events was finally adopted.[25]

President Millard Fillmore's response would not be long in coming. In a sense, it had been in the works for months, ever since Fillmore had been pressed to deploy federal troops to aid Philadelphia's federal marshal in one of the earliest cases under the new Fugitive Slave Law. After that case Fillmore had grudgingly consented to the use of federal military force to assist a federal marshal who requested help, but only after the marshal's request had been reviewed by a federal judge.[26] In the Crafts case, too, the secretaries of war and the navy had been ordered to supply troops if the U.S. marshal called for assistance.[27] In the current crisis over Shadrach Minkins' rescue, pro-Unionists had some expectation that Fillmore, pushed by his secretary of state, Daniel Webster, would finally call out troops. Ever since the news of the rescue first broke, Fillmore had been closeted with his cabinet and a select handful of advisers. "No man in that Cabinet stands up for the South in a manner more decided, and prompt and efficient, than Mr. Webster," one report asserted.[28] A rumor circulated that Webster had even threatened to resign within twenty-four hours if the president did not take suitably strong action.[29]

But by the time the Senate debate took place on Tuesday, assurances from Boston that the rescue had been an isolated incident and that the city was not in a state of insurrection had given the president the option of following the conservative course he preferred. Instead of calling out troops, Fillmore merely issued a proclamation calling for "all well disposed citizens" to obey the law and for all military and civil authorities in Boston to prevent further rebellious acts and to assist in recapturing the fugitive. "I do especially direct, that prosecutions be commenced against all persons who have made themselves aides or abettors in this flagitious offense," the proclamation stated.[30] The secretaries of war and the navy had already ordered their forces stationed in Boston to be available to the federal marshal if the latter's request was accompanied by a certificate that forces "too powerful to be overcome by the civil authority" were involved.[31]

The presidential proclamation, issued on February 19 under the signatures of both Fillmore and Webster, was largely a symbolic gesture, hardly what Webster desired. Yet it did create the impression that the president would use the army, if absolutely necessary, to enforce the Fugitive Slave Law. In his personal reply to the Senate Fillmore underscored his determination to see the law executed "to the fullest extent."[32] Webster busied himself assuring his fellow citizens that the stigma placed upon the city was not deserved. "Shame will burn the cheeks, and indignation fill the hearts of nineteen-twentieths of the people of Boston," he asserted confidently.[33] His Boston friends echoed his words. "The feeling of the community here in Boston is just as it should be . . . We are deeply mortified," industrialist Amos A. Lawrence wrote.[34] On Tuesday Boston's Board of Mayor and Aldermen passed resolutions supporting "the integrity of the laws and dignity of the Commonwealth" and ordering the city marshal, when "properly informed," to assist the U.S. marshal "faithfully and truly, with the whole police force under his control." Shortly afterward Boston's Common Council passed similar resolutions.[35]

Even before the president's proclamation was issued, Boston's federal officials had been busy demonstrating their loyalty and efficiency. On Monday, two days after the rescue, the U.S. marshal's men arrested *Commonwealth* editor Elizur Wright and Charles G. Davis, one of Minkins' lawyers. Both men, who were being escorted from the courtroom when the rescue took place, were charged with giving the signal that started the attack. J. Thomas Stevenson, the merchant prince and Webster supporter who had tried to contribute to purchasing the Crafts' freedom, posted the $3,000 bail for Davis, an act that faintly hinted that Boston's leading commercial men might yet be brought around to the abolitionist side.[36]

On Tuesday morning Saturday's excitement was renewed when Marshal Devens' officers seized John Foye (or Noye), a sturdy, intelligent-looking black truckman. Rumors spread quickly. One report circulated that another fugitive slave had been arrested. Another report got abroad that Minkins had been recaptured. Within an hour a crowd of several hundred was milling about the Court House.[37] Inside, twenty-five city watchmen kept order.

When Foye was brought in, Commissioner Curtis had just reconvened the hearing adjourned the previous Saturday. Abolitionists who had managed to be admitted watched an entertaining spectacle unfold. First Seth Thomas, DeBree's attorney, called for Shadrach Minkins to be brought before the commissioner, which was of course manifestly impossible. U.S. Marshal Charles Devens, just back from Washington, awkwardly reported that Deputy Marshal Riley was still preparing his explanation. In a few minutes Riley appeared and read his deposition, which blamed the events of the previous Saturday on Mayor Bigelow's refusal to cooperate. During an argument between Minkins' lawyer and Commissioner Curtis, Foye was brought into court by his armed guard and placed in the prisoner's dock. Finally, during a break, the charges against Foye were heard. It was alleged that Foye was the man who had taken the marshal's ceremonial sword. After a brief hearing, Foye was bound over for a full hearing the following Tuesday and ordered to give bail.[38]

On Wednesday, February 19, the day of Fillmore's proclamation, there was a brief flurry of excitement when black clothing merchant James Scott was arrested at his shop on a charge of participating in the rescue. A large crowd of blacks quickly materialized. "Though a rescue was threatened, and excited cries were made," according to the *Boston Daily Mail*, Scott was hustled to the Court House by half a dozen officers armed with short clubs and described as "determined."[39] At the Court House the noisy, threatening crowd was barred at the door. The only black allowed in the courtroom was Scott's lawyer, Robert Morris.[40] "The Ringleader Arrested," crowed the *Boston Daily Times* prematurely.[41] Accused of leading the rush on the door, Scott was ordered to post bond for his appearance at a hearing the following Tuesday. Three black clothing merchants, Jonas W. Clark, John P. Coburn, and Coffin Pitts, posted the required sum of $3,000.

By the middle of the week, calm had gradually returned to Boston and the nation. Wright, Davis, Foye, and Scott had been arrested.[42] The exaggerated reports of the number of rioters, which had undoubtedly increased tensions, were laid to rest. President Fillmore's official proclamation announced, at least in theory, the federal government's determination to see that violations of the Fugitive Slave Law did not go unpunished. Conciliatory gestures by local officials also had a calming effect. All this led the Washington correspondent for the Philadelphia *Public Ledger* to conclude confidently, "the attempt to make a national affair out of a local riot has entirely failed."[43]

The initial hearings of the accused rescuers, which would run for two weeks, were just the forum the Webster-Fillmore forces needed. A decisive show of federal judicial authority would go a long way toward restoring the tarnished reputation of Boston and her federal authorities. But Charles G. Davis' hearing, the most thorough of the initial hearings, revealed many difficulties ahead. Davis' examination began on Thursday, February 20, five days after the rescue, in the U.S. Circuit Court Room, with the presidential proclamation still ringing in the ears of the nation.[44] Benjamin F. Hallett, U.S. commissioner, judge, and ardent Webster sympathizer, presided. George Lunt, U.S. district attorney for Massachusetts and a longtime Whig opponent of the antislavery movement, stood for the prosecution.[45] On the defense side, Davis acted as his own counsel, with Richard Henry Dana, Jr., assisting him. Although Richard Henry Dana,

Rescue case defense attorney Richard Henry Dana, Jr., 1849.

Sr., worried that his son was irreparably injuring his legal career by taking the case, he wrote to a friend that he felt "gratitude toward God who had given me a son with the moral principle & courage to take his stand (when not a man of weight at the bar could be found to do it) against the wealth and rank of this overbearing city—a young man with a large & growing family, & working like a slave to support it."[46]

As a succession of witnesses against Davis stepped to the stand on the first day of the hearing, the flimsiness of George Lunt's case rapidly became apparent.[47] The prosecution attempted to portray Davis as the key figure in the rescue, responsible both for keeping the crowd in the hallway informed about the situation in the courtroom and for giving the signal for the assault to begin just after he was escorted from the courtroom. Lunt had no difficulty establishing that Davis was indeed at the door or had just gone through it when the assault began. No one disputed that. But beyond that point the prosecution's case foundered. Assistant Deputy Marshal Charles Sawin could offer little more than a recollection that Davis had said that Minkins' arrest was "damned dirty business" and that the officers "ought to have your throats cut"—proof of strong feeling but hardly of active participation in a conspiracy.[48]

Potentially damning testimony against Davis came from Assistant Deputy Marshal Frederick D. Byrnes, who had been escorting Davis and *Commonwealth* editor Elizur Wright out of the courtroom at the time the attack began. According to Byrnes, the moment before the crowd began forcing its way into the room Davis had slipped through the narrowed opening and was standing in the hallway against the wall. At that point, Byrnes claimed, Davis had uttered the words, "Take him out, boys—take him out," whereupon the assault began. But under cross-examination Byrnes soon hemmed his certainty with qualifications. A dozen other voices had also been calling out at the same time, he admitted. Moreover, the voice he heard uttering the words "Take him out" he merely "took to be Mr. Davis's." He had not seen Davis' lips move, but he "thought it was him who spoke the words, and I think so now," because he was "familiar" with Davis' voice.[49]

Even if Byrnes's statements had been accurate, they hardly proved that Davis was part of a conspiracy. In fact anyone who heard the testimony could reasonably have concluded that Davis, if he had uttered the words Byrnes claimed he did, had done so spontaneously, encouraging the crowd only after the assault had already begun. There was no evidence that the people there had been waiting for his signal. No connection had been established between Davis and anyone who invaded the courtroom.

Moreover, none of the other officers could offer an iota of direct support for Byrnes's view of events. One officer, Calvin Hutchins, did note that in going out Davis had put his back against the door jamb and pushed the door with his left hand, opening it "more than was necessary." But so much pushing and shoving had been going on at the door that it was easy to believe that Davis had merely been protecting himself from being wedged in the narrow opening between the jamb and the door. A bystander testified that Davis had come out of the courtroom and gone back in "by the east door" just a few minutes before the rescue, suggesting the possibility—remote at best—that Davis had been communicating with the crowd in the hall and perhaps coordinating the rescue attempt.[50] No one else had seen Davis do this, and the marshal believed it impossible for anyone to have used the east door, which had been locked.

Under further cross-examination by Dana, Byrnes's testimony grew even weaker. Yes, Byrnes admitted, the hallway had been filled with shouts and cries, and yes, he was hard of hearing. "My deafness," Byrnes called it. All he could offer to shore up his assertion that he had heard clearly was, "I think Saturday was one of my hearing days." When Dana wondered how it was possible to be certain that it was Davis, and not another man, who had uttered the words "Take him out," Byrnes answered lamely, "It was not the voice of a colored man."[51]

If the district attorney had planned to regale the court with accounts of Davis's complicity in intrigue, subterfuge, deception, and lawlessness, Deputy Marshal Byrnes, his star witness, had served up only the weakest of fare. No other prosecution witness was able to add any meat to Byrnes's weak broth. A string of defense witnesses, testifying that Byrnes was a disreputable character, further diluted his testimony. In the end, the government's case against Charles Davis was hopeless. No one had seen Davis conferring with a single person accused of being part of the assault. No one but Deputy Byrnes had heard Davis say anything, and what Byrnes had heard was suspect.

In his closing on Monday, February 24, District Attorney Lunt concentrated on Davis' *lingering* about the courtroom and on his *strong expressions* against the law and the proceedings. He reminded the judge that according to the Fugitive Slave Law, persons "directly *and indirectly*" engaged in "aiding, abetting, or assisting" were to be subject to penalty. Dana, in his closing, hammered away mercilessly at the vagueness of the evidence and ridiculed the testimony of the government's chief witness, Deputy Byrnes. The evidence, Dana declared triumphantly, "is reduced to an exclamation on the stair-case, sworn to, not very confidently, by a deaf man, who was too far off to hear well at any rate of hearing, denied by three officers, with good hearing, two of whom were outside, while a dozen voices were calling out the same thing at the same moment."[52] Privately Dana ridiculed the district attorney and the commissioner. "Lunt is the oddest mixture of obstinacy, ignorance of legal principles, vanity & Irritability I ever met with in such a place," Dana fumed, calling

Lunt's conduct of the case "extreme, inquisitorial, ill-tempered, incredulous, conceited . . . intolerable." Dana heaped scorn equally on Commissioner Benjamin F. Hallett: "His almost incredible ignorance of law, & his mock dignity, the ludicrous manner in wh[ich] he is swayed about from one absurd decision to another, makes great sport for the bar."[53]

In the end, however, Hallett exceeded Dana's expectations. In delivering his judgment the commissioner explained that he had been careful "not to confound an indiscretion or . . . mere expression of opinion, however gross, with a wilful act constituting legal guilt."[54] Hallett ruled firmly for the defense: "It was made clear there that there was no plan or premeditation, even among the negroes . . . [and] that the rescue was a sudden thing, done by not more than twenty negroes."[55] For the "ill-bred District Atty," as Dana's father called George Lunt, the result was a sharp defeat.[56] For Webster and the Unionists, it was an even greater defeat, one more humiliation in a long, frustrating series.

Richard Henry Dana, Jr., savored the victory over Lunt and Webster. "We had the audience & the public with us," Dana would write triumphantly.[57] Yet neither Davis' release nor Webster's defeat gave Boston's black community much comfort. Arrests for aiding the escape continued. On the afternoon of Friday, February 21, Joseph K. Hayes, superintendent of Tremont Temple and member of the Vigilance Committee, had become the third and final white person to be arrested. The case against him was "weaker than water," the *Commonwealth* alleged.[58] Friday also brought the exciting arrest in Salem of nineteen-year-old Alexander P. Burton, a local black barber. According to hastily written stories in the pro-Compromise Boston newspapers that night and the following morning, Burton was arrested "with much difficulty," and the mayor had had to "read the riot act" to keep order.[59] The *Boston Daily Journal* claimed that "nearly three thousand persons . . . expressed their determination to rescue him from the officers." The *Boston Daily Courier* account added that the captain of the Salem Artillery had volunteered his services and that the Artillery and the Independent Cadets "met at their quarters and were in readiness to respond with energy." Salem weeklies and biweeklies, however, objected strongly to the accounts of "zealous cooperation" printed in Boston, describing them as "most exaggerated," "intentionally magnified," and "ridiculous."[60]

Once Burton had been delivered to Boston, the pro-Compromise script created by Boston dailies broke down rapidly. The warrant proved to be for Andrew J., not for Alexander P., Burton.[61] Boston tax records for 1850 and 1851 show the error of the officers. According to these records, Andrew J. Burton could be found, not in Salem, but living barely a dozen blocks from the Boston Court House, at 2 Second Place, in the Fifth Ward.[62] In court, U.S. District Attorney George Lunt lamely admitted that Alexander Burton was not the person named in the warrant and made a motion to dismiss the charges.[63] "Some of the anti-law-and-order persons . . . seemed highly delighted, and appeared disposed to manifest their feeling by applause," the *Boston Daily Journal* reported.[64] A relieved Burton returned to Salem on the next train.[65]

More arrests followed. On Saturday, a week after Minkins' arrest and rescue, Thomas Paul Smith, a black secondhand clothing dealer and community leader, was apprehended for aiding in the rescue. The *Boston Daily Journal* described Smith as "a very intelligent and influential man among our colored citizens." Once again there was "some commotion" on the occasion of the arrest, but again a show of force by the officers prevented any violence. At the hearing in the Court House, one witness claimed to have seen Smith in the hallway acting "as a sort of leader of the mob" just before the rescue began, several witnesses placed Smith among the group of rescuers leaving the courtroom, and still another witness recollected seeing Smith with the rescuers in Cambridge Street. After two days of hearings, Smith was bound over for trial.[66]

Also on February 22, federal officers seized Lewis Hayden at the *Liberator* offices at 21 Cornhill Street. Hayden later "complained bitterly" that the officers "took hold of him" and handled him roughly, but in the marshal's office he joked with James N. Buffum of Lynn, an abolitionist who was there to post Hayden's bail. "I always thought you were a pretty clever fellow," Buffum said. "You know, it takes a pretty clever fellow to do such an act," Hayden replied, smiling.[67] The tone of Hayden's hearing was more subdued, however. Witnesses identified Hayden at almost every stage of the rescue, and he was bound over for trial.

On Saturday, March 1, two more blacks were arrested for "aiding and abetting," bringing the total number of arrests to ten. These two were John P. Coburn, a well-known clothing merchant, and Robert Morris, the second of Minkins' lawyers to be charged. Both arrests attracted small crowds but produced no real disturbance. At the hearings, witnesses identified Morris as one of those who had escorted Minkins through the streets of the West End. The evidence against Coburn was merely that he had been seen in the hallway making inflammatory remarks shortly before the rescue began. Both men were bound over for trial.[68]

Thus, two weeks after the glorious rescue of Shadrach Minkins, Boston's blacks had little to rejoice over. Although the rescue had been successful, the escape had been uncomfortably close. Boston federal authorities had cooperated fully with the slaveowner's agents. The Vigilance Committee had failed to learn that a warrant had been issued. A fugitive had actually been arrested and taken to court. True, lawyers on the Vigilance Committee had succeeded in delaying court proceedings, giving Hayden and the others time to act. But what if Deputy Marshal Riley had received the help he requested from Mayor Bigelow, or if the U.S. officers had been armed, or if federal troops had been in readiness to support the marshal? What would happen the next time? The presidential proclamation, the resolutions of Boston's Board of Mayor and Aldermen and of the Common Council, the pledges by "respectable citizens" to aid the U.S. marshal, the "proper orders" to the federal forces in the area—all this told Boston's fugitives that their enemies were more numerous and more powerful than ever.

Unnerving news and rumors continued to circulate freely. According to one story, the U.S. marshal had purchased sixty pistols and distributed them among his men. Another rumor told of a company of marines dispatched to Boston to hunt down and imprison the rescuers.[69] Still another report claimed that clerks at the Custom House were being asked to sign their names to a paper volunteering their services to assist the U.S. marshal in capturing fugitive slaves. The *Boston Daily Evening Transcript* printed a story that "a number of our most respectable citizens" had gone to the marshal's office to offer to assist in executing the laws.[70] A letter from "Signer of the call for the Union Meeting" called on fellow Union-savers "to put our shoulders to the wheel for the execution of this law . . . [with] a phalanx of a thousand strong."[71] "We shall not be content with mob law alone, we shall have the real Lynch law added," Boston industrialist Amos A. Lawrence blustered.[72]

Stories of Southern agents sighted on the streets and of new warrants against fugitives were common. On Thursday, February 20, the *Common-*

wealth reported that warrants were out for several fugitives and that authorities had already attempted to arrest two the day before. A week later, a *Commonwealth* report warning blacks to "Look out for the Kidnappers" claimed that Virginia agents had tried unsuccessfully to have "no less than three" fugitives arrested. Wendell Phillips wrote a friend that the loose tongue of a U.S. officer was responsible for one fugitive's lucky escape. Another fugitive, Phillips wrote, had disappeared after spotting his old master on a Boston street.[73]

The Boston Vigilance Committee met feverishly through the end of February and the first weeks of March. "Long evening sessions—debates about secret escapes—plans to evade where we can't resist—the door watched that no spy may enter—the whispering consultations of the morning . . . intimates forbearing to ask the knowledge which it may be dangerous to have"—all this, Wendell Phillips wrote, reminded him "of those foreign scenes which have hitherto been known to us . . . only in books." "We enjoy ourselves richly," Phillips confessed, adding that he doubted "whether more laughing is done anywhere than in anti-slavery parlors."[74] Of course predominantly white Vigilance Committee members could enjoy their flirtation with lawlessness "richly" because the color of their skin insulated them against many of the dangers faced by black Bostonians. Still, they took their duty to Boston's frightened fugitives seriously, forming two new standing committees to meet the crisis while continuing to dispense advice and aid. One committee was "to advise colored persons supposing themselves to be in danger, as to the expediency of their remaining in or leaving Boston." The other, a ten-man "minute man" team, was to stand ready "for services on any emergency."[75]

According to one estimate, within a week of Shadrach Minkins' rescue 100 fugitives had fled from Boston.[76] Boston Vigilance Committee financial records for late February document numerous expenditures to move fugitives to safer locations. "[To] Lewis Hayden carriage hire to send John Armisted [Armstead?] and other fugitives out of the city," reads a typical entry, for February 22.[77] On February 23 a payment was recorded for "passage to St. Johns" for Henry Watson, his wife and child. Two days later Reverend Leonard Grimes was reimbursed seven dollars "for passage of Wm. Ringold, Isaiah Gaiter, Wm. Peters to Southboro & James Peters to Halifax."[78] Boston social worker Abby Alcott, the wife of philosopher Bronson Alcott, wrote to her brother on the twenty-eighth, "I have sent 20 colored women to service in the country—where for the present they will be safe—[I] may yet have to meet the penalties of the law—I am ready."[79] Even Lewis Hayden felt compelled to send his wife, a fugitive, out of the city into hiding.[80]

"It is horrible to see the distress of families torn apart at this inclement season, and the working head forced to leave good employment," wrote an anguished Wendell Phillips.[81] Although benevolent-spirited white citizens visited black neighborhoods to dispense "pecuniary aid and friendly counsel," relief efforts were necessarily hit-or-miss, with some needy families inevitably passed by.[82] "Never was a darker day in our Country's history," Abby Alcott confided to her brother.[83]

10 North Star

Late on the night of February 15, 1851, while Henry Thoreau slept in his parents' house just down Concord's Main Street, three men in a wagon turned into the yard of blacksmith Francis Edwin Bigelow. The late hour and their dark skin meant only one thing—more fugitive slaves had stopped to rest on their way north. For years Concord had been a haven to fugitives following the North Star, part of the loose network of friends known somewhat inaccurately as the Underground Railroad. No one will ever know how many fugitives passed through the town, but according to the estimate of Ann Bigelow, wife of the blacksmith and founder of the Concord Women's Antislavery Society in 1837, Concord averaged one a week.[1]

In Concord, as in hundreds of other small towns and villages throughout the North, fugitive slaves had to look mostly to local whites for any assistance they received. In towns like Concord, the few blacks were usually too poor and too vulnerable to provide substantial help.[2] Among the whites who joined in Concord's fugitive relief efforts were Ann Bigelow, Mary Rice, and Henry Thoreau's mother and sisters, assisted by the "perfectly fearless" Mary Brooks and other women.[3] "Mr. Nathan Brooks and Mr. Ralph Waldo Emerson were always afraid of committal, we women, never," Ann Bigelow remembered proudly at the end of the century, notwithstanding Emerson's many brave pronouncements against slavery.[4] That the women of Concord were not entirely on their own, however, is well known. Prominent among the Concord men who helped fugitives were Dr. Josiah Bartlett

House of Concord blacksmith Francis Edwin Bigelow and his wife, Ann.

and Henry Thoreau. Both drove fugitives to the West Fitchburg railway station, and Thoreau sometimes even escorted them in the railway cars. A visitor to Concord wrote admiringly of Thoreau's "tender and lowly devotion" to a fugitive staying in the Thoreau family home in the 1850s.[5]

That February night, the wagon in the Bigelows' yard held a single fugitive, the most famous of all Concord's clandestine visitors: Shadrach Minkins. Only a dozen hours before, he had been in the custody of Boston's federal marshal. Almost certainly the news of Minkins' late-night arrival was whispered among the Emersons, the Whitings, the Thoreaus, and others among the Bigelows' antislavery friends, but for good reasons no contemporary record of the event appears to have been made. "Aiding and abetting" a fugitive in any way could have led to fines of $1,000, plus additional $1,000 penalties to compensate owners for each unrecovered fugitive. It could also have led to imprisonment for six months. President Fillmore's proclamation calling for the speedy capture and prosecution of those responsible for Minkins' escape had put Northern federal authorities on notice that failure to enforce the law would not be tolerated. Within days of Minkins' visit, those authorities made the first of nearly a dozen arrests. So, wisely, Concord lawbreakers kept silent.

More than twenty-five years passed before many of the stories of the fugitive slaves in Concord and throughout the North were finally written down. In that great gap of years, many memories had grown dim or been blotted out entirely, or else had been preserved second- or thirdhand, recounted to historians (or, more often, newspaper reporters) by the children or grandchildren of the original participants. Some stories had been richly embroidered in a succession of tellings. Others were woven entirely out of fancy. In few cases was any witness alive to correct exaggerations, errors, and falsehoods.

The story of Minkins' visit to Concord was not immune to error and mythologizing. One much-repeated account credits Mary and Nathan Brooks, not the Bigelows, with putting Minkins up for part of the night.[6] Another credits a white abolitionist, not Lewis Hayden or John J. Smith, with driving Minkins to Concord.[7] And the record of Minkins' flight after he left Concord is even more vague and contradictory, if not fanciful.

For Minkins' few hours in Concord, however, an unusual array of firsthand testimony and corroborating evidence has survived. Chief among these are Ann Bigelow's four separate reminiscences of that February night. Recounted over a span of twenty years toward the end of the century, her separate memories are like fragments of a broken vase. The earliest, and the only one to appear in print, is part of Harriet J. H. Robinson's opening section of *"Warrington" Pen-Portraits*, a selection of her husband's pseudonymous contributions to the *Springfield Republican* and other newspapers. An active member of the small Concord Women's Antislavery Society and one of the original Lowell Mill literary girls, Harriet Robinson must have heard the story of Shadrach Minkins many times from her Concord friends before she included it in her book. The story, appearing in distinctive type prefaced by the words "Mrs. Bigelow's account of this historic affair is as follows," described how Lewis Hayden and Minkins rode to Concord

in a carriage drawn by a black horse and a white one, and driven by a Mr. Smith. They arrived at Concord at three o'clock Sunday morning, and drove into Mr. Bigelow's yard. Mr. Bigelow, hearing the carriage, opened his door, and let in the poor fugitive, though the penalty was a thousand dollars, and

Ann Bigelow in old age.

six months' imprisonment, for "aiding and abetting" a slave to escape. The blinds of the house were at once shut, and the windows darkened, to evade the notice of any passers-by; and breakfast was prepared in the bedchamber (by Mrs. Bigelow), on an air-tight stove, with the bureau for a table. Mrs. Brooks, an antislavery neighbor, was sent for, and came, accompanied by her husband, Hon. Nathan Brooks. Mr. Brooks, though an abolitionist, did not go so far as his wife in advocating radical antislavery measures; and he had warned her that he should not countenance any such "aiding and abetting." But when he saw the poor fugitive, so frightened and forlorn, his kind heart made him forget the majesty of the law; and he did his part by furnishing Shadrach with a hat of his own with which to disguise himself,— the hat of a law-abiding citizen! As soon as Shadrach was refreshed (he was so fatigued with loss of sleep, and anxiety, that he could hardly keep awake while eating), Mr. Bigelow, in a wagon hired for the purpose, drove him to the house of Mr. Drake in Leominster, another station on the "underground railroad." From there he was carried to Fitchburg, and thence by rail to Canada.[8]

Each time Ann Bigelow retold the story of that night, she emphasized different details dredged up from her memory. The earliest of the three additional records was made almost twenty years later by Dr. Edward Waldo Emerson, son of the transcendentalist, shortly after an interview with Ann Bigelow on December 13, 1892. Though interested primarily in Henry Thoreau's involvement with fugitives, Emerson took down additional information, including Ann Bigelow's brief but vivid recollections of Minkins' visit. Her dating was slightly in error, but in general the details of this retelling correspond closely with the version of twenty years before.

In retelling the story in 1892, Ann Bigelow focused more on the character of lawyer Nathan Brooks. Known as a judicious man who "carefully read, examined, and considered all sides of social, religious, and political questions," Brooks was caught, like Harriet Beecher Stowe's Senator Bird, between his reverence for the law and his reverence for liberty.[9] And like Stowe's ambivalent senator, Brooks (whose story may have influenced Mrs. Stowe's characterization) chose the "higher" rather than the lower law when confronted with a fugitive in the flesh. Brooks's dilemma endows Emerson's notes of Mrs. Bigelow's story with dramatic tension and unity:

> At three in the morning of March [February] 17th [16th] a little before dawn, Shadrach was brought to the Bigelows' house. Mrs. Bigelow was not well. Her husband, however, made a fire in the air-tight stove in her room to get the slave and his rescuer some breakfast, and meanwhile went over to get Mrs. Brooks, a most ardent abolitionist, though law-abiding Squire Brooks said, "But if she is very sick they may want me for something, so I'll go over with you." When there, the door opened, [and when] Mr. Bigelow heard Mr. Brooks' voice down stairs with his wife's, he said, "What shall we do now?" But Mrs. Bigelow said, "There must be no concealment: let Mr. Brooks come up." Mr. Brooks with his wife entered Mrs. Bigelow's chamber and to their surprise found Mr. and Mrs. Bigelow, Mr. —— and Shadrach the fugitive. Squire Brooks saw what was going on at once, but here was an abstract matter hitherto now presented to him in the most concrete form.
>
> They were fitting Shadrach out with clothes. Mr. Bigelow's hat wouldn't fit him, but the man of law straightway zealously ran across the road to his house and fetched his own hat, sheltered by which Shadrach departed for the North Star, driven by Mr. Bigelow with a horse got from the stables near by (his own horse was white, well known, and hence unadapted for contraband service) in the wagon of Lowell Fay, another near neighbor.

Next day Mr. Cheney, a Webster Whig, said sharply to Mr. Brooks, "Shadrach was brought to Concord," which statement the Squire had to bluff off as best he might, but he was now liable to fine and imprisonment for violating the sacred law of the land.[10]

By the end of the century, the story of Minkins' surreptitious visit had clearly become a family treasure, to be passed from generation to generation. In 1893, in response to Professor Wilbur Siebert's advertisements for information about Underground Railroad activities, Ann Damon, a niece of Ann Bigelow, took down the story from her aged aunt. By then, according to her niece, Ann Bigelow was "almost totally blind and deaf . . . [but] more and more able to perceive by the mind alone." In Damon's letter to Siebert accompanying the page of notes, she offered to question her aunt further on special points. However, there appears to have been no further correspondence. According to Damon's notes,

> Shadrac[h] came here (to Mrs. Bigelow's house),—rescued from Court house in Boston by Lewis Hayden. The two ate from plates spread on her bureau in her room, at $3\frac{1}{2}$ A.M. Then her husband Francis E. Bigelow got a carry all & took S. to Leominster where a convention was in session. Friends forwarded him, & Mr Hayden drove back to Cambridge with his hired span (one black & one white horse) after going first to Sudbury. He was arrested.[11]

The final recording of Ann Bigelow's reminiscences takes the form of a handwritten school report titled "Inside History of Shadrach Fugitive Slave Case," written in 1905, seven years after her death. A sheet attached to the front reveals that the author spent approximately twenty hours preparing the report and received a grade of B. Largely derived from printed sources, the document could be easily dismissed except that its author was Theron J. Damon, the son of Ann Damon. In the margin next to the brief section dealing with Concord a note states: "Personal recollections—given orally by Mrs. Ann H. Bigelow, taken down by my mother Mrs. A. E. Damon." According to Damon's report, Hayden hired a two-horse carriage in Cambridge and,

> putting Shadrach inside, drove in the evening to Concord. The horses were badly matched . . .
> Soon after midnight Hayden arrived at the home of Mrs. Ann H. Bigelow, a zealous worker on the "underground railroad." Mr. Bigelow heard the

doorbell and spoke from the window. Hayden asked if Mrs. Ann Bigelow lived there. "What do you want?" was Mr. Bigelow's reply. "I want to see Mrs. Ann Bigelow." "You can trust me" said Mr. Bigelow, upon which Hayden told his errand. The fugitive was taken in, trembling from hunger, cold, and fear. He was fed and put to bed for a short while, during which time Mr. Bigelow hunted up a carriage. Bigelow then drove Shadrach to Sudbury.[12]

On the strength of the consistencies in these four separate retellings, Ann Bigelow's story bears more weight than almost all other late-century fugitive slave stories. Still, all four reports come from but one source, and each one is substantially different. In 1877, when the first version was printed, all the original Concord participants had died except Ann Bigelow, so there was no one to correct her. Two later accounts, however, support the broad outline of her story. Late in the century Reverend A. P. Putnam of Concord wrote that "it was there [the Bigelows'] that 'Shadrach' was secretly brought by Lewis Hayden and a Mr. Smith." Putnam, who apparently knew all the participants, added that Minkins was cared for by both the Brookses and the Bigelows. More important than Putnam's statement, which is at best secondhand, is a brief notice of the events by the black leader of the rescue and escape, Lewis Hayden. Before he died in 1889, Hayden revealed to a friend that he and John J. Smith had driven the fugitive to Concord on the night of the rescue, stopping "at Mr. Bigelow's house, where we were visited by some female anti-slavery friends."[13]

Several postscripts are necessary to complete the record of Shadrach Minkins' connection with Concord. In April Lewis Hayden came to Concord to address an antislavery gathering. Although his speech to the meeting is lost, presumably he did not reveal any details of the night visit to Concord in February. At the time, Hayden and six others were under indictment for the rescue and were awaiting trial in the coming months. But the *Liberator* reported that Hayden's words seemed "to echo the shriek of the arrested man."[14]

On February 16, the day after Minkins' nighttime visit to Concord, Henry Thoreau wrote in his journal:

Do we call this the land of the free? What is it to be free from King Geo[rge] the IV. and continue the slaves of prejudice? What is it [to] be born free & equal & not to live? What is the value of any political freedom, but as a means to moral freedom. Is it a freedom to be slaves or a freedom to be free, of which we boast. We are a nation of politicians—concerned about the outsides of freedom, the means and outmost defenses of freedom.[15]

Although Thoreau does not explicitly mention Minkins' visit, the entry is suggestive that he had heard about the rescue and the visit, perhaps even while it was occurring. Entries earlier in the month show Thoreau occupied with observing the effects of an unusually long midwinter thaw and with increasingly strained relations with his Concord neighbor and longtime friend Ralph Waldo Emerson. Suddenly on this day something set him musing on the meaning of freedom and slavery. Theodore Parker would express the same sentiment, but more bluntly, when he said, of another case, that assenting to the Fugitive Slave Law made Northerners the slaves of Virginia just as certainly as the law made slaves of hundreds of thousands of blacks.[16] Thoreau is clearly more interested in spinning out the implications about the personal meaning of intellectual freedom. The debate about real versus apparent freedom runs like an anthem through Thoreau's journals and books. The coincidence of date and subject in February 1851, as well as lengthy journal entries following the two later fugitive slave cases in Boston, suggests that Minkins' visit stimulated Thoreau's return to this favorite theme. During and after each of the later fugitive slave cases in Boston, Thoreau's journal entries crackle with bitterness as he explores the ironies of the "Cradle of Liberty" rocking to the tune of "Carry Me Back to Old Virginny." After the Anthony Burns case in 1854, Thoreau's anger boiled over: "Who can be serene in a country where both the rulers and the ruled are without principle?"[17]

Two other incidents connected Shadrach Minkins and Concord. In the fall of 1851 a fugitive named Henry Williams rested temporarily at the Thoreaus' house. On October 1 Henry Thoreau wrote in his journal: "5 P.M. Just put a fugitive slave, who has taken the name of Henry Williams into the cars for Canada. He escaped from Stafford County Virginia to Boston last October, has been in Shadrachs place at the Cornhill Coffee-House . . . "[18] A year later Concord and Shadrach Minkins were linked again during the trial of Elizur Wright, the final trial of Minkins' alleged conspirators, when Francis Bigelow somehow managed to be seated on the jury.[19]

*   *   *

A number of stories purport to describe Shadrach Minkins' movements
after leaving Concord, but many seem to belong to the shadowy realm of
anecdote and oral folk tradition. Some seem to contain germs of truth;
others are entirely incredible. Most were not recorded until the end of the
nineteenth century, and one detailed account did not appear until 1928.
Although they may reflect the facts only dimly, if at all, they do reflect the
underlying *meaning* of the events connected with Minkins' flight, meaning
that was inspired by passionate feelings and filtered through the imaginations of several generations. Some contain mythic elements that link the
stories to great cultural heroes or symbols. Others contain elements of the
mysterious. And at least two seem to be the product of fertile imaginations
of men who, fearing no contradiction, seized the opportunity to paint
themselves in heroic roles and to take a shortcut to immortality.

The evidence is quite reliable that the next leg of Shadrach Minkins'
journey took him to Leominster, a manufacturing town just south of
Fitchburg, thirty miles west of Concord.[20] One report suggests that he
traveled on the Fitchburg Railroad and was taken off the train in Leominster, just outside Fitchburg, where authorities were suspected to be waiting.[21] It is more likely, however, that the journey to Leominster was
accomplished entirely by carriage.

Minkins' stopover in Leominster is confirmed by a variety of sources,
including the last firsthand reports of his flight. We know with near certainty
that Minkins left Concord in a carriage driven by Francis Edwin Bigelow
and that he was taken into the Leominster home of Garrisonian abolitionists
Frances Drake and her husband, Jonathan, a shoemaker.[22] In 1854, when
the Boston Vigilance Committee appealed to the towns of Massachusetts to
form similar fugitive-protection committees, Frances Drake wrote to report
that although Leominster was unwilling to form such a committee, she and
her family were ready to shelter any fugitives who reached them. In this
letter she proudly proclaimed that she had "had the honor of sheltering
Shadrach when his pursuers were searching for him."[23]

The Drake home in Leominster is apparently the setting for a story that
appeared in the Boston *Commonwealth* just four days after the rescue. The
Commonwealth reported that Minkins spent Sunday morning quietly in an
unidentified town "less than 100 miles from Boston," arriving while the

family was eating a late breakfast. Refusing to join the family in their meal, he accepted only a glass of water "and then, falling on his knees, thanked God for his deliverance, and prayed most earnestly for a continuance of His mercies."[24] The account of the prayer made for effective abolitionist propaganda—the more devout Minkins appeared, the more abominable the attempted enslavement would seem.

Leominster is also the setting for one of the most entertaining, and probably more fanciful, anecdotes connected with the fugitive slave days. According to this story, which appeared in the *Commonwealth* on February 22, Shadrach Minkins arrived in Leominster on the very weekend a little antislavery rally and fair was being held. On Sunday evening an antislavery lecture was to be delivered—this much is in fact confirmed by a variety of sources. According to the story, Minkins wished to attend, but it was feared that even among the antislavery converts his safety would be in jeopardy. Finally his friends dressed him up as a woman and ushered him into the gathering. "He enjoyed the meeting highly," the *Commonwealth* stated gleefully in its report, "it being the first Abolition gathering he had ever seen." In June the abolitionist James Buffum, testifying at the trial of one of the alleged rescuers, confirmed the story of the Leominster meeting and, indirectly, Minkins' presence at it. Asked if he had seen Minkins "on the road to Canada," Buffum said that he had heard later that Minkins "had been present [at the Leominster meeting] a part of the evening dressed in woman's clothes."[25]

A later retelling of the Leominster stopover, nearly seven decades after the original events, is at best a second- or thirdhand story and has no credibility. But as an instance of the *process* by which legends accumulated around a seed of history and of people's desire afterward to identify themselves with the "right" side of the fugitive slave issue, it is very revealing. In 1928 a letter in the *Leominster Daily Enterprise* recounted the story of Minkins' visit to the Drakes in the kind of intimate, precise detail that only a firsthand observer could have known. The letter writer reported having heard her abolitionist father, identified only as a "Mr. Yeaw," tell "many stories of the exciting times of those days." According to the writer, her father had told her that it was Frances Drake who suggested a disguise and dressed Minkins in women's clothes. The writer went on to provide very precise details about the night of Minkins' visit: Minkins had sat "between Mrs. Drake and my grandmother," wearing a disguise of "widow's weeds" belonging to Frances Drake's recently deceased mother—a "long flowing black skirt and mantilla cape, a big Poke bonnet and long heavy crepe veil which was draped over the bonnet covering the face and extending below the waist . . . [and] black gloves." Afterward

> a little company met in the [Drake] house, where he spent the night, and at the close of the evening, Sherwood [Shadrach] sang a hymn, and again prayed in an earnest and impressive manner. He is said to [have] be[en] very calm, and to have expressed his perfect confidence in the protection of God. He declared that, at the worst, his claimant should have nothing but a dead body to carry from the state.[26]

This story, had it been recorded in 1858 instead of 1928, and by an actual witness, would automatically have some credibility because of its extraordinarily vivid details. Only one of Ann Bigelow's reminiscences of events in Concord contains anything as precise. But the 1928 story of the Leominster visit is at best secondhand and is uncorroborated by other testimony. It is far more likely that a personal and family mythology is being built. In the letter the writer's father and an unnamed grandmother become participants in a great moral event. For all these reasons, the "women's garb" story belongs to legend, not to history.[27]

The main facts concerning the Leominster episode are supported by other evidence. A letter from Frances Drake to William Lloyd Garrison, dated Wednesday, February 19, substantiates the occurrence of the antislavery meeting, although it contains no mention of Minkins. In the letter Frances Drake reported her disappointment with inclement weather and fair-weather abolitionists: attendance was poor because a week of rain had left water shoe-deep in the streets; moreover, four of her women committee members had withdrawn "for fear of being associated with the pulling down of churches, etc."[28] Mrs. Drake thanked the speakers, Wendell Phillips, James Buffum, and Thomas Russell, who had made the journey from Boston on the Fitchburg Railroad, for having roused the enthusiasm of the dampened crowd. When Buffum was later called on to testify about having seen Minkins in Leominster Sunday night, and having heard that Minkins attended the evening meeting in disguise, District Attorney Lord was to ask, "Did you know that he was present?" No, Buffum answered, adding that he could not tell one person in female attire from another, "the Bloomer costume not having been adopted at the time."29 A roar of laughter erupted, but the district attorney was not amused.

One Leominster report contains the most mythic story connected with Minkins' flight toward Canada. The earliest version appears to have been in circulation within days after the events it purports to describe. It reports that while Minkins was eating at the Drake house, news of his presence leaked out, and the townspeople eagerly flocked to meet him. After he had finished his meal, the townspeople "broke bread into small pieces and handed [them] to him, that each might have the satisfaction of saying *he or she had violated the infamous law* by giving aid and comfort to a fugitive slave."30 Another version of this story is embellished with additional details. It reports that at the Drakes' house, Minkins was sitting by the fire when Judge Thomas Russell, "knowing it was in direct violation of the law . . . begged the privilege of offering Shadrach a piece of bread." Minkins then "took the bread and broke it, and, repeating words of the communion service, passed it to the friends assembled." The same ritual was followed with a glass of water, the fugitive adding afterward "a most fervent and affecting prayer."31

The details of this Last Supper tableau in Leominster are not implausible. It is easy to imagine the abolitionists self-consciously enacting this religious ritual. It is a little more difficult to imagine Minkins' having the self-confidence at this point in his flight to engage in or even to initiate a bit of symbolic role-playing. But it is far more likely that none of the story is true, that it is a translation, conscious or unconscious, of *feeling* into *narrative.* As the story passed by word of mouth and in various versions in the columns of antislavery newspapers, details could have been added and changed. Just how rapidly this story was initially transmitted says something about how much was invested in it. The version involving only the communal breaking of bread appeared in the *Burlington* (Iowa) *Hawkeye* on March 20, 1851, little more than a month after Minkins had been in Leominster. All of these circumstances reveal an imagination hungry for raw material upon which to work. The story of Shadrach Minkins, like the stories of hundreds of other fugitive slaves, offered the combination of deeply felt significance and lack of verifiable hard facts that fosters mythmaking.

A few unverifiable reports claim to chart Minkins' progress beyond Leominster. One from the late nineteenth century traces him to Fitchburg and Ashburnham, a tiny town five miles northwest of Fitchburg and only five miles south of the New Hampshire border:

> From Leominster he went to Mr. Snow's at Fitchburg. The following evening a little company of friends had gathered at the home of Mr. C[rocker], to pay the family a visit. Among them was the venerable and good deacon L, a conservative anti-slavery man like many others in the Baptist church . . . [who] meekly and piously went for obeying the law. This good deacon had a good deal to say about the majesty of the law. "We must sustain the majesty of the law" were words always and ever upon his lips . . . Later, when the company were about to leave, a carriage drove to the door, and lo and behold! There was Mr. Snow with the fleeing Shadrach. He was taken into the house by the side door as quietly as possible . . . All were acquainted with the circumstances . . . Everyone was anxious and earnest to see him. After much persuading and promises of secrecy, he reluctantly went into the room where the people were. They were all much pleased with his appearance, and felt disposed to converse a long time. After the prolonged interview with him, Mr. C. said to the friends, "this poor fellow is destitute, it is cold weather, and he is going to Canada to a colder climate. Can't we make up a little purse of money for him?" A hat was passed and every one put into it. Those who had no money borrowed of their neighbor, and a nice little sum was given him.
>
> . . . Later on that night Mr. Crocker sent Bolivar Crane, one of his workmen, with his team and Shadrach up to North Ashburnham to Mr. Wood's.[32] Mr. Wood was a friend and helper of the fugitive. At his home he was taken sick and remained secreted in his attic for some time. When sufficiently recovered, he went on to Canada.[33]

According to the article, a few months later Minkins sent back "a little article of Indian work" in thanks, and the horse that pulled him was ever after known by the name Shadrach.

As is clear from his later timetable, Minkins must have crossed the New Hampshire border on February 17 or 18. Exactly where that crossing took place is unknown. He may have continued on a roughly northwest bearing, heading toward northern Vermont. This route would have had the advantage of keeping him fairly close to the railroad line that led northwestward to Keene, New Hampshire, so that at almost any point he could have been put on a train for a relatively comfortable journey farther north.[34] Another possibility is that he was taken overland on a more westerly route to Brattleboro, Vermont, just across the Connecticut River from New Hampshire and about a dozen miles north of Massachusetts. There he would have had access to a rail line coming north from central Massachusetts.

The likeliest scenario has Minkins passing through Burlington or St. Albans, in the northwest corner of Vermont, by midweek. Burlington, a substantial town of 6,000 about thirty-five miles south of the Canadian border, was reportedly a regular stop for fugitive slaves. Burlington's small black population was organized and militant, having vowed "to resist the outrageous [Fugitive Slave] law to the death," and among the city's whites there were a number of outspoken antislavery advocates.[35] From Burlington fugitives could take the train north to St. Albans, and thence to St. Johns, in what is now Québec Province, along a rail line that cut across the northern bays and inlets of Lake Champlain. In mild weather fugitives could be taken by boat across the lake to the New York shore and put on the trains to Rouse's Point and the Canadian border just beyond. They could also take a steamer or other boat up the lake to St. Johns or Rouse's Point, a route that would make it nearly impossible for them to be detected before they reached the border. In deep winter fugitives could also cross over on the ice from Vermont to New York. According to an 1893 letter from Reverend Joshua Young of Burlington to Wilbur Siebert, the Underground Railroad historian, railroads were the principal means of flight. Young tells of fugitives regularly being shipped northward by the Vermont Central Railroad through Burlington or, when Burlington did not seem safe, being driven twenty-five miles farther north to St. Albans to be put on the train there.[36]

In Vermont Minkins "fell down upon his knees & poured out his fervent thanksgiving to God in a manner to draw tears from the eyes of my informant who was with him."[37] So wrote Samuel Gridley Howe to Charles Sumner. If this rather doubtful report is true, it describes the last sighting of Shadrach Minkins in the United States.

On Thursday or early Friday, Minkins crossed into Québec Province (then known as Canada East or Lower Canada before the 1867 Confederation) heading for La Prairie, a hamlet fifteen miles north of St. Johns. The sublime, rugged landscape of the Vermont mountains was replaced by a frozen plain that swept almost unbroken to the horizon in all directions. The preceding summer, following nearly the same route into Canada, Henry Thoreau had noted the dullness of the border crossing, with only the flat, reedy Lake Champlain shoreline and a plain, barnlike railway station at St. Johns to mark the transition into a new country.[38]

But Shadrach Minkins did not need sublime landscapes to make his border crossing dramatic. For him, the nondescript political boundary loomed larger than the Alps. Behind him, on the U.S. side of the border, the law of the land made him liable at any moment to be seized, bound, and, after a brief hearing, stripped of his human and political rights and declared a mere piece of property, a thing. On the Canadian side, regardless of the color of his skin or the "condition" of his parents, he was free. The laws of this new land, derived from England, protected his life and his liberty.

Although fugitive slaves were known to have been kidnapped in Canada or tricked into recrossing the border, only one had been returned to the United States by a Canadian governmental action, in 1842, and since then Canadian laws had been strengthened.[39] It was thus with good reason that fugitive slaves, when first reaching Canadian soil, often whooped and hollered and danced for joy. Perhaps Shadrach Minkins, exhausted as he undoubtedly was after his weeklong flight, celebrated aloud or said a prayer. For the first time in nearly a year, he was safe. For the first time in his life, he was completely, unequivocally free.

MONTREAL

11 "Please to Remember Me Kindly"

Shadrach Minkins probably crossed the Vermont border into Canada East, or Lower Canada (now Québec Province), on Thursday, February 20, 1851, in the bleakest of late-winter weather. On Friday, six days after being rescued from the U.S. marshal at the Boston Court House, he reached a point opposite Montreal—undoubtedly at the hamlet of La Prairie, on the southern bank of the St. Lawrence. The towering peaks of the Adirondacks and the Green Mountains, the last visible reminders of the land from which he had fled, had long since disappeared behind him. Ahead, a mile across the swath of the frozen St. Lawrence, lay the city of Montreal, the largest city in British North America (the collective name for the provinces of Canada until the 1867 Confederation created a single nation).

Minkins' first view of Montreal surrounded by a vast collar of ice had to be forbidding. No bridge yet spanned the St. Lawrence, a mile or more wide where it embraced the island city. The last ships had long since departed to reach the Atlantic, leaving the docks and warehouses waiting for "the business season," as the months from April to November were called, when the St. Lawrence was free from ice. All these circumstances underscored the great distance Minkins had traveled and the remoteness of this place of sanctuary.

But if Shadrach Minkins was not too preoccupied with his own private uncertainties and fears, he may also have shared the wonder felt by other travelers on first seeing Montreal. From a

"Montreal from the Mountain" (1851), lithograph by E. Whitefield

distance, the island city presented a striking view. "Exceedingly imposing," exclaimed English traveler James Bryce Brown. Everywhere Brown
looked, he found "evidences of material prosperity"—in "the massive and
elegant stone-built wharfs of the city lined by ocean vessels, steam-boats,
coasting and other craft of every description"; in the "substantial warehouses, hotels, and public buildings" along the wharves; in the "towers
and spires diversifying the mass of houses, and displaying the importance
of place," backed by a "picturesque mountain" with "finely sloping base,
luxuriant in orchards and gardens, and sprinkled with stately seats and
villas."[1] Other travelers were also bewitched by Montreal's limestone
stateliness and its metal roofs gleaming in the sunlight. The whole undu-
lating panorama of stone, garden, and forest gave the city the appearance
of a Camelot.

In leaving the United States, Shadrach Minkins joined the thousands
upon thousands of blacks who had already left their country of birth in
search of freedom and a better life. In Canada they found other blacks,
some descended from slaves brought by English and French settlers in
the eighteenth century. They also found West Indians (the beginning of a
migration that a half-century later would become the main source of
Canada's black population). But in 1850 most blacks in Canada had come
from the United States, and many were fugitive slaves.[2]

Enactment of the Fugitive Slave Law in September 1850 dramatically
increased the flow of fugitive slaves and their families to Canada. Within
weeks as many as 2,000 reportedly crossed the border seeking the
Queen's protection. In 1860 some observers claimed that as many as
100,000 blacks from the United States were living in Canada, but such
figures undoubtedly reflect exaggerations by partisans on both sides of the
slavery argument. Robin Winks, author of the authoritative study, *The
Blacks in Canada* (1971), concluded that no one will ever know the actual
size of the black population of Canada for any time in the nineteenth
century. Winks's best guess is that by 1860 there were something like
60,000 in all of Canada, only a portion of whom were fugitive slaves and
their families.[3] Michael Wayne's recent study of the 1861 manuscript
census for Ontario suggests that there may have been only half that
number, and that fugitive slaves may have made up as little as 20 percent
of that population.[4]

In the four decades before the U.S. Civil War, the vast majority of fugitive slaves headed not for Canada East, or Lower Canada, as Québec was then known, but for Canada West, or Upper Canada (Ontario). By 1850 large numbers of U.S.-born blacks had already settled in Windsor, Sandwich, Amherstburg, Colchester, Chatham, and the towns and villages clustered near the shores of Lakes Erie and Ontario.[5] At the eastern end of Lake Erie, primarily on the Niagara peninsula, there were substantial numbers at Niagara Falls, Niagara-on-the-Lake, St. Catharines, Brantford, and Hamilton.[6] Hundreds had crossed Lake Ontario by steamer to settle in Toronto. Coburg, Kingston, and other towns near the lakeshore also attracted sizable numbers. Some fugitives had fled to the black communal settlement at Wilberforce, established in the 1820s, and to Dawn, begun in 1842. A smaller number of refugees lived in New Brunswick and Nova Scotia, where many black communities traced their ancestry to black Loyalists resettled by the retreating British after the Revolutionary War. A remnant population descended from English and French slaves was also scattered across Canada. There was still a handful of slaves in Canada at the beginning of the nineteenth century. As late as 1832 an illegal sale of a slave was recorded.[7]

Despite Montreal's reputation as a major terminus for fleeing fugitive slaves, only an unnamed Georgia fugitive and two or three nameless others are known to have come to Montreal before Shadrach Minkins.[8] Reports of several fugitive slaves traveling through northern Vermont hint of more arrivals, but their ultimate destinations remain unknown.[9]

If Shadrach Minkins could have selected his Canadian destination, he almost certainly would have chosen Toronto over Montreal. Though smaller than Montreal in 1851, Toronto was more accessible and offered far more support to fugitive slaves. In Toronto Minkins would have found many acquaintances from the Norfolk/Portsmouth area as well as numerous fugitives with Boston connections.[10] One Boston antislavery figure, Caroline Healey Dall, ministered to fugitive slaves in Toronto in the early 1850s. By 1857 Toronto's estimated 1,200 to 1,600 free blacks and fugitive slaves would nearly equal the black population of Boston.[11] As early as 1838, Toronto's African-Americans had met to protest against slavery. By 1851 several black churches and a well-organized program of assistance were aiding fugitives arriving from the states. Later in 1851, when the interracial Anti-Slavery Society of Canada was founded in Toronto, two houses were set aside to shelter new arrivals, who were given "wood-saws, axes, washing-tubs, smoothing irons, &c. according to their capabilities."[12] Benefit concerts and other Anti-Slavery Society fundraising activities supported these efforts.

The circumstances that led Shadrach Minkins to Montreal rather than Toronto were heavily ironic. The Fugitive Slave Law had been forged, in part, to satisfy the commercial interests that linked Southern cotton producers, Northern manufacturers, and railroads and merchants both North and South. These commercial forces, so eager to sacrifice fugitive slaves on the altar of national harmony, prosperity, and profit, built the railroads that helped speed Minkins and other fugitives northward to safety and freedom. When Shadrach Minkins arrived, the final dozen miles of track linking northern Vermont with Montreal were less than a year old.[13] This rail link drew Montreal more firmly than ever into the circle of Boston commercial success. A later list of owner John DeBree's investments shows that he owned stock in the Vermont Central Railroad.[14]

With the exception of a hundred or so Canadian fugitive slaves who were interviewed or who happened to be mentioned in newspaper stories or surviving letters, we do not know the names or origins of the thousands of African-American refugees arriving in Canada. Shadrach Minkins would have been one of these anonymous thousands if his arrest and dramatic rescue had not made headlines in a hundred newspapers across the continent. The day after Minkins had crossed the Canadian border, the Boston *Commonwealth* printed a brief announcement of the fact.[15] Over the next few weeks and months a number of unfounded stories about Minkins appeared in U.S. newspapers, some of them quite erroneous or fantastic. One story claimed that Minkins had gone to Toronto, not Montreal. Another claimed that he was to be exhibited at the world's fair in London. A report was printed that the Boston marshal had purchased his free papers so that he could return to Boston to testify at the trial of his rescuers. One newspaper reported that Minkins—and his mother!—had found employment as servants in the Montreal House hotel. Still another report circulated that he was "in a state of great destitution" and had written a Boston merchant a letter "begging a small sum of money to support life until he could get employment."[16] One story of uncertain date even reported that Minkins had settled on a farm in Buxton, Canada West, and that he was later aided in going back to Georgia to rescue his family.[17]

Minkins himself laid to rest some of the rumors about his whereabouts and circumstances in a short thank-you note to an unidentified recipient, written after he had been in Montreal for barely a week. Because he was illiterate, the letter must have been written for him by a friend. The formal, stilted phrasing indicates that the friend may also have assisted in composing the brief note, the only extant communication from Shadrach Minkins:

MONTREAL, FEB. 28TH, 1851.

Dear Sir:

   I feel it my duty to forward you the account of my arrival in this city. I reached here last Friday evening, a journey of four days. The weather was very severe during the time, and we had to cross the ice twice; once the distance was nine miles. My health is not so good as when I left, but I hope a few days will restore me. I am at a loss for words to express the gratitude I feel to those kind and dear friends in Boston, and believe me I shall always consider it my duty to pray for their health and happiness. Please to remember me kindly here,—and to the ladies. And in conclusion, permit me to subscribe myself,

Your grateful servant,
Frederick Minkins[18]

Although Minkins signed himself "Frederick," the name he had adopted in Boston, crossing the border had made it possible for him to resume using his old given name of Shadrach—but with a difference.[19] In slavery he had been merely "Shadrach" to his owners and other whites. In Boston he had concealed his true identity, adopting the name Frederick Minkins (or Wilkins). But after arriving in Canada he joined "Shadrach" and "Minkins," symbolically appropriating his full identity.

Although the published Canadian census for 1851–52 listed no blacks in Montreal, when Minkins arrived the city was home to several dozen blacks of various origins.[20] Minkins would have found at least four households headed by U.S.-born blacks, presumably refugees from slavery like himself. James Smith, who had been in Montreal since at least 1843, was operating a hairdressing salon in the 100-block of Notre Dame Street with his white, English-born wife, Louisa.[21] A second household was headed by

Isaac Taylor, a coachman, who lived with his wife, Harriet, a Québec-born black. Another U.S.-born black householder, Peter Dago, worked as a dyer and scourer. Dago had been living in the city since at least 1847.[22] Evidence also suggests that when Minkins arrived, William F. Jones, a barber in his forties, was living in the city with his wife, Ann Queen, and their three children, James H., George E., and Sarah L. Freeborn blacks from Annapolis, Maryland, Jones and his wife had left the state with their family about 1849. Apparently they stopped briefly in Troy, New York, where daughter Sarah was born. From Troy the family went on to Montreal. Descendants of the Jones family can be found living in the Montreal area today.[23]

In addition to U.S.-born black householders and their families, at least three dozen other blacks were living in the city when Shadrach Minkins arrived. Five heads of household had been born in England, the West Indies, or the Canadian Maritimes: James Grantham, a young English-born tobacconist; carpenter James Carpenter, the sole male member of a household of six blacks; John Grantiers, another carpenter, born in St. John, New Brunswick; James T. Nurse, a native of the West Indies who had begun to work in Montreal as a cabinetmaker by 1847; and Mary Ann Grant, a native of the West Indies.[24] Other blacks living in Montreal cannot be identified with certainty because most of the 1851–52 manuscript census has been destroyed. Nevertheless, some of the thirty unnamed single blacks recorded in the 1842 manuscript census must still have been living in the city when Minkins arrived.[25]

Everything in Shadrach Minkins' experience in the United States had taught him to think of the color of his skin as the main (though hardly the only) source of his identity in the larger white-dominated world. In the new Montreal environment, where religion, national origin, language, social class, and occupation all competed as sources of identity, and where the issue of race was diluted by the tiny numbers of African-Americans and the very different cultural milieu, he must have felt a strange disorientation. In a city where English/French and Protestant/Catholic cultural differences were the main sources of tensions, the few blacks in French-speaking households, together with the handful of West Indians and blacks born in England, had little experience to link them with the U.S. refugees.

Moreover, U.S.-born black immigrants themselves could be separated from one another by multiple cultural and social barriers. An extreme case is found in the example of the Healy family. In the early 1850s at least five of the Healys—the children of a light-skinned slave mother and a white Georgia planter—were in Montreal under the care of various Catholic orders. When Shadrach Minkins arrived, the oldest brother, James, was studying for the Catholic priesthood at the Sulpician Seminary, and his fourteen-year-old sister Martha was also in Montreal. Other Healy siblings soon followed.[26] The world of the Healys—that of French Catholicism and of upper-middle-class, very light-skinned African-Americans—was remote indeed from the one Shadrach Minkins would know in Canada. James Healy would later become bishop of Maine, an unthinkable attainment for the average African-American in the white world of the nineteenth century. The Healys and fugitive slaves like Shadrach Minkins might as well have been living on different planets.

Although Montreal did not offer Shadrach Minkins the transition houses, ready-made black community, or other attractions of Toronto, the city did seem to promise several advantages. The absence of an established black community meant that Minkins entered an environment uncomplicated by long-standing jealousies and animosities, social reputations and protocols, or tight kin or neighborhood networks. Adversity, dislocation, and shared experience provide occasions for unusual camaraderie. Not only Minkins but nearly every African-American refugee would have been looking for new bonds to replace the old ones that had been severed upon leaving the United States. And for African-Americans in a new setting, being a *visible* minority—so often a disadvantage—became an advantage insofar as it made for nearly instant recognition among the refugee group. African-Americans like the Healys may have remained aloof from the refugees, responding to class and status markers that in established black communities made for complex social networks and barriers; but for refugees like Shadrach Minkins, the Montreal world brought new social possibilities.[27]

Montreal refugees also benefited from a largely sympathetic Canadian press. Montreal's English and French newspapers had been attacking slavery fiercely. With the passage of the Fugitive Slave Law in 1850, their animosity toward slavery and their sympathy toward the fugitive slave intensified. "A curse, a robbery, a sacrilege, a blasphemy," the *Montreal Gazette* called the law.[28] The reformist *Montreal Pilot* had labeled Northern Congressmen who supported it "betrayers of the liberties of mankind" and worried that "the coloured population generally will be exposed to great oppression."[29] The smaller French-language press of both Montreal and Québec City, led by *Le Canadien,* also condemned the Fugitive Slave Law and sympathized strongly with African-Americans' plight. These feelings were heightened by a perception that the scorned African-Americans paralleled the subordinate position of French Canadians in Canadian society.[30]

The Montreal press promised fugitive slaves like Shadrach Minkins a warm welcome. "Oh! We don't advise any one to come here slave-hunting, unless they have an insurance against tar and feathers," the *Courier* boasted.[31] Commitment to fugitive slaves like Minkins led the *Witness,* heretofore an ardent supporter of the movement to annex Canada to the United States, to declare itself "willing, not only to forego all the advantages of annexation, but to see Canada ten times poorer and worse governed than she is."[32] Other English- and French-language papers similarly declared their cordiality toward the black refugees.

But despite the warm assurances of the press that fugitive slaves would find Montreal whites eager to assist them, in Canada as in the United States antislavery rhetoric often concealed complex and ambivalent attitudes toward African-Americans. As historian Robin Winks has shown convincingly, the black immigrants to Canada frequently encountered the same "patterns of prejudice found in the North, although . . . muted."[33] Jason Silverman's study of the white response in Canada West, where black immigration was heavy, reveals considerable hostility toward the refugees. Canada West black refugee Samuel Ringgold Ward even claimed that "Canadian Negro Hate, is incomparably *MEANER* than the Yankee article."[34]

Shortly before Shadrach Minkins arrived in Montreal, several expressions of deeper anxiety about black immigration appeared in Montreal newspapers. One *Courier* writer lamented that Canada was becoming "a *cul de sac* for undesirable races" and ended with a stark threat: "let the colored race who migrate to Canada, feel that this land cannot be their permanent home." A few days later the *Courier* warned American blacks to avoid "contending with a people who look upon him as an alien, and treat him as a nuisance."[35] In the spring of 1851 a letter to the same paper denounced the newly formed Anti-Slavery Society of Canada for encouraging black immigration.[36] And although a writer in the *Montreal Gazette* acknowledged that collecting money and clothes for fugitives slaves already in Canada "forcibly commends itself to the public benevolence," he added that it was "one thing not to refuse them shelter, and quite another . . . specially to invite them."[37]

Despite this evidence of racial animosity, Shadrach Minkins and other fugitives soon found examples of the "public benevolence" called for by the *Gazette* writer. Evidence of support appeared almost immediately in the form of advertisements for work placed in a variety of newspapers through the help of unidentified benefactors, including, presumably, the newspapers themselves. In early March, two weeks after Minkins arrived, the "Want Situations" columns of the *Transcript, Pilot,* and *Gazette* carried the following notice:

> SEVERAL YOUNG MEN OF COLOUR, for a long time residing in and near Boston, but on account of the Laws recently passed by the United States Government, have been forced to leave, and come to the True Land of Liberty, wish to meet with employment in Canada, and are willing to accept Situations as COACHMEN, COOKS, WAITERS in PRIVATE HOUSES, or in HOTELS.
>
> Should this meet with the eye of any person wanting such men, their orders will receive immediate attention by applying at the Pilot Office.
>
> Newspapers in the city of Montreal will do a great kindness, by giving this a few insertions in their respective journals.[38]

Another advertisement seeking "Men of Colour, who understand working in tobacco" may have been aimed at the fugitive slaves.[39]

A brief *Pilot* editorial accompanying the first advertisement announced that "among these colored persons is *Shadrach*" and explained that the fugitives had "found it necessary to leave Boston through fear of Southern vengeance" and were "anxious to find employment as servants or in stores." The notice added, "they need help, as their resources are very limited. Information will be given at this office, and contributions thankfully received." A follow-up appeal indicated that three of the fugitives had found work, adding that the two remaining "have been accustomed to porter's work in dry good stores, and are very anxious to obtain employment."[40] Overall the editorial gives an impression of ready sympathy and support for Minkins and the others.

These advertisements for work provide evidence that Shadrach Minkins and other fugitives received some assistance, although who placed the ads or what additional aid was provided is not known. Six whites living in the city in the early 1850s are among the likely benefactors. D. S. Janes, a flour merchant who became one of the vice-presidents of the Anti-Slavery Society of Canada when it organized in Toronto in March, later was so closely connected with the fugitives' cause that he earned the nickname "the African consul."[41] Ira Gould, a U.S.-born owner of a flour mill, was to hire several fugitives, including one of the earliest arrivals. John Dougall, editor and publisher of the *Montreal Witness,* and ministers Henry Wilkes and William Bond also sympathized strongly with the antislavery cause.[42] A sixth known sympathizer, young Frederick Frothingham, a native of Canada with Boston family connections, would be described years later by his abolitionist cousin Reverend Samuel May, Jr., as "one of the few men in the American pulpit who never blinked the question of slavery, nor shunned to tell his hearers of the true character of the system."[43] In the early 1850s, while Frothingham was in Cambridge part of the year attending the Harvard Divinity School, he was the only regular Montreal subscriber to Garrison's *Liberator.*[44] Although Frothingham may have been too young and inexperienced to have been active in aiding the fugitives at the time Shadrach Minkins arrived, he was shuttling back and forth to Boston in these years, and with his family connections to the antislavery movement, he could have been a valuable assistant.

Shadrach Minkins and the others were soon promised aid from an unlikely source. In the first week of March, while Minkins and the others were still looking for work, a black minstrel group called Butler's Real Ethiopian Serenaders arrived in the city for a series of concerts at Odd Fellow's Hall and the Garrick Club Theater. By 1851 minstrelsy, the combination of low comedy, music, and dancing that the Real Ethiopians brought to the Montreal stage, was already decades old. It had become so popular in the United States that some minstrel companies had even built their own theaters. As early as 1837 minstrelsy had been exported to England. Jim Crow and Zip Coon, the archetypal black bumpkin and city slicker, and a host of other grotesque characters began to appear on the Montreal stage a few years later. By 1850 a succession of troupes with names like "Sands' American Minstrels," "Lowerre's Original Sable Melodists," "Fisher's Original New York Melodists," "Mower's Harmonian Troupe," and "Conlisk's Ethiopian Warblers" crisscrossed eastern Canada annually.[45]

J. H. Butler's group was unusual in that it was composed of "five *colored* men from Philadelphia"—hence the "Real" in the group's name—rather than whites in blackface.[46] They were soon delighting Montreal audiences with their trademark piece, the "Laughable Burlesque of the BLACK SHAKERS," mocking the strange and oft-ridiculed religious dances of the United Society of Believers in Christ's Second Coming, and with other sketches, songs, stories, gags, dances, and instrumental performances.[47] Although one high-minded paper deplored the Ethiopians' Shaker piece ("we do not wish to see the peculiar religious observance of any denomination . . . serve to pander to low vulgarity") and found a "Lucy Long" piece tasteless, the same reviewer nevertheless described the company as "the best that have visited us." The writer singled out bones player D. Fitzgerald for his "tasteful execution of many feats . . . hitherto unseen in this city."[48] The minstrel troupe guaranteed an evening "well spent, to anyone who loves music with a strong vein of fun pervading it," one reporter remarked.[49]

For Shadrach Minkins and the other fugitives, there was heavy irony in the popularity of the performances of the Real Ethiopian Serenaders and other minstrel troupes. Minstrel caricatures exploited the interest in slavery generated by the controversy and at the same time seemed to justify the subjugation of blacks. Peopling the stage with jig-dancing, spiritual singing, clownish "negroes," minstrelsy presented the reassuring picture of the plantation and of the benighted, childish Negro character that slavery apologists loved. Runaways, whose desire to flee gave the lie to the myth of a paternalistic plantation paradise, were rarely depicted in minstrel shows, and when they were they tended to be homesick repentants longing for the golden plantation days, or else to be buffoons, pretentious dandies, or incompetents—personifying the prejudiced view that free Negroes, unsupervised by whites, turned rotten—were lazy, foolish, thieving, dependent, arrogant knaves.[50]

Parodies like the Ethiopian Serenaders' "Shaker Burlesque" or the standard comic lecturer who spouted gibberish played flagrantly to white racist beliefs in the intellectual inferiority of blacks. The demeaning subtext was that when blacks aspired to high-brow and middle-brow white culture, only a clownish, clumsy imitation resulted. Blacks could merely "ape" the outward form. This demeaning message was intensified by the fact that Montreal audiences came away from the sketches of the "Negro

THEATRE ROYAL.

FOR THE BENEFIT OF THE
FUGITIVE SLAVES.

BUTLER'S
REAL ETHIOPIAN SERENADERS,

FROM PHILADELPHIA,

Consisting of Five Colored Men,

RETURN their sincere thanks to the Ladies
and Gentlemen of Montreal, for the very
liberal patronage bestowed on them during their
short stay, and beg to announce that they will
give their FAREWELL CONCERT, at the
above place of Entertainment, for the Benefit of
Messrs. SHADRACK, WILLIAMS, JOHNSON, TYBOLD
and SCOTT—five Fugitive Slaves—(who have
lately escaped from bondage, and are now in this
city, destitute of the means of subsistence,)
THIS EVENING, (Thursday,) the 13th March,
when they trust that a generous public will sustain them in this effort to relieve their unfortunate
Fellow-Countrymen.

SHADRACK will appear in the course of the
evening, and relate the circumstances of his wonderful Escape from Boston, and other incidents in
his life.

Admission:—Boxes, 2s. 6d.; Pit, 1s. 3d.; Gallery, 7½d. Doors open at SEVEN o'clock; Concert to commence at EIGHT o'clock.

Tickets may be procured at all the principal
Hotels, Book and Music Stores.

March 13.

Notice of the Real Ethiopian Serenaders' benefit concert,
Montreal Pilot, March 13, 1851. Similar advertisements
appeared in several other papers.

delineators," as the minstrel performers were often billed, with a "true
portrait" of American blacks firmly etched in their minds. One Montreal
reporter, for example, praised a blackface performer named Mulligan as
"a most amusing delineator of Negro oddities," adding that "a gentleman
who resided some years in the South told me that his imitation of the
Southern Negro is to perfection," as if that settled the matter.[51]

Butler's Real Ethiopian Serenaders arrived while Shadrach Minkins and the other Boston fugitives were struggling to fit themselves into their strange new environment. So when Butler offered to assist them, they could hardly have refused. On March 13 Montreal newspapers (including the French-language *La Minerve*) announced that the Real Ethiopian Serenaders' final concert would be a benefit for five newly arrived fugitive slaves. The advertisement for the event gave their names as "Messrs. Shadrack, Williams, Johnson, Tybold and Scott" and promised that "Shadrack . . . will appear in the course of the evening, and relate the circumstances of his wonderful Escape from Boston, and other incidents."[52] "It would be well if a slave-catcher or two could be there, to hear and see for himself," the *Pilot* added boastfully.[53]

If the slavecatcher had been there, he would have heard Minkins' words join the Serenaders' nostalgic "Pompey from Home," their cheerful "Have a Little Dance Tonight," and their raucous "Stop Dat Knockin' at the Door."[54] The master and the slave, in the spectral form of the grinning minstrel show gargoyle, had followed Shadrach Minkins to Montreal.

No report of the evening's performance has been found, but a notice printed in the newspapers four days later tells the outcome of the show:

TO THE CITIZENS OF MONTREAL

We, the undersigned Fugitives from the United States, beg to state to the Citizens of Montreal, that the benefit given for them by Mr. Butler's Ethiopian Serenaders was an imposition upon the public, as none of them received any thing from Mr. Butler or any other person. They may try to play the same game in some other City of Canada if it was not made known to the public.

Charles Williams
Stephen Tidball
Minken Shadrach
James Scott
Henry Johnson

Upper Canada papers will do a great kindness by giving this a few insertions.—March 17.[55]

Soon afterward, however, the newspaper reported having received a letter from J. H. Butler accusing James Scott of being the real scoundrel. Butler claimed that he had in fact given Scott $7.50 to divide with the four other fugitives.[56] Butler's unsubstantiated countercharge may have been nothing more than a smokescreen, but Montreal papers gave it credibility just by reporting it. By casting suspicion on one of their fellow fugitives, Butler left Shadrach Minkins and the others to contend with an unwanted and unpleasant complication. It was not the new beginning the refugees would have wished for—nor was it the only trial that Minkins and the others were to face.

12 A Home Far Away

A book published in 1852 describes the home of a Montreal black family:

> The scene now changes to a small, neat tenement, in the outskirts of Montreal; the time, evening. A cheerful fire blazes on the hearth: a tea-table, covered with snowy cloth, stands prepared for the evening meal. In one corner of the room was a table covered with green cloth, where was an open writing desk, pens, papers, and over it a shelf of well-selected books.

This passage is part of the conclusion to Harriet Beecher Stowe's best-selling novel, *Uncle Tom's Cabin.* Readers of Stowe's work will remember the scene as the home of fugitive slaves George Harris, his wife, Eliza, and their son, Harry, who, in one of the novel's most memorable episodes, has been nimbly carried to freedom by his mother across Ohio River ice floes. The Harrises' Montreal home, with its tea-table, its pens, paper, and writing desk, and its bookshelf of "well-selected" volumes, is part of Stowe's vision of the place of blacks in a land of racial equality. The details speak of the possibilities for middle-class aspirations and upward mobility. George's self-reliance and "zeal for self-improvement," Stowe suggests, provide a model of individual initiative that alone would be sufficient to elevate African-Americans.

Although Stowe claimed that the concluding scene of her novel had been inspired by a report of an actual reunion of a fugitive slave with his wife in Montreal, Stowe's imagination could hardly have been expected to capture the reality of the lives of Shadrach

Minkins and other black refugees in Canada.[1] The world in which they lived was remote from her experience. It was more complex and more contradictory than the one she imagined for the talented mechanic George Harris and his family.

Adjusting to life in Canada would prove to be no easy task for Shadrach Minkins and thousands of other black refugees. The harsh climate, the unfamiliar culture, the loss of friends and family, of jobs and possessions, must have been overwhelming to many of them. Fugitives who had given up nearly everything found that they had traded legal for economic insecurity. Work was scarce. In Canada West some of the black settlers found themselves in communities that were not self-sustaining, depending on annual fundraising expeditions—"begging," their critics called it—for survival.[2] "Times are very hard in Canada . . . Every thing are so high and wages so low They cannot make a living," one Norfolk fugitive later wrote from New Bedford to explain why two friends had just returned from Canada.[3] Other fugitives were simply overwhelmed by separation from loved ones. In an 1851 letter to the *Liberator,* Nova Scotian refugee Thomas H. Jones aptly summarized the feelings of many others in his circumstances. "So long as nature prompts me . . . I shall look back to my native clime with anxiety, sorrow, and devotion. My personal friends, my flesh and blood, are there . . . I am now in exile."[4]

For these and other reasons, including the unpleasant discovery that racial prejudice was not restricted to the United States, an unknown number of fugitives returned across the border, willingly trading legal freedom in a cold sanctuary for the uncertainties of warmer and more familiar surroundings. Even among those who stayed, there was not unanimous sentiment that life in Canada was clearly preferable to life in the United States. Some refugees undoubtedly stayed because they had neither the energy nor the resources to leave.

Soon after the incident with the Ethiopian Serenaders in mid-March, a visitor from the South discovered Shadrach Minkins operating a small business in Montreal. A friend of the Southerner sent a report of the meeting to the Boston *Commonwealth:*

GEORGETOWN, MARCH 27, 1851

Messrs. Editors:—You will be pleased to hear that Mr. Charles Boynton, of this place, saw the famous Shadrach, in Montreal, on Saturday last.—Mr.

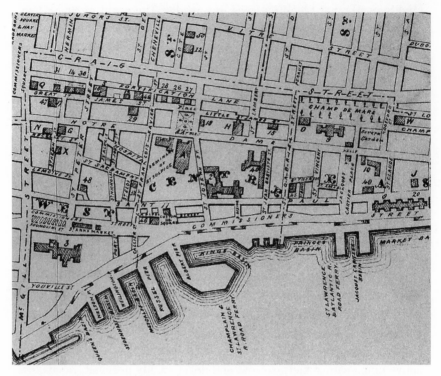

Detail of 1851 map showing the Old Montreal section, where Shadrach Minkins and other African-American refugees lived.

Boynton had quite a long conversation with him; he looked quite well, declared he had no desire to return to "The land of the *free* and the home of the *brave.*" He has opened a barber's shop in the city. He also told Mr. Boynton that he had received fifty dollars from a lady in Boston a few days ago.

Yours respectfully,
John McCourly.[5]

By the summer Minkins was living and working near the custom house, in the section of the city now known as Old Montreal. Bordering the dock district along the St. Lawrence River, the location would have put Minkins at the center of Montreal's business life. The docks and surrounding streets bustled with activity eight months of the year. Boisterous cabmen were known for fighting for the business of disembarking passengers. Hundreds of carts and wagons—and in winter, sleighs—carried dry goods and various supplies through the streets and lanes to the warehouses and businesses that lined St. Paul, Notre Dame, and Commissioners Streets.

For a time Minkins was one of the Old Montreal "sights" for U.S. visitors. Southerners sought him out, looking for evidence that his escape had ruined him. (Southerners or their friends were undoubtedly behind a story that claimed Minkins was living in dire poverty, able to sustain himself only by the aid of donations from Boston.)[6] Abolitionists sought him out as a kind of living shrine to the antislavery movement.

Visitors' reports provide the main details of Minkins' first year in Montreal. At the end of the summer of 1851 Minkins told another visitor from the United States the story of his difficult first months. Life in Montreal had been a struggle at first, Minkins said. He "knew no one, and no one knew him."[7] For nearly two months he had been ill. He had earned his meals waiting tables at the small Montreal House hotel at Commissioners Street and Custom House Square. The hotel, "kept by a live Yankee," was, according to one visitor, "pleasantly located, not large, with good rooms and table—assistants obliging, &c." Minkins had been "much liked by his employer," another report claimed.[8] He changed jobs several times to improve his position, and by summer, apparently with the help of at least one contribution from Boston, had saved a small sum, which he and a partner used to open a small restaurant. The venture soon collapsed, however, when the partner disappeared, taking with him most of their funds.[9]

By the end of the summer Minkins had got on his feet again and opened a second restaurant, the West End Lunch, at 172$\frac{1}{2}$ Notre Dame Street. In August the Montreal correspondent of the *Cleveland Democrat* visited Minkins at his "small lunch shop" and found him "doing well." The writer's companion on the visit, a "gentleman from Mississippi," thought he would not want Minkins on his plantations. "He is a smart fellow, but he knows too much," the Mississippian observed.[10]

In September Northern papers published two more reports from visitors who had made their way to Minkins' lunchroom. One, a correspondent of a Maine newspaper, described Minkins as "a bright, intelligent negro, [who] seems quite happy, though he likes Boston better as a place of residence."[11] The other visitor provided the most vivid of all the accounts of Minkins. "Having returned to the Montreal House," wrote this un-named visitor,

> I determined upon making my next sally for the purpose of calling upon Shadrach, the fugitive, and accordingly directed my steps to a saloon, called the West End Lunch in Notre Dame street. I entered and found a hearty good-natured looking negro within, talking with the captain of an English vessel. Having ascertained of the negro, that he was indeed Shadrach himself, I heartily congratulated him upon his escape from his enemies, and his safety in a land of freedom.[12]

This was the visitor to whom Minkins told the story of his early difficulties in the restaurant business. "He . . . thinks the lesson he learned from the conduct of his intended partner, no mean part of his capital," the visitor reported.

Although few of Minkins' words were recorded, the visitor's comments tell us that he talked enthusiastically of finding peace and freedom in Canada. "Notwithstanding his misfortunes, he is in excellent spirits, and feels what he never felt previous to his residence in Canada, that he owns himself, and is perfectly safe from the impious clutch of the man-hunter." His feelings toward the United States were decidedly cool, if not bitter. He told the visitor that "friends in the States have held out various inducements" to come back, but he had refused. "Worlds would not induce [me] to again set foot on American soil, until slavery is abolished," he reportedly said. He added that he had jokingly instructed his friends to shoot him if he were ever crazy enough to start back toward the U.S. border.

Clearly, Shadrach Minkins was turning away from the country of his birth. Although he had been forced to flee from the United States, he now accepted and even welcomed that step and had therefore come uncon-sciously into harmony with black emigrationist thinkers like Martin De-lany and Mary Ann Shadd.[13] At least for the time being, Canada was his country of choice.

The fate of the Boston fugitives who arrived about the same time as Shadrach Minkins is uncertain, but indications are that they, too, had trouble adjusting to the new environment. Three of the fugitives named with Minkins in the advertisement for the Ethiopian Serenaders' benefit concert simply vanished. Their names never appeared in the census, public records, tax records, or city directories. They may have moved about Canada seeking better prospects, or died, or even lived for a number of years in Montreal in the households of others. As with the vast majority of Canada's African-American refugees, we simply do not know what happened to them. However, the lack of evidence tells us that they were either unwilling or unable to put down even shallow roots.

Besides Shadrach Minkins, the only other early fugitive who can be traced in the city is Charles Williams. Williams had originally fled to Montreal immediately after the Fugitive Slave Law took effect, possibly arriving with a group reported on October 30, 1850.[14] Apparently he later returned to Boston to be reunited with his wife, only to flee again to Montreal in February 1851, after being warned through a friend of his employer that agents for his master were looking for him. Soon after arriving the second time he found work, probably as a servant, with U.S.-born flour mill owner Ira Gould. Documents in the papers of Caroline Healey Dall show that abolitionist intermediaries tried unsuccessfully to negotiate Williams' freedom with his owner, a man named Ridgley from Washington, D.C., from whom Williams had fled sometime before 1845.[15]

In the meantime Charles Williams' personal life in Montreal rapidly grew more complicated. He met a young Irish woman, Margaret Maguin. About nine months later, the young woman bore a son, and "Charles Williams, waiter," was entered in the birth record as the father.[16] What all this means is not hard to guess. It was not an unfamiliar story. Adult male fugitives who found themselves isolated and alone in strange surroundings naturally looked to local women for companionship, and some inevitably ended up in Williams' situation.[17] The days stretched into weeks, the weeks into months, and the months into years. Back in Boston Mrs. Charles Williams waited for him at 4 Southac Place, and in 1852 and 1853 the Boston city tax collector's entry for the Williams' house included the notation "Canada" next to Charles Williams' name.[18] On March 22, 1851, the Boston Vigilance Committee gave Mrs. Williams money to pay for fuel for wives bereft of their fugitive husbands. Later in March and again in April, June, and July, the Vigilance Committee reimbursed her for expenses connected with "destitute fugitives."[19]

Charles Williams may have fully intended to return to his wife in

Boston, but the birth of a son in Canada complicated matters. In the end he took what probably was the path of least resistance; a later census record shows that he and Margaret Maguin had other children and continued together for many years.[20]

In March 1851 Shadrach Minkins and other Montreal black refugees were apparently too caught up in the struggle to meet their own needs to participate in the founding of the Anti-Slavery Society of Canada in Toronto. Perhaps they were not even aware of the event. And in the fall of 1851, when forty-six black U.S. and Canadian representatives convened in Toronto to invite U.S. blacks to "come out from under the jurisdiction of those wicked laws," no Montreal blacks were in attendance. About the same time, black abolitionist Samuel Ringgold Ward, passing through Montreal on his way to Toronto, met Shadrach Minkins and several local abolitionists but found that Montreal blacks knew almost nothing of the activities of blacks in Canada West.[21]

After the fall of 1851 Minkins disappeared from sight for many months. Events in Boston in the year following his escape make it unlikely that he returned to the United States, however. In March, on the heels of his escape, Boston's U.S. marshal had made a major effort to recover fugitive slaves from New Bedford, but a terrific storm at sea apparently forced the mission to be canceled. Then in April 1851 Thomas Sims, a twenty-three-year-old fugitive slave from Georgia, was arrested in Boston. A bricklayer by profession, Sims had escaped by stowing away aboard a Boston-bound vessel from Savannah on February 21, the same day Shadrach Minkins was crossing over into Canada. After narrowly escaping being returned by the captain of the vessel, Sims took lodging in a black seamen's boarding-house. Later he telegraphed his free wife for money, and the telegram giving his address was intercepted. Agents soon arrived in Boston, and Sims was arrested only a few hours later—testimony to the Boston federal officers' zeal to make a good showing. Despite a week of agitation and threats of rescue and riot by Boston's abolitionists, Sims was judged a "chattel personal" and remanded to the custody of his owner on Friday afternoon, April 11. Before daylight the next day, a brigade of two hundred Boston police and watchmen and a hundred volunteers formed a hollow square around the diminutive fugitive and marched with him from the Court House to Long Wharf, where Sims was placed aboard the brig *Acorn* for the voyage back to Georgia.[22] Boston's abolitionists stood by helplessly as the procession passed.

To nearly everyone but the most adamant Compromise supporter, Thomas Sims's forced return to the South from the city of Paul Revere, the Boston Tea Party, and black martyr Crispus Attucks of Boston Massacre fame was a painful irony. The machinery of both state and nation had been grotesquely turned against a Massachusetts man whose only crime had been to seize his liberty for himself. Even the ordinarily apolitical Henry Thoreau, writing in the security of his Concord home, filled his journal with angry words about the Bostonians who had assisted in the deed, calling them *homines ad servitutem natos*—"men born to be slaves"—after Tiberius' famous complaint about the Roman senators. "A government which deliberately enacts injustice—& persists in it!—it will become the laughing stock of the world," he fumed.[23]

New reports and rumors suggested that Boston was an increasingly dangerous place for fugitive slaves. The Vigilance Committee learned that federal authorities were apparently quietly assembling a force of a hundred men to assist in future cases.[24] In early May two agents from Georgia and another from New Orleans were reportedly prowling Boston in search of fugitive slaves. Warrants were said to have been issued for several fugitives, one of them named Joseph Russell, "a resident of twenty years with a business in the basement of the Brazier building."[25] The Vigilance Committee warned Russell and, through J. B. Smith, gave him $7.50 to speed him by rail to Canada. Account books from mid-April to mid-May show that the Vigilance Committee treasury also paid the railway fares to Canada for at least 10 other fugitives and family members.[26] Reports of slaveowners' agents, of warrants, and of flight continued to fuel the exodus from Boston. Reverend Theodore Parker claimed that by the end of May more than 350 had fled from Massachusetts since the passage of the Fugitive Slave Law, most of them, presumably, from Boston. "One man, Mr. Caswell, the city missionary—has aided 93 to escape from the clutches of the kidnapper since last September, & has 8 or 10 more on his hands," Parker noted.[27] The Boston *Commonwealth* (perhaps deliberately underestimating the numbers to protect those remaining) predicted that by the second week in May there would be no more than ten fugitives left in the city, and those were "pretty wide awake."[28] So were Boston's free black citizens, as several arrests for carrying concealed weapons revealed.[29]

At the end of April a thousand Vigilance Committee handbills posted throughout the city screamed out the most famous warning issued during the fugitive slave days:

CAUTION!!
COLORED PEOPLE of Boston, ONE AND ALL
You are hereby respectfully CAUTIONED and advised,
to avoid conversing with the WATCHMEN and Police Officers of Boston
For since the recent ORDER OF THE MAYOR & ALDERMEN,
they are empowered to act as
KIDNAPPERS and SLAVE CATCHERS,
and they have already been actually employed in
KIDNAPPING, CATCHING, AND KEEPING SLAVES.
Therefore, if you value your LIBERTY, and the WELFARE OF THE FUGI-
TIVES among you, *shun* them in every possible manner, as so many HOUNDS
on the track of the most unfortunate of your race.
Keep a Sharp Look Out for KIDNAPPERS, and have TOP EYE open.[30]

For Shadrach Minkins the Boston news—avidly reported in the Montreal press—was bleak. It meant that there was no prospect of an immediate return—or perhaps of any return. Further warnings against his return were the trials of his accused rescuers, which began at the end of May. James Scott, the young black clothing merchant, was the first to go to trial. The prosecution was led by U.S. District Attorney George Lunt, a fact that left Daniel Webster in despair. Webster had wanted "the best talent & experience of the bar" for the prosecution, but Lunt, whom Webster hated for professional as well as personal reasons, was a given commodity.[31] "He is not a good lawyer, theoretic or practical; and at the same time he is opinionated, self-willed, & obstinate," Webster wrote despairingly to President Fillmore. "The members of the Bar feel that he has no right to hold the office."[32] Webster's contempt for Lunt was exacerbated by the fact that at the 1849 Whig convention Lunt had been the sole Massachusetts delegate to abandon candidate Webster for Zachary Taylor. Compounding the insult, Taylor, on assuming the presidency, had rewarded Lunt by appointing him U.S. district attorney for Massachusetts despite Webster's intense lobbying—almost begging—to have his son, Fletcher, appointed.[33]

Still, the defense team of Richard Henry Dana, Jr., and John Parker Hale, New Hampshire's antislavery senator, had a tough assignment. Five officers positively identified Scott, who towered over most men, as one of the persons who had fought their way into the courtroom to rescue Minkins.[34] "Scott had on a rubber overcoat, and a Sou-wester cap," Assistant Deputy Marshal Frederick Byrnes added definitively. Dana and Hale brought forward several persons familiar with Scott who had not seen him among the rescuers and two who swore that Scott was in his shop around the time of the rescue.[35] None of this testimony was very persuasive, but it proved to be enough to keep at least two jurors from voting for conviction. Scott was released but remained liable for retrial.[36] "A legal farce," predictably declared the South Carolina *Charleston Mercury*.[37]

Lewis Hayden's case presented even greater difficulties for the defense. On the first two days of his trial in early June, a procession of prosecution witnesses all swore positively that they had seen Hayden with, or leading, the rescuers every step of the way. On the final day of testimony Thomas Murray, the cabdriver who had transported Minkins and Hayden from the city, even testified that before the trial began, Hayden had offered him a bribe of "from $50 to $100 . . . [to] clear out and stay till this trial was through."[38] Yet Hale and Dana's witnesses who claimed to have seen Hayden elsewhere about the time of the rescue, together with Lunt's bumbling attempt to prove involvement in a conspiracy, apparently prevented Hayden from being convicted. His jury reportedly stood nine for conviction and three for acquittal, and Hayden was dismissed (although, like Scott, he remained liable for retrial).[39]

Apparently undaunted, the U.S. district attorney pressed forward with the other cases. Whether Lunt really believed convictions possible, whether he was just making the best show he could for Southern audiences, or whether he had been ordered to proceed with the prosecutions regardless of their outcome is difficult to know. Some believed Lunt's main motivation in pursuing the cases was to multiply his fees.[40] A year and a half later Lunt told Richard Henry Dana, Jr., that Webster had "taken these cases into his own hands" and had decided which ones to prosecute.[41] Although there is no direct evidence to support Lunt's claim, the charge is undoubtedly correct. Webster clearly was trying to stage-manage the Boston fugitive slave cases—and Massachusetts Whig politics and policy—in order to keep his presidential campaign on track. In April, shortly before the rescue trials began, he wrote to Fillmore, "It is of great importance to convict [Elizur] Wright," and a few days later he again wrote to the president about the need to convict "some" rescuers in order to demonstrate Boston's allegiance to the Compromise.[42] At the same time he was trying to prevent the Massachusetts Whig Party from nominating anti-Compromise candidate Robert Winthrop for governor. Being linked to Winthrop on the party ballot, Webster feared, would weaken his own chances.[43] He personally supervised arrangements for the hearing and return to slavery of the fugitive slave Thomas Sims.[44] "The great point, at present," Webster wrote in June, "is to let it be known, in Massachusetts, & *else where,* that the friends of Union in Mass. are determined, & *will not take any backward step, under any circumstances.*"[45] By then Webster-for-president petitions were in heavy circulation. The rescue trials were simply one more political front in his campaign for the nomination.[46] Nothing he said or wrote suggests that he saw them in any other light.

In November George Lunt brought lawyer Robert Morris to trial, and again the black community worried that one of their leaders would be imprisoned. Again the prosecution had many witnesses who claimed to have seen Morris with Minkins during the rescue, including sixteen-year-old Newell Harding, who stated that Morris had been going down Southac Street with his arm either "laid on the fugitive's back" or around his waist—he could not remember exactly.[47] But again, defense witnesses provided contradictory testimony. And again, as in both previous cases, Lunt failed to produce any evidence of a premeditated conspiracy among the rescuers. The jury voted unanimously for acquittal.[48]

The unresolved cases (four men—two black and two white—had not yet been tried, and two, Scott and Hayden, were liable for retrial) were postponed again and again through the remainder of 1851 and into 1852. Incredibly, in 1852 George Lunt brought Elizur Wright to trial—twice. Lunt's case was flimsy, and Wright was almost certainly innocent. "I have actually done nothing and *said* nothing so far as the rescue of Shadrach is concerned," Wright reassured his anxious brother privately a month after being arrested. "I merely witnessed the rescue of Shadrach without lifting a finger or uttering a word to aid it."[49] The first trial, in which Wright stubbornly insisted on conducting his own defense, ended in a hung jury; the second, defended by Richard Henry Dana, Jr., and George Farley, in an unambiguous acquittal.[50] "The bar ought to vote Farley & me a service of plate, for demonstrating the importance of professional services," Dana wrote with self-satisfaction in his journal.[51] What he did not note, and apparently did not know at the time, was that one juryman assuredly would have prevented a guilty verdict and probably had much to do with bringing about the verdict of innocent. He was a man who knew the case intimately, the very man who had harbored the fleeing Shadrach Minkins under his roof on the night of the rescue over a year and a half before—Concord blacksmith Francis Edwin Bigelow.[52]

Elizur Wright's second trial proved to be the government's last bid for a conviction in the rescue cases. Lunt carried the five unresolved cases over onto the 1853 docket, over Dana's protest.[53] Lunt agreed that the delay had been exceedingly lengthy ("they have already been punished enough," he told Dana, prompting the angry comment in Dana's journal, "What right has he to punish?"), but he refused to drop the remaining cases entirely, saying that he might yet prosecute one of them in May.[54] Apparently he decided otherwise. The last reference to the cases in the Circuit Court docket books is the May 1853 notation "nol. pros."—*nolle prosequi,* meaning that the prosecution had decided to pursue the cases no further.[55]

In the final tally, the trials of Shadrach Minkins' alleged rescuers proved to be an enormous failure for Daniel Webster. Even with Benjamin R. Curtis, a staunch ally, presiding over the Circuit Court in the final three rescue cases, the government had been unable to secure a conviction.[56] The trials were thus a fitting symbol for Webster's political hopes. His dream of leading a Union party to save the nation had never come close to materializing.[57] In June 1852, in three days of balloting at the national Whig convention in Baltimore, Webster never finished more than an embarrassingly distant third behind Fillmore and General Winfield Scott, the eventual nominee. By the fall the Whig Party was in collapse, and a dispirited Webster was dying.[58] Elizur Wright's acquittal came, symbolically, within days of Webster's death at his Marshfield estate on October 24. Webster's friends mourned the loss of the great man, the voice of New England for nearly half a century. Even Webster's opponents felt "an irreparable loss," Dana wrote, because "they feel that this great sun has gone down in a cloud."[59]

Luckily for James Scott, Lewis Hayden, Robert Morris, and Elizur Wright, juries had not shared Webster's view of the Fugitive Slave Law or of the need to appease the South. But for the defendants and for Boston's black community, the trials—especially of community leaders Lewis Hay-

den and Robert Morris—had been intimidating. And for Shadrach Minkins, the whole inept affair of the drawn-out trials contained a bleak
personal warning. To be a fugitive slave, pursued by an owner and his
hirelings, was one thing. But to be the potential sacrificial lamb on the
altar of national harmony and Union—that was another thing entirely.
Boston was not safe; he could not return. Fortunately, by 1853 Shadrach
Minkins had already found another life to live.

Minkins was almost certainly counted with Montreal's other blacks in a
census taken by the city in 1852. That census showed a total of 80 blacks
living in Montreal: 18 in St. Louis Ward, 15 in West Ward, 26 in St. Antoine
Ward, with the others scattered through four of the six remaining wards.[60]
Many of these 80 blacks were probably fugitive slaves like Minkins, but
there must also have been a smattering of free black Americans, West
Indians, and descendants of black Canadian slaves or of black Loyalists.
As only the numerical totals survive, it is impossible to know their origins.

What seems fairly clear from the 1852 census and from other sources,
however, is that in the early 1850s few fugitive slaves were joining
Shadrach Minkins in Montreal. Fugitives from Boston and coastal New
England continued to flee elsewhere, often by ship. The Boston Vigilance
Committee account book mentions fugitives fleeing "to St. Johns" and "to
Halifax."[61] No Québec localities are named.

Apparently, however, a trickle of blacks—fugitive and otherwise—continued to arrive. When British traveler William Chambers stayed at the
Montreal House in 1853, where Shadrach Minkins had worked briefly
soon after his arrival, he noted that "all the waiters in the establishment,
about a dozen in number, were negroes, being probably refugees from the
South."[62] In the fall of 1851 the *Montreal Transcript* carried the notice
"SITUATION WANTED BY A FUGITIVE SLAVE," which read:
"Wanted, a SITUATION as Groom or Coachman, or as Waiter in a Gentleman's Family, or in a Hotel, by a Coloured man, who has been forced
to leave the United States or go into Slavery."[63] Several U.S.-born blacks
who arrived about this time are known by name, although it is impossible
to pinpoint the year of their arrival. John Watkins, a waiter in 1852,
probably arrived at least as early as 1851. Joseph Wright, who would be
listed as a boot- and shoemaker several years later, also apparently
reached the city in the early 1850s.[64]

By 1853 Shadrach Minkins had settled in and begun to put down roots. He had met and apparently married a young Irish woman named Mary— last name unknown—and sometime in 1853 or early 1854 Mary gave birth to a daughter whom they named Eda. Within two years a son, William, would be born. The *Liberator* in September 1853 reported that Minkins was operating an "eating house."[65] The following year itinerant Unitarian minister Charles Dall went hunting for Minkins when he visited Montreal. As Dall reported in a lecture a short time later, "after going through several narrow streets, and examining all the signs, but finding no 'Shadrach,' [I] finally went into a small shop over which was a little sign with 'S. Makins, Victualler &c.' " He asked the black man he met inside where he could find Shadrach. "I am Shadrach," came the reply. Dall told the audience that he had gently scolded Minkins for lacking "Yankee calculation" in naming his establishment so obscurely: "The man had a fortune in his name, and did not know it—else he would surely have signed himself 'Shadrach.' "[66]

While Shadrach Minkins struggled to adjust to his new life in Canada, fugitive slaves in the United States continued to be harassed. The Fugitive Slave Law had given the green light to many Southerners eager to recover assets they had written off. From the time of its enactment through 1854, owners and hired assistants made several hundred attempts to seize individual fugitives or groups of runaways in nearly every Northern state, where many had resided in relative safety for years, even decades. Fugitive slaves were returned to Southern owners from Massachusetts, New York, Pennsylvania, Ohio, Indiana, Illinois, Iowa, and Michigan. Many attempts and seizures, especially along the Mason-Dixon line and the Ohio River, bypassed judicial procedures and public notice altogether. The system of slavery was once again forcibly separating families, leaving children and spouses to grieve for their lost family members. This time, however, many of the forced separations were taking place not on the auction blocks of Mississippi or Virginia or South Carolina but in the federal courtrooms of the North.[67]

Some fugitives escaped capture by resisting with violence. The most famous incident was the Christiana Riot, in southeastern Pennsylvania, on September 11, 1851. When a Southern posse attempted to capture a fugitive slave, armed local blacks fought back, mortally wounding the slaveowner and injuring several others. The cost to Christiana blacks was high. Several lost their lives, others had to flee, and still others were arrested and put on trial. Before the month had ended, another dramatic case occurred in Syracuse, New York. William Henry, known as Jerry, was arrested as a fugitive slave at a time when a Liberty Party meeting had drawn many abolitionists to the city. The abolitionists, together with local blacks, attacked the police station and rescued the fugitive, who was sent to Kingston, Ontario.[68]

The vast majority of fugitive slave cases occurred in the border states from Pennsylvania westward, but there were enough in New York and Massachusetts to keep Boston fugitive slaves and their friends on guard. Boston continued to be the prize target of Southerners' efforts to exert their "rights" even in the heart of the North. Thomas Sims had been captured and returned to his Georgia owner in 1851, and in 1854 another Boston fugitive, Anthony Burns, was seized. After a halfhearted, poorly coordinated attack on the Court House by abolitionists, for a second time, with enormous expenditure, a fugitive slave was marched to the Boston docks and put aboard a ship bound for the South.[69]

For Shadrach Minkins and other fugitive slaves from Boston, the cases of Thomas Sims and Anthony Burns contained special warnings. Even stronger personal warnings for Minkins were the continued attempts by Norfolk and Portsmouth owners to recover fugitives from Boston and elsewhere in New England. In January 1854 several Portsmouth and Norfolk owners, possibly with hired assistants, arrived in Boston to enlist the U.S. marshal for an expedition against their fugitive slaves, believed to be in New Bedford. (These may have been the same owners involved the alleged 1851 failure of a naval raid on New Bedford's fugitives.) When, impatient with the slow pace of the marshal's investigation, the owners began to make inquiries themselves, the scheme was revealed and the fugitives apparently went into hiding.[70] Nevertheless, the attempt carried the unmistakable message that Massachusetts would continue to be targeted by owners of fugitive slaves from Shadrach Minkins' Virginia neighborhood.

Five months later two black men from Lowell, Massachusetts, arrived in Manchester, New Hampshire, with news that kidnappers were seeking to capture Edwin Moore, a fugitive of eleven years from a master in Norfolk. The Southerners reportedly had obtained a warrant for Moore and were preparing to arrest him. According to the *Montreal Pilot,* Moore was sent immediately to Montreal, where he found work as a barber in St. James Street. "We can confirm all that is said of Moore's ability and intelligence," the newspaper added, noting that the fugitive had had to leave a wife and three children behind in Manchester.[71]

None of the attempts on fugitive slaves in the United States would have generated as much discussion or worry as an attempt in 1855 to lure fugitives from Montreal itself. Not that the fugitives in Canada had ever been able to relax their vigilance totally. All through the 1850s, rumors and reports circulated of attempts to entice or force fugitives across the border so that they could be arrested on U.S. soil. In 1855 a notice from Toronto warned fugitives throughout Canada that fraudulent offers of employment in Detroit, Philadelphia, and other Northern cities had been made to a number of Canadian blacks. "You are in Canada," the notice warned, "and let no misplaced confidence in this or the other smooth-tongued Yankee, or British subject either, who may be mercenary enough to ensnare you into bondage by collusion with kidnappers in the States, deprive you of your liberty."[72]

Although several incidents in the Niagara Falls area put Shadrach Minkins and other black refugees on alert, no black was known to have been returned to slavery from Canada since the Fugitive Slave Law of 1850 had gone into effect. Nor had any Southerner been audacious enough to attempt a wholesale effort to recover Canadian fugitives. That is, no one until John H. Pope, an enterprising policeman from Frederick, Maryland, came along. In January 1855 a letter from Pope was delivered to the Montreal chief of police.[73] In the letter Pope explained that, fearing to cross over into Canada to capture fugitive slaves, he needed "a good assistant" in Montreal to help him lure fugitive slaves to the border. "I would be there to pay cash," Pope added enticingly.[74] Similar letters were sent to Toronto, Kingston, and possibly to other Canadian towns and cities.[75]

Fortunately for Shadrach Minkins and Montreal's other blacks, the police chief immediately exposed this enterprising plot by sending Pope's letter to the newspapers. "Triple shame on the people whose laws sanction such conduct!" thundered the *Gazette,* adding with familiar self-satisfaction, "and we may thank God, once more, and rejoice, that their country is not ours,—that we have no share or participation in their sin." Another letter from Pope, however, may have stripped away any comfort that the police chief's response had given to Shadrach Minkins and other Montreal fugitive slaves. In the letter, Pope boasted that publication of his original letter had in fact attracted the assistance he sought. "Long before this letter [dated January 16] reaches its destination," he bragged, "Officer Pope will have secured eight of her Majesty's loyal black subjects."[76] Whether Pope's claim was true or not, it would have had a chilling effect in Montreal's black homes.

In the later 1850s the small black population of Montreal and the rest of Canada East remained almost invisible. Black abolitionist minister John Lewis, traveling in 1855 through the "eastern townships" bordering Maine, New Hampshire, and Vermont as an agent for *Frederick Douglass's Paper*, met few black refugees in the small villages such as Coaticook, the first important depot of the Portland and Montreal Railroad on the Canadian side. Lewis admitted that deplorable racial attitudes had spilled over from the United States into the eastern townships. Nevertheless, he assured black refugees that if they came to Coaticook, they "would meet with all the hospitable kindness that heart could wish."[77]

Only a handful of African-Americans who reached Montreal in the mid to late 1850s can be identified. One was Edwin Moore, the barber from New Hampshire. Another fugitive, John Scott, traveled directly to Montreal in 1857 after escaping from Richmond, Virginia.[78] Thirteen additional individual black immigrants or families can be identified between 1853 and 1860 by working backward from identifications in the 1861 census. Many of these newcomers gave a Southern state as their place of birth, a fact that does not automatically mean they were fugitive slaves but certainly increases the likelihood that they were. These newcomers were distinguished by the number who had a skill or trade. Among them were Matthew Bell, a carpenter; John Wilson, a brickmaker, first noted in marriage records for 1854; Thomas Cook, listed variously as a whitewasher, a cook, and a coffeehouse operator beginning in 1856; and six barbers, William Briscoe, David Johnson, William Medley, Edwin Moore, Isaac Newton, and Clarence F. Selden. In 1842 Selden had been one of the secretaries of a Troy, New York, meeting of black citizens protesting a U.S. Supreme Court decision (*Prigg v. Pennsylvania*) regarding fugitive slaves.[79] Nothing is known about the U.S. lives of the others except their places of birth.[80]

*   *   *

During the mid-1850s Shadrach Minkins operated several restaurants at various locations in Old Montreal. The city directory for 1856 shows that he had moved to 27 St. Paul Street, perhaps the location where Reverend Charles Dall had stumbled upon him two years before. It was an area crowded with other restaurants and inns—twenty-one of the first hundred addresses on St. Paul Street alone. Tax records indicate that in 1856 Minkins paid an innkeeper's tax of forty dollars. Sometime in the next year, perhaps to escape the intense competition along St. Paul, Minkins moved again, this time to St. Alexis, a short cross-street running between Notre Dame and St. Sacrament just two blocks from the great cathedral opposite Place d'Armes. Minkins' "Yankee ingenuity" would have pleased Charles Dall now, for he had named his new venture after Harriet Beecher Stowe's 1852 bestselling exposé of slavery, "Uncle Tom's Cabin."[81]

Despite its famous name, Minkins' restaurant apparently did not prosper. For part of 1857 he tried to earn a living as a trader at the St. Alexis Street address, apparently without success. The next year Minkins' name is absent from both the tax records and the city directory. Failing in business was not the only hardship that Shadrach and Mary Minkins endured that year. Records of the new Protestant cemetery on the northwest side of Mount Royal reveal that William Minkins, who was only three or four years old, died on October 11, 1857. On his burial record is written a single word of explanation: "croop."[82] On April 7, 1858, William's older sister, Eda, died of "consumption" (tuberculosis) and was buried near her brother. The deaths of the two children left the grieving parents alone, but soon Mary would be pregnant again.[83]

By 1859 Shadrach Minkins was again on his feet, operating a barbershop at 75½ Commissioners Street, in the heart of the commercial district along the waterfront. Another black barber, Isaac Newton, operated a shop just a few doors away.[84] The proximity of Newton's barbershop is one of several hints that Minkins and the other black refugees built relationships with one another in the late 1850s.[85] In 1858 Clarence Selden and fellow black barber William Briscoe witnessed the burial certificate of the infant daughter of Samuel Williams.[86] When Williams died a few months after his daughter, William Briscoe was once again a signatory to the certificate.[87] The signatures of fellow black refugees George Anderson and barber Clarence F. Selden on the burial certificates of Minkins' two children in the mid-1850s tell us that the two men were there to offer comfort and support to the grieving father and mother.[88] In 1859 William Henry Medley, a twenty-three-year-old black barber from Baltimore, Maryland, witnessed the marriage of barber Henry Barr, a U.S.-born black, and Angélique St. Louis, a French Canadian.[89]

A single surviving letter from an African-American refugee in Montreal in the late 1850s confirms this impression of interaction and mutual support. In the letter to Philadelphia Vigilance Committee chairman William Still, fugitive slave John Scott attempted to arrange for his wife to find him upon arrival in Montreal by contacting fellow refugee Edmund Turner:

> MONTREAL, SEPTEMBER 1ST, 1859
>
> Dear Sir:—It is with extreme pleasure that I set down to inclose you a few lines to let you know that I am well & I hope when these few lines come to hand they may find you & your family in good health and prosperity. I left your house Nov. 3d, 1857, for Canada I Received a letter here from James Carter in Peters burg, saying that my wife would leave there about the 28th or the first September and that he would send her on by way of Philadelphia to you to send on to Montreal if she come on you be please to send her on and as there is so many boats coming here all times a day I may not know what time she will. So you be please to give her this direction, she can get a cab and go to the Donegana Hotel and Edmund Turner is there he will take you where I lives and if he is not there cabman take you to Mr Taylors on Durham St. nearly opposite to the Methodist Church. Nothing more at present but Remain your well wisher
>
> John Scott[90]

It is not known whether Scott's wife ever reached the city.

Although evidence of contact and assistance among the African-American refugees is spotty, it bears a whispered witness to a network of friendships and shared responsibilities. The connections that wove together the lives of Shadrach Minkins and the other fugitive slaves and freeborn blacks in Montreal made a protocommunity if not an actual community. Faint though this testimony is, it offers hints of a group solidarity growing out of shared needs and experiences. How many black refugees were included in the developing network of relationships, or whether non-U.S.-born blacks were included, is unclear. Nor is it clear whether the relationships were strong enough to form a foundation upon which a lasting community could be built.

13 "Free at Last! Free at Last!"

In the United States, the end of the 1850s brought dark clouds presaging a great storm. The war between slavery and free-soil settlers in "Bleeding" Kansas, Preston Brooks's murderous assault on Charles Sumner on the Senate floor, and John Brown's ill-fated 1859 raid on the federal arsenal at Harper's Ferry were the first thunderclaps. The presidential campaign of 1860, culminating in the election of Abraham Lincoln without a single Southern electoral vote, was one long sustained rumbling. The storm that broke over Fort Sumter in Charleston Harbor the next year would sometimes sweep before it a tide of fire and blood, sometimes stall into a slow, cold, murderous sickness. For four agonizing years the war smoldered and raged, leaving a weary, wounded, devastated nation in its wake.

All of Montreal, indeed all of Canada, would watch this appalling denouement to the slavery controversy with fascination and concern, and no Canadians followed events in the United States with more interest than Shadrach Minkins and Montreal's other African-American refugees, the living links to this ferocious conflict. From that distant place they shared in the disappointment and frustration of all African-Americans when the war dragged on and still President Lincoln issued no proclamation of freedom for the slaves. When the Emancipation Proclamation took effect on New Year's Eve 1862, welcomed by dozens of freedom-night watches through the North, it was no less glorious to African-Americans in both Canada and the United States for being a practical act of Union desperation designed to reinforce a failing Union campaign.[1] In Boston a tumultuous celebration that began at the Tremont Temple continued through the night at the Twelfth Baptist Church, the "Church of the Fugitive Slaves."[2] That night, as Frederick Douglass wrote, "Joy and gladness exhausted all forms of expression."[3]

Undoubtedly Montreal's refugees knew something of the raising of the first black regiments and of the movement of the fronts. They may also have heard of the terrible loss of life among the black troops of the Massachusetts 54th Regiment who stormed Fort Wagner, and of the race riot that terrorized New York City's blacks, leaving half a dozen dead by lynching.

The war news spurred African-Americans across Canada to form a more powerful group identity. It also forced them to confront a disturbing question: Who were they? Were they Canadians, rooted in the land that had given them sanctuary and to which they owed their lives? Or were they merely exiles, waiting for the chance to return "home"? Was their identity indissolubly linked to the terrible struggle for freedom? Did they belong only among the friends and family they had left behind? As the decade wore on, these questions became ever more insistent.

While events in the United States accelerated toward civil war, Shadrach Minkins' life quietly changed. He had tried operating a restaurant, trading (very briefly), and barbering at a variety of addresses. By 1860 he had moved southwest from Commissioners Street in the old city to the St. Antoine Ward.[4] There he rented 81 St. Antoine Street for forty-eight dollars a year and opened another barbershop. The following year he moved close by to 83 Montagne Street (now known by the English form Mountain), perhaps to accommodate his growing family: a daughter, Mary, had been born in 1858 and a son, Jacob, in 1860. Both children were to prove hardier than the first two: a decade later, their names would appear in the census, and Jacob Minkins would live to the age of seventy-five.[5]

By moving to Mountain Street Shadrach Minkins put himself in the center of the most dynamic area of the city. Though lacking the brokerage firms, commission merchants, importers, and other businesses that typified Old Montreal, the St. Antoine Ward was the center for the new industrial economy and the immigrants who supplied its labor.[6] Between 1851 and 1861, when the city grew by more than 50 percent, the St. Antoine district absorbed a large share of Montreal's 32,000 new residents.[7] "Works" by the dozens sprang up in Montreal's "Little Lowell," the St. Anne Ward along the Lachine Canal just to the south—iron works, flour mills, the Chemical and India Rubber Works, the Oil and Colour Works, the Candle Works, and the Canada Marine Works, among others.[8] Lighter industries producing shoes, clothes, tobacco products, and other consumer goods became increasingly common in the St. Antoine Ward, later the center of Montreal's shoe industry.[9]

Shadrach Minkins could hardly have chosen a more active location. The cobblestone street in front of his barbershop-home rumbled with the carts and wagons of market vendors, carters, teamsters, and cabmen. To all this traffic was added the flow of goods and laborers to and from the Lachine Canal manufacturing district half a dozen blocks south. Soon a new markethouse a block north added even more traffic past his door. With the 1858 opening of the Victoria Tubular Bridge, the first bridge to span the St. Lawrence River at Montreal, Grand Trunk Railroad traffic from the east was added to an already flourishing east–west traffic. A Grand Trunk Railroad yard soon grew up barely a block from Minkins' establishment, filling the air with the screeching, the smoke, and the soot of progress.[10]

The house on the little block where Shadrach Minkins lived has long since been demolished, but where St. Antoine and Mountain Streets intersect, a few of the simple two-story brick structures like the ones that were part of his street could still be seen in the early 1990s. An old city directory reveals that this working-class neighborhood was an ethnic and occupational mosaic. Minkins' immediate neighbors on one side were Irish workers, William Doyle, a laborer, and Miss Bridget Murphy, a dressmaker, and on the other side French Canadians Jean Baptiste Richot, a laborer, and François Richot, a carriagemaker. The whole street echoed with the accents of French, English, and Irish neighbors: Lamoureux, Falex, Mooney, and Riordan (carters); McGiven, Gauthier, Gougon, Killy, and Legget (laborers); Tollert (trader), Prendergast, Cousineau, Savard, and Dowian (grocers). There were Spring (dealer), Guy (notary), Lawson & Company (boots and shoes), Gregoire (carpenter), Prance (joiner), Lesperance (turner), Macdonald (bookkeeper), Ashton (hatter and furrier), Koester (saloon), and Gravelle (hairdresser).[11]

"The colored population of Montreal has greatly increased of late," said the *Witness* early in 1860, adding that "so far as we have the means of judging, they appear to be a sober, industrious, respectable class of the community."[12] But just how many African-Americans joined Shadrach Minkins in Montreal, or where they came from, is unclear. Although the *Gazette* argued that there were more than four hundred, the published census of 1861 indicated only 46 black residents. Manuscript census slips, however, show 228, and since this figure almost certainly represents an undercounting, the actual numbers may have been fairly close to the *Gazette* estimate.[13] Nearly three-quarters of the adult blacks (89 of 124) identified in the manuscript census reported having been born in the United States. Of the 44 who gave their state of birth, 24, including Shadrach Minkins, named Virginia, followed by Maryland (10), Florida (4), Pennsylvania (2), and Delaware, Kentucky, New Jersey, and Ohio (1 each).[14] Although Southern birth did not necessarily mean that refugees were fugitive slaves (William F. Jones of Maryland, for example, was free and his wife freeborn), the great distance and the expense of traveling to Montreal make it likely that many were.

The lives of Shadrach Minkins and his fellow African-Americans emerge faintly in the 1861 Canadian census, tax records, and city directories. These sources show that Montreal's small black population was dispersed through the city. The largest number, 46, lived in the St. Antoine Ward. St. James Ward, a predominantly French-speaking area on the opposite side of the city, was a close second, with 43 blacks, followed by the more central wards of St. Louis (30), St. Lawrence (27), and Centre (17). Smaller numbers lived in the St. Anne and St. Marie wards at the extreme ends of the city and in the two wards (East and West) that, with Centre, made up the old city. Rarely did the same block contain two black households. Adjacent black households were even rarer. As far as we can tell, Shadrach Minkins' closest black neighbor lived more than a block away.

Although Montreal's blacks were not tightly clustered as they would have been in Boston and most other northern U.S. cities, a loose residential grouping hints at a pattern of mutual assistance and shared responsibilities. Fourteen black refugees shared their homes with one or more unrelated blacks (most of these were widows and young single men living with families, although several households consisted entirely of unrelated adult men).[15] Four loose clusters of black homes also tell of developing interrelationships among the refugee blacks.[16] One cluster of twenty black addresses was at the eastern end of the city, bounded by St. Mary,

Amherst, Lagauchetière, and Voltigeurs Streets. A second group consisted of a handful of barbershop-residences—about one per block—along Notre Dame Street beginning a block east of Place d'Armes. In the southern part of the city there were a number of residences scattered widely along St. Antoine Street and side streets to the south, beginning from about St. Margaret Street. It was in this third, very loose cluster that Shadrach Minkins settled with his family on Mountain Street about 1860.

Although Shadrach Minkins' St. Antoine Ward housed the largest number of blacks in 1861 and would become the thriving center of Montreal's late-nineteenth-century black community, in the early 1860s a fourth cluster of addresses in the center of the city, bordered by Dorchester, St. Constant, Craig, and St. Urbain, was probably the real center of Montreal's refugee black population. The first block of St. Urbain Street, just across Place d'Armes from the Cathedral of Notre Dame, was home to Florida-born whitewasher P. Thomas and his family of four. Nearby lived U.S.-born "washer" Claban Bibb at 2 St. Urbain, and the family of H. Smith at number 4. Other African-Americans lived on Scotch Lane, off St. Urbain, and on streets close by.

The key St. Urbain Street residence, number 13, was the home of thirty-nine-year-old Thomas Cook, a native of Virginia.[17] The 1861 city directory listed Cook as a whitewasher and colorer (dyer of fabrics), but informally he was the operator of a boardinghouse and, probably, an unlicensed tavern (it would be twenty years before the city directory finally designated him by the title "hotelier.") Cook was also something of a one-man social service agency. Young black refugees came to his house for lodging and boarding, and through him began to make contacts with the larger community. When the 1861 census was taken, the house was occupied by his wife, Anah, a native of Pennsylvania, their daughter, Carolyn, born in New York, and six unrelated persons—four young black men (two from Virginia), a white adult male, and a young woman who was also probably black.[18] A note in the manuscript census shows that Charles Van Schaick and William Briscoe, two black barbers who resided elsewhere, also gave their census information at 13 St. Urbain, where they were apparently operating a barbershop.[19]

For Shadrach Minkins and many of Montreal's other black refugees, the difference between starting a new life or simply biding time in Montreal hinged principally on two things: finding a marriage partner and finding steady work. With the exception of about a dozen men who came to Montreal with their wives, fulfilling the first requirement for stability was difficult. Although there were few young, single black women to choose from, seven men somehow managed to find black partners, all of them born in Canada. For the vast majority of single male refugees, however, finding a partner meant finding a white partner. Twenty-nine men, including Shadrach Minkins, were able to do so. Of those women whose place of birth is known, six had been born in Lower and one in Upper Canada, eight in Ireland, five in England, and two in Scotland.

The refugees also needed steady jobs to help anchor them in their new environment, and Minkins and other black immigrants appear to have had substantially greater occupational success in Montreal than blacks typically experienced in Northern U.S. cities. From 1860 to 1862 well over half of the adults whose occupations are known were skilled, semiskilled, or small entrepreneurial workers—a percentage that compares favorably with every Northern city in the United States, where the overwhelming majority of blacks worked as laborers, the lowest and least descriptive occupational category.[20] There were 21 black barbers, 9 tobacconists, 7 whitewashers, an upholsterer, a brickmaker, a clothes cleaner, a caterer, a carter, 3 carpenters, a fireman, a porter, a paperhanger, a shoe- and bootmaker, a tailor, and a groom who soon became the operator of the Prince of Wales Livery Stable.[21] Black men with the lowest employment status—waiters, servants, and laborers—accounted for less than a quarter of working blacks. What little information the census yields about women's occupations reveals, predictably, that black women were almost entirely confined to menial work as laundresses, servants, and cooks. One woman, twenty-nine-year-old Emily Watkins, supported herself and two children as a dressmaker.

Although racial barriers almost certainly played some role in funneling Shadrach Minkins and other black refugees into certain types of work, many other factors also played a part, including urgency, availability, experience, self-confidence, and personal preference. When Shadrach Minkins first arrived, he apparently sought work as a waiter, the occupation by which he had supported himself in Boston. Perhaps he thought that such work was all that would be available to him. But certainly he was in no position to debate his prospects, especially in a land where temperatures could reach −40 degrees Fahrenheit and winter could drag on almost endlessly. In most years the ice on the St. Lawrence River held until May. Until the ice broke up, food and other supplies grew scarce and dear, and the captain of the first oceangoing ship to reach the city each spring was an instant hero.[22]

The work that Shadrach Minkins finally settled into—barbering—was something of a privileged occupation among blacks. Minkins and the twenty other black barbers and hairdressers accounted for almost 25 percent of Montreal's working blacks (Boston black barbers were a mere 10 percent of Boston's black work force).[23] Because many barbers were independent shop owners with greater economic autonomy than most other workers and because the demand for barbers' services was steady, not seasonal or sporadic, their numbers indicate both acceptance by Montreal's white population and a degree of economic success, as the ambitiously named "Shaving and Haircutting Emporium" of black barbers George E. and James H. Jones on McGill Street hints.

Together with the other two categories of small entrepreneurs—whitewashers and tobacconists—but more important because of their numbers, barbers and hairdressers helped create the city's stable core refugee group.[24] Barbering and hairdressing were the foundation of a stable social network. Barbering creating an interracial intimacy that helped to anchor Shadrach Minkins and other black barbers more firmly into the larger community of neighbors and customers—often overlapping categories— than most other occupations. By playing body servant and confidant, therapist and adviser, moderator and friend, barbers built important bridges between blacks and whites.

The numerous interracial marriages, the dispersed housing, and the low percentage of blacks in jobs at the bottom of the employment scale all suggest that Shadrach Minkins and Montreal's other black refugees were less affected by racism than were blacks in many other parts of Canada. Still, several incidents suggest that the newcomers did not find Montreal an interracial paradise. Two examples in the 1861 census slips hint that racism was widespread. After recording the usual data for the household of a white widow and her daughters, one census enumerator glossed the absence of marks in the column for "Colored Persons, mulattoes, and Indians" with the comment, "none, thank God."[25] Another entry, for the house of a Florida-born whitewasher, included the notes "1 male over 30 nigger," "1 female over 20 nigger," "3 males under 5 niggers," and still another entry, on the census slip for George Anderson's house, included the comment "1 nigger."[26]

In 1862 two cases of assault provoked by racial slurs reached the Montreal courts. In the first case, a black named Wilkinson prosecuted an Irish carter named Dooner for striking him. According to reports, the dispute between the two men had escalated after Dooner called Wilkinson "Sambo."[27] In the other case, an Irishman named William O'Brien prosecuted black carpenter Matthew Bell for assault. Apparently angry about a sign Bell had made for him, O'Brien "used a great deal of abusive language, capping the whole by calling him a 'bloody common nigger,' " at which point Bell ordered the Irishman out of his shop, followed him into the street, and struck him twice. Although the judge ruled for O'Brien, he noted that Bell had been given "much provocation" and called O'Brien's conduct "very lamentable . . . in a free country, where all classes and origins are entitled to equal liberty."[28]

These incidents document isolated examples of racial prejudice. Nevertheless, experience as well as historical studies suggest that for every documented incident there were hundreds of undocumented ones.[29] Fortunately for Minkins and the others, the sympathetic attitudes expressed by authorities and the press, the widespread English-French and Catholic-Protestant tensions, and the very small numbers of black immigrants appear to have kept antiblack racism in check. In fact Montreal's small band of fugitive slave refugees soon became something of a source of local pride.

From 1859 on, records of births, deaths, and marriages continue to indicate informal relationships among Shadrach Minkins and other black refugees. But now, for the first time, they began also to have a public community identity. The prelude to a more visible identity came as part of the Canadian response to John Brown's ill-fated 1859 attempt to liberate the slaves of the South. In Montreal Brown's daring raid, capture, and plight struck a responsive chord.[30] A meeting of sympathy for Brown, then awaiting trial, drew a crowd of 1,000 whites, and various newspapers, led by the *Witness,* solicited contributions for the Brown family.[31] At an antislavery rally a month later, speeches were made by several local whites, including flour merchant D. S. Janes, chairman of the meeting and founding member of the Anti-Slavery Society of Canada. Two blacks, a minister named Wood who had been in Sierra Leone, and a Mr. Anderson, identified merely as a "colored minister," addressed the meeting. Anderson recounted the horrors of slavery to which "he himself was an eyewitness" and drew considerable applause in concluding that he "rejoiced that he had come from under the claw of the eagle, and placed himself under the paw of the lion."[32]

These meetings in response to John Brown's capture and execution were among the first indications of an antislavery movement in Montreal. By the late 1850s antislavery consciousness had been regularly heightened by visits from antislavery lecturers and agents such as black editor Henry Bibb and Reverend Henry J. Young, a black Delaware-born minister who visited the city soliciting contributions for a church in St. Catharines, Ontario, "chiefly used by refugees from slavery."[33] In 1857 the Montreal Young Men's Christian Association had voted against Richmond, Virginia, as a convention site because they "could not meet slaveholders in a slaveholding locality." The group had also voted to suspend all relations with Southern YMCAs because "they refuse membership to Christian colored men on account of color."[34] In June 1859, a few months before the raid on Harper's Ferry, Reverend John Wood lectured at the Mechanics' Institute on the native tribes of Sierra Leone.[35] A little later the *Witness* was helping him promote a plan "to get up a reading room and evening classes for the colored population of this city."[36] This effort, whether or not it was successful, inevitably attracted new attention to Montreal's blacks.

The John Brown episode proved to be a rallying point for Shadrach Minkins and Montreal's other black refugees. In late November 1859 they organized a gathering to express their sympathy for Brown and his fellow martyrs. This meeting, the first known instance of a black community event in Montreal, began with a morning prayer meeting at Bonaventure Hall, where "a number of the white race united with them in special prayer for John Brown, and for the freedom of the oppressed." According to the *Witness*, the prayers, especially the ones by the blacks, "were intensely earnest and touching . . . The hearty responses and moistened eyes showed the depth of sympathy."[37] In the evening U.S. abolitionist Samuel Gridley Howe and others addressed a large public gathering at which a collection was taken for Brown's family.

A thin sheaf of documents in the National Archives at Ottawa contains the most dramatic evidence of a growing collective identity among Montreal's refugee blacks. The chief item is a petition, dated February 19, 1860, requesting permission to form "The Colored Company of Montreal Volunteer Rifles." (See pages 227–228 for the complete text of the petition.) As proposed, the unit was to consist of a captain, a lieutenant, an ensign, three noncommissioned officers, a bugler, and fifty rank-and-file members.[38] In the United States, where black militia companies had to overcome local and state prejudice, such petitions were part of the campaign for equal rights.[39] The petition is signed by thirty-eight blacks, including Shadrach Minkins and a number of other longtime residents.

Documents in the archives show that the militia petition was rejected, at least partly on the grounds that there were already too many such companies and partly on the grounds of insufficient numbers of blacks (only 38 signed the petition). But racial prejudice also played an active role. "I can speak positively as to the dissatisfaction it would be likely to cause amongst the Officers & Men under my command, with whom doubtless such a Corps would expect to amalgamate," the local commander wrote in a letter marked "Private." "To isolate them on occasions of Parade or Duty, would be extremely inconvenient, & hurtful to their own feelings," the commander explained.[40]

Despite the negative response, the petition itself was an important event in the lives of Shadrach Minkins and Montreal's other black refugees. It focused their efforts on a common goal and helped to develop a community spirit. Key figures were barbers and tobacconists, who made up nearly half the thirty-eight signers. Barber Clarence Selden, one of the cosigners of the letter forwarding the militia petition, appears to have been the central figure. Selden's carefully wrought signature headed the list of names. Other barbers who signed the petition were William Armstead, James Jones, John Jones, William Medl[e]y, William H. Smith, Edmund Turner, and Charles Van Schaick.[41] Shadrach Minkins' name—written S. Minkings—is eleventh on the list, the signature painstakingly traced in the crude script of a novice writer. Tobacconists were represented on the list by William H. Bowles, B[enjamin] F. Brothers, James Grantiers, Fleming W. Jackson, Cornelius H. Johnson, William Mosby, and Jesse Trueheart. Longtime residents Thomas Cook, carpenter Matthew Bell, and clothes cleaner and dyer Charles Williams were also signers.[42] Nearly all the signers (twenty-three men and one woman) who can be traced in other sources had been residents of Montreal for at least five years, and all but one had been born in the United States.[43]

The militia petition expressed not only public community identity among the U.S. refugees but also a strong identification with the government and institutions of British North America. The accompanying letter declared Shadrach Minkins and the other signers to be "loyal and dutiful subjects of Her Gracious Majesty Queen Victoria . . . desirous of proving their attachment to the British Crown under which they hold their rights and privileges as Free Citizens, in common with their brethren of European origin." To prove their own ability, they cited as precedent the distinguished service of black West Indian regiments in India. Later in the year they made a similar commitment as British citizens when they met to prepare an address to the visiting Prince of Wales and to plan their part in the procession in his honor.[44] Clearly, Montreal's U.S.-born blacks had begun to see themselves not simply as refugees. Phrases in the militia petition like "loyal and dutiful subjects," "attachment to the British crown," and "rights and privileges as Free Citizens" show that they were constructing a new identity as British and Canadian patriots. Furthermore, the language of the petition declares their status as expatriates, symbolically repudiating any vestigial affiliation with the United States.

During 1861 and 1862 Shadrach Minkins and his fellow African-Americans remained a visible presence in the city both because of their increased numbers and because the Civil War and other events focused attention on them and on their race. In 1861 they joined with Montreal whites and with blacks and whites all across Canada to protest the attempt to extradite fugitive slave John Anderson. Anderson, who had killed one of his master's friends during a fight occasioned by his escape, had fled to Canada West, and American authorities sought to have him extradited not as a fugitive slave but as a murderer. On these grounds a Canadian court ruled against him, but a tremendous public outcry eventually led to a reconsideration and eventually a reversal of the decision. Afterward Anderson spent several weeks in Montreal waiting for the ice to break up on the St. Lawrence so that he could sail for England, where he was to receive an education. At an interracial meeting to raise funds for his support in England, an unnamed Montreal black spoke feelingly about how "great a protection the British Government was to the colored race throughout the world."[45] Later in the year, black barber William Briscoe helped organize a meeting to raise additional funds for Anderson.[46]

In 1862 Shadrach Minkins and Montreal's other African-Americans further proclaimed their communal expatriate identity as well as their growing Canadian identity when they held what appears to have been their initial August First celebration of England's 1833 emancipation of slaves in the British West Indies (an interracial celebration had been sponsored by the white YMCA the year before). Meeting at Bonaventure Hall, the U.S. refugees offered prayers and hymns to commemorate the day on which slavery had been abolished throughout the British Empire.[47]

What part Shadrach Minkins played in the activities of Montreal's emerging expatriate black community is not known, but it is likely that he attended the John Brown and John Anderson meetings, the Emancipation Day ceremonies, and other events. That he identified strongly with the activities of his fellow African-Americans can be inferred from his signature on the militia petition and from the interrelationships indicated by signatures of fellow African-Americans on burial records for his first two children.

For many blacks throughout Canada, the Civil War era signaled a call to return home. Once the war had begun, fugitives began to retrace their steps, lured by the promise of a quick end to slavery and the prospect of being reunited with family and friends. Still others, exasperated by the twin curses of prejudice and poverty that dogged them even in supposedly color-blind Canada, chose to face these obstacles on warmer, more familiar soil. In August 1863, when President Abraham Lincoln opened the ranks of the Northern army to blacks, a new impulse like an electric current suddenly ran through the black communities across Canada. The trickle of returning blacks soon swelled to hundreds as men crossed the border to join the battle against the slave states. Agents for black regiments visited Toronto and other Canadian havens, and at the Elgin settlement in Canada West a community meeting resulted in about forty Union recruits (later followed by another thirty).[48] Canada West leaders like Martin R. Delany and Mary Ann Shadd returned to the United States as recruiting agents for the black regiments. The black British Methodist Episcopal Church in Canada endorsed joining the Union army.[49] One black Canadian leader, Josiah Henson, recruited soldiers while pocketing the bonus money, ostensibly for "safe keeping."[50]

At the war's end in 1865, the siren call of the United States grew even more alluring as U.S.-born blacks in Canada were caught up in the euphoria that followed the extinction of slavery. Burning desire to be reunited with family and friends, together with rumors that ex-slaves were being given land confiscated from Confederates, and the pervasive, badly mistaken belief that ex-slaves would all be given forty acres and a mule made the appeal of return nearly irresistible.[51] A growing sentiment among some white Canadians, especially in Canada West, that the refugee blacks had overstayed their welcome and no longer had an excuse not to return "home" provided further impetus.[52]

Just how many fugitives and free-born blacks returned from Canada is impossible to determine with any precision. Historian Robin Winks has estimated that within a short time of the war's end, as many as two-thirds of the U.S.-born Canadian blacks had returned to the United States. Although Michael Wayne's recent work suggests that the percentage of returning blacks may have been much lower, there is no question that returnees numbered in the thousands.[53]

Shadrach Minkins and Montreal's other African-Americans clearly shared these impulses. Even as they celebrated their Canadian citizenship on August 1, 1862, one speaker worried that the lure of the States was already exerting too powerful a magnetic pull on them all. Warning the assembled refugees against the temptations of "the flesh-pots or onions and garlic of the Egypt from which they had been delivered," he called for renewed "diligence, piety, contentment, and thankfulness, in this land of freedom."[54]

Evidence from the next few years suggests that the fleshpots, onions, and garlic of the United States were simply too attractive for many of Montreal's black refugees to resist. Nearly a third of the signers of the 1860 militia petition never appeared in any city directories or tax records, and the names of U.S. blacks who had been listed in these sources during the 1850s and early 1860s disappeared at a rapid rate. Of forty-one adult blacks who first appeared in 1860 or 1861 records, only ten would be listed in the city directory half a dozen years later. Although natural attrition—death or normal patterns of transience—can account for some of these disappearances, most were probably the result of migration back to the United States.[55] Additional indirect evidence of an exodus comes from the number of names missing from the 1870–71 census.[56]

One return migrant who can be identified was fifty-year-old Maryland-born barber James S. Smith. The 1870 U.S. census shows Smith living in Boston with his eighty-two-year-old mother and two sons. The older son, fifteen-year-old Samuel J., had been born in Canada East (almost certainly in Montreal), and the younger, seven-year-old Joseph L., had been born in Massachusetts; thus the Smiths must have moved to Boston sometime before 1864.[57] Although it is impossible to match their names with those of known Montreal blacks, several other black Bostonians who listed Canada (rather than the Maritimes) as their place of birth or as the place of birth of wives or children may also have lived in Montreal.[58]

Despite the returning flow of exiles, as late as 1866, the year before the Confederation of Canada created a single nation, Montreal's black community was still vigorous enough to support an August First celebration. Three of the four organizers of the event—Thomas Cook, Charles Williams, and John Watkins—were longtime U.S. expatriate residents, and most of the participants undoubtedly were antebellum immigrants as well.[59] The black population was still so small that almost all of Montreal's African-Americans must have attended, else there could hardly have been a celebration at all. Shadrach Minkins, Charles Williams, and others who had fled from the United States many years earlier were still living in the city and certainly would have attended the historic festivities. "Let the friends of Philanthropy and Mercy rejoice," the advertisement for the gathering announced, referring to the end of the Civil War the previous year. At the meeting, held at the YMCA, Montreal's black expatriates celebrated "the entire abolition of Slavery . . . by prayers and addresses."[60] And celebrate they might. At long last, Shadrach Minkins and many of Montreal's other African-American expatriates were fugitive slaves no more.

Epilogue

For African-Americans throughout the United States and Canada, the great day of jubilee when the slaves were freed in the South came and passed. Soon after the speeches and the cheering and shouting from the hundreds of Freedom Night celebrations had died away, blacks were forced to confront the fact that equality and freedom would not be achieved by proclamation or law. The Emancipation Proclamation, the collapse of the Confederacy, and then the Thirteenth Amendment were only the first steps on a long, long road. Before a new day of racial justice and equality dawned, there would be thousands of dark nights.

For many African-Americans in Canada and the United States, North as well as South, the end of the Civil War came as a beacon of hope. In the South tens of thousands of slaves set off on innumerable dusty roads and lanes to rejoin or hunt for lost family members, or to put distance between themselves and their old masters, or simply to test their new condition. In the North and Canada, free blacks and refugees like Shadrach Minkins felt the temptation to join in these vast movements of searchers and seekers. Strong attachment to their old kin networks and "home" locales led many Northern refugees to return to the South. According to historian Elizabeth Pleck, return migration from Boston to Virginia was common. Other prewar refugees who did not return permanently made periodic visits, and still others at least kept up contacts. Newcomers to Boston brought fresh news from back home.[1]

Shadrach Minkins' old Norfolk home had an especially magnetic appeal. During the war thousands of "contraband" slaves had sought refuge in Norfolk, and the city had become a center of black activity behind Union lines. After the war, spurred by returning fugitives from the North like Thomas Bayne, the dentist's assistant who had helped slaves escape from Norfolk before himself fleeing to New Bedford, Norfolk became a center of black political activity. In their *Equal Suffrage Address* of 1867, Norfolk blacks declared their determination to be included on an equal footing with whites in rebuilding a new Virginia. The *Address* was a milestone in black aspirations during the postwar era. For a time, the dream of equality and full citizenship appeared to be within their grasp.[2]

If the initial postwar euphoria among Norfolk blacks failed to entice Shadrach Minkins back home, subsequent events were not likely to. Over the next two and a half decades, Norfolk's ex-slaves and free blacks managed to make steady political and social gains, but those gains were exceedingly fragile and were often sustained only by the presence of federal troops. After federal troops withdrew from Virginia and white conservatives regained voting rights, the backlash against blacks rapidly intensified. A brief political alliance with a "Readjuster" party of Norfolk whites in the early 1880s gave blacks eight seats on the city council and a share of political appointments. These triumphs, however, merely postponed, and indeed made even more inevitable, black losses.[3]

During the final decades of the nineteenth century—later than to many areas of the South, but just as inexorably—Jim Crow came to Norfolk. Through violence and intimidation, through subterfuge and deceit, blacks lost nearly all of their newly won political gains, and many of their social and economic gains as well. Segregation in housing and jobs increasingly confined most of Norfolk's blacks to second-class economic and social positions.

Boston also appealed strongly to many postwar refugees—both those who had been forced to flee from the city by the Fugitive Slave Law and new immigrants from the liberated South. By 1870 more than 400 Canadian-born blacks—almost all of them from the Maritimes—had migrated to Boston.[4] Many undoubtedly were the children of U.S.-born refugees who had fled before the Civil War. At least a few Montreal blacks must have been part of this immigrant stream, but barber James S. Smith and his eldest son are the only ones who can be identified with certainty.

If Shadrach Minkins had returned to the city he had fled so precipi-
tously more than a dozen years before, he would have found Boston
swollen with friends and neighbors from Norfolk. During and immediately
after the war a flood of blacks from throughout Virginia had headed to
Boston to be reunited with family members and friends already there or
simply to try their fortunes in a Northern setting. These arrivals were new
links in the chain of migrants that had drawn Shadrach Minkins and other
Norfolk slaves and free blacks to the city. By 1880 Boston's growing black
community would be almost one-third Virginia-born.[5]

But if Shadrach Minkins had returned to Boston, he would also have
found his fellow African-Americans beset by a pattern of racial tensions
and disappointed hopes similar to that experienced by Norfolk blacks—a
pattern of initial gains followed by relentless erosion. For a time the
legacy of black activism and white sympathy sustained the hopes of the
prewar generation. Lewis Hayden remained a key figure in Boston's black
community and in the struggle for black rights until his death in 1889.
Hayden, John J. Smith, J. B. Smith, and several other Boston blacks were
elected to seats in the Massachusetts House of Representatives. Hayden,
Charles Lenox Remond, and others also served in the federal and local
government in elected or appointed positions. Several black newspapers
gave voice to black aspirations, and black political clubs promoted black
interests.[6] But these advances would prove ephemeral. Through redis-
tricting and other tactics, Boston's blacks were to lose most of their
political gains by the end of the century. Black Bostonians increasingly
found themselves unable to rise out of poverty. Increasingly they were
segregated, mainly in the traditionally black neighborhood in the West
End, and increasingly they were limited to menial work, especially the
newest immigrants from the South.[7]

In the 1871 census of Montreal, Shadrach Minkins' name appeared with
the names of a dozen other black householders who had fled to sanctuary
a decade or more before: Thomas Cook, John Scott, Clarence Selden,
James Smith, John Stewart (or Stuart), Isaac Taylor, John Thomas, William
Thomas, Jesse Trueheart, Charles Van Schaick, Emily Watkins, and Charles Williams.[8] These thirteen and members of their immediate families
account for roughly two-thirds of only fifty-eight adult blacks who can be
identified in 1871.

Barbering and other employment familiar to African-Americans continued to provide Minkins and other expatriate blacks and their families with modest economic success. In 1871 Shadrach Minkins and six other blacks were barbers. By then some expatriates had risen from laborers and waiters to work as whitewashers, tobacconists, or in other more stable and lucrative jobs and businesses. Charles Williams, who had worked as a waiter in the 1850s, was operating a clothes cleaning and dyeing business. Isaac Taylor, a carter in 1861, had become a miller by 1871. Thomas Cook, after many years as a whitewasher and an apparently unsuccessful 1858 attempt to operate a coffeehouse, had opened a small hotel business. Some of the sons of the antebellum refugees had been able to find work as drivers and even as clerks.[9]

Shadrach Minkins and the other Montreal black expatriates were part of a core of black expatriates across Canada—no one knows how many—who held fast. Whether they were too knowing to indulge in the soaring dreams of their fellow former slaves in the United States, too wise to believe that the United States could be easily reformed and transformed, too satisfied with their circumstances, or simply too poor, or too tired, to uproot themselves once more, is not known. Undoubtedly a complex mixture of motivations and realities played a part. For many, time had played a key role, eroding their U.S. identities. "I am a regular Britisher . . . I have lost my American taste," explained fugitive slave minister Alexander Helmsley, interviewed in St. Catharines, Canada West, more than ten years after fleeing from New Jersey.[10] Like Helmsley, Shadrach Minkins and many other Montreal expatriates had been in Canada long enough to have completed this process of erosion and accretion. Montreal had become what Minkins and his fellow African-Americans *knew*. It was their world, their familiar *reality*. Shadrach Minkins had married and his children grown up in this world. Minkins' family and friends, neighbors and work, made up his web of immediate experience.

Moreover, the reality that Shadrach Minkins found in Montreal was a reality that, ultimately, he had seized for himself. The Canadian experience was enabling, but it was Minkins' conscious decision to identify with the new country that proved to be transforming. Operating in somewhat the same way as Frederick Douglass' English experience in the mid-1840s, the Canadian experience reshaped Minkins' and other refugees' sense of identity. This effect is seen most clearly among Montreal blacks in their militia petition of 1860. In portraying themselves as "loyal and dutiful subjects," in declaring their "attachment to the British Crown," and in celebrating their "rights and privileges as Free Citizens," Montreal's African-Americans proclaimed both their political and social identity. This identity-making, community-making, profoundly creative process of acculturation and redefinition also constituted a rejection of the U.S. culture that had refused to accord them full citizenship. Ultimately, remaining in Canada was an act of continuing resistance to the failed promise of U.S. egalitarian ideology. It was a continuing protest against the yawning gap between U.S. ideology and U.S. reality. Once before, they had voted for Canada with their feet. Now they voted again with their feet—by planting them.

For reasons simple and complex, Shadrach Minkins and other African-American expatriates resisted the "onions and garlic" of the United States. But remaining in Canada did not protect them against the narrowing of opportunities and the epidemic of racism that afflicted blacks throughout the United States in the closing decades of the nineteenth century and the early decades of the twentieth. Even in Montreal they felt the effects of the increasing racial hatred of the Reconstruction period. More and more, the conservative press across Canada carried stories of black violence against whites that were staples of reactionary papers in the United States. Blacks were stereotyped as lazy, dirty, illiterate, and untrustworthy. By the early twentieth century Canadian authorities would be actively excluding blacks from the immigrant stream, largely by unwritten authority.[11]

Even in Montreal, where this new, more virulent strain of racism was somewhat muted, newspapers increasingly identified blacks by race in crime statistics, and the word "nigger" began appearing with some frequency in English-language papers.[12] New black immigrants were more and more likely to find themselves relegated to menial labor.[13] U.S.-style racial hatred was to dominate racial attitudes throughout Canada for several generations. Not until a labor shortage during World War II did the door of economic opportunity finally begin to open to blacks, and then it opened only a crack.[14]

Shadrach Minkins did not live to experience the intensifying racism of the last quarter of the nineteenth century and the early twentieth century. He died on December 13, 1875, in the middle of a long, hard winter. "Disease of the stomach," the handwritten burial record explains, noting his age as sixty-three.[15] On the afternoon of December 15 friends gathered to console his widow and children before following the coffin two miles to the Protestant Cemetery on Mount Royal for the burial.[16]

With Shadrach Minkins' death, the fugitive slave era in Montreal was nearing its end. Over the next few years migration, illness, and death inexorably reduced the tiny band of black men and women and children from the slavery era. In 1881 Clarence F. Selden was still cutting hair, Charles Williams was still running his clothes cleaning business, and Thomas Cook was still operating a restaurant and hotel. But over the next dozen years all three disappeared from the city directories.[17]

By the turn of the century the antebellum black expatriates had been replaced by a new group of black immigrants from the United States. Arriving to work on the trans-Canada railroad, they became the nucleus of a larger, more permanent community. The Union United Church, Montreal's first black church, was established soon afterward in the vicinity of Shadrach Minkins' barbershop. This area, known variously as the "West End" and "little Burgundy," was the main black neighborhood in the first half of the twentieth century.[18] By then the memory of the fugitive slaves was rapidly fading. The few children and grandchildren who were the links to the older generation may have kept the stories alive in their homes and their consciousness. Shadrach Minkins' son Jacob, who worked first as a waiter and then for many years as a hotel bellboy and porter, lived for more than two decades on St. Felix Street, only a few blocks from his boyhood home on Mountain Street. Jacob Minkins knew his father's story and could have passed it along to his children, but he died childless in 1935.[19] But even if he had had children, he might have kept silent. Until Alex Haley's *Roots* gave African-Americans new reason to feel pride in their slave ancestors, many blacks wished simply to forget. "Don't ask me nothing about those old slaves," Robert "Bud" Jones, a fifth-generation descendant residing in the St. Hubert suburb of Montreal, remembers hearing old people say.[20]

Montreal's black community today is primarily of West Indian origin, and the fugitive slave era has been all but forgotten. But Bud Jones, former flyweight Canadian boxing champion and a veteran of World War II and the Korean War, remembers. He was one of the people for whom Alex Haley's *Roots* came as a revelation. It changed his life, he says.

Today Bud Jones is a one-man African-American heritage center. The hundreds of photographs and documents displayed in his tiny basement study—or wherever he is invited—tell an eloquent story of the Jones family going back to the days of Shadrach Minkins' fearful flight.[21] He has traced his heritage back to his great-great-grandfather William Francis Jones, the free black barber from Annapolis who settled in Montreal with his wife and children around the time Shadrach Minkins arrived in the city. One of William Francis' sons, Bud Jones's great-uncle George E., was Shadrach Minkins' friend.

The Protestant cemetery on the northwest side of Mount Royal seems steeped in silent, inscrutable memories. The visitor who enters at the

Barber George E. Jones, who came to Montreal with his family around 1850. In 1875 he signed Shadrach Minkins' burial record.

north gate and follows the curving gravel path past Lilac Knoll soon comes to the old B-2 section, surmounted by an ancient white birch of gigantic proportions. Here, at his gravesite, Shadrach Minkins' memory once again comes alive. No stone marks his grave; only the yellowing three-by-five-inch card in the records office at the gate commemorates his burial here. But on a darkening late spring afternoon, among the mossy stones over-grown by the spirea and lilac and yew planted long ago to memorialize the dead, it is possible to conjure up the memory of the fugitive slave who lies here with two of his children.

Treading the earth here, it is easy to remember that Shadrach Minkins and other antebellum black expatriates found in Montreal something more than temporary refuge. Like other U.S.-born blacks across Canada, Shadrach Minkins found not a color-blind paradise but the haven and home that the United States of slavery and Daniel Webster, Compromise and commerce, had been unwilling to provide to people of African descent. In Boston as well as in Norfolk, African-Americans were aliens, estranged from many of the privileges of citizenship and equality enjoyed by white Americans. Another century would pass before genuine efforts were made to bring U.S. practice regarding race into line with the nation's ideals. Shadrach Minkins' unmarked grave in Montreal, and thousands upon thousands of other African-American graves across Canada, in England, in Liberia and Sierra Leone, and elsewhere around the globe, as well as the living communities they established, testify both to this long failure and to an equally sustained determination and resilience.

Militia Petition by Black Residents of Montreal

The following petition was submitted under a cover letter to Colonel Ermatinger, "Inspecting Field Officer," dated Montreal, February 29, 1860.[1]

To His Excellency Sir Edmund Walker, Head, [?] Governor General of British North America and Captain General and Governor in Chief of the Provinces of Canada, New Brunswick, Nova Scotia and the Island of Prince Edward, &c. &c.

The humble Petition of a number of the Colored Inhabitants of the City of Montreal, Canada East,—

MONTREAL, 19TH FEBRUARY, 1860.

Respectfully Sheweth,

That the undersigned Petitioners, loyal and dutiful subjects of Her Gracious Majesty Queen Victoria, and residing in the City of Montreal, Canada East, are desirous of proving their attachment to the British Crown under which they hold their rights and privileges as Free Citizens, in common with their bretheren of European origin, humbly and most respectfully solicit the Authority of Your Excellency as the Representative of Her Majesty in this part of Her Dominions, to allow your Petitioners to raise and organize from amongst themselves a Volunteer Militia Company of Foot, in class B, to be denominated, if it should so please Your Excellency, the Colored Company of Montreal Volunteer Rifles; to be drilled & exercised in conformity with the regulations of the Service in all respects.

That Your Petitioners pledge themselves should Your Excellency feel disposed to favor their views, to clothe themselves at their own expense, in a neat and appropriate uniform (subject to the approval of Your Excellency), and to conform in every way to the Militia Rules & Regulations,

That Your petitioners venture most respectfully to bring to Your Excellency's notice, that in the West India Islands belonging to Her Majesty, there exist many Companies of Militia composed entirely of the Colored population, who have at all time been found ready to do their duty when called on; and that the Regular Colored Colonial Regiments in the West Indies volunteered their Services to a man on the outbreak of the Indian Mutiny; thus proving that the Colored race, under a free and enlightened Government like that of Great Britain, are second to none in loyalty, fidelity and truthfulness to their Country and their Queen.

Your Petitioners, in conclusion, would most respectfully entreat Your Excellency to grant them a favorable reply to this their earnest Petition, to be allowed to participate as Citizens, in the duties of the Militia Force of this valuable Colony; and should your Excellency under all the circumstances of Your Petitioners case, view the same in a favorable light, they, as in duty bound will ever pray—

Proposed Strength of Company

1 Captain	3 N.C. Officers
1 Lieutenant	1 Bugler
1 Ensign	50 Rank & File

[Signed]

Clarence F. Selden	Isaac Taylor	James Grant[res?]
Matthew Bell	Edgar R[ankin?]	William H. Smith
Samuel Eustis	Edmund Turner	George Anderson
Fleming W. Jackson	Alexander W. Thompson	William H. Bowles
William Mosby	A. Brown	B. F. Brothers
Isaac Turner	Joseph Craig	Leonard L. Bownte[rs?]
Beverly S. Jones	Edward Ran[ce?]ls	William Medly
Jesse Truehart	Thomas Thompson	John Jones
Cornelius H. Johnson	Charles W. Van Schaick	James Jones
Henry Lewis	Charles Mead	David Johnson
S[hadrach]. Minkings	Charles Clifton	Thomas Cook
William Barber	John [L.?] Dunmoore	Wil[burn?] Armstead
Henry Ross	Joseph W. F. Jackson	

Notes

Abbreviations

BAP   *Black Abolitionist Papers*, ed. C. Peter Ripley et al., 5 vols. (Chapel Hill: University of North Carolina Press, 1985–1992)

CCEM61   Manuscript Census, Canada East, Montreal, 1861, Public Archives of Canada, Ottawa

DWC   *The Papers of Daniel Webster, Series One: Correspondence*, ed. Charles M. Wiltse, et al., 7 vols. (Hanover, N.H.: University Press of New England, 1974–1985)

mDW   Microfilm edition of *The Papers of Daniel Webster*, 41 reels (Ann Arbor: University Microfilms, 1971)

BPL   Boston Public Library

HL   Houghton Library, Harvard University

MHS   Massachusetts Historical Society, Boston

1. "Han't Got No Self"

1. From Calvin Fairbank's *Autobiography*, quoted in Charles T. Davis and Henry Louis Gates, *The Slave's Narrative* (New York: Oxford University Press, 1985), p. xxx.

2. On the development of an African-American subculture in eighteenth-century Virginia (including how blacks influenced white culture), see Mechal Sobel, *The World They Made Together: Black and White Values in Eighteenth-Century Virginia* (Princeton: Princeton University Press, 1987).

3. Thomas J. Wertenbaker, *Norfolk: Historic Southern Port*, ed. Marvin W. Schlegel, 2nd ed. (Durham, N.C.: Duke University Press, 1962), pp. 82–94.

4. Thomas C. Parramore, with Peter C. Stewart and Tommy L. Bogger, *Norfolk: The First Four Centuries* (Charlottesville: University Press of Virginia, 1994), pp. 137–142; John P. Kennedy, *Memories of the Life of William Wirt*, 2 vols. (Philadelphia: Lea & Blanchard, 1949), 1: 99.

5. Wertenbaker, *Norfolk*, p. 88; Tommy Lee Bogger, "The Slave and Free Black Community in Norfolk, 1775–1865" (Ph.D. diss., University of Virginia, 1976), p. 151, n. 5; *The Norfolk Directory, 1806–1807* (Norfolk: A. C. Jordan, 1806), pp. 44–45; Parramore, *Norfolk*, pp. 102–105, 118.

6. Parramore, *Norfolk*, pp. 112, 125.

7. Moreau de St. Méry, *Moreau de St. Méry's American Journey [1793–1798],* trans. and ed. Kenneth Roberts and Anna M. Roberts (Garden City, N.Y.: Doubleday, 1947), p. 60.

8. William S. Forrest, *Historical and Descriptive Sketches of Norfolk and Vicinity, including Portsmouth and the Adjacent Counties, during a Period of Two Hundred Years* (Philadelphia: Lindsay and Blakiston, 1853), p. 419.

9. Peter Randolph, *From Slave Cabin to the Pulpit* (Boston: James H. Earle, 1893), p. 191; Charles L. Perdue, Jr., Thomas E. Barden, and Robert K. Phillips, eds., *Weevils in the Wheat: Interviews with Virginia's Ex-Slaves* (Charlottesville: University Press of Virginia, 1976), p. 234.

10. Richard C. Wade, *Slavery in the Cities: The South, 1820–1860* (New York: Oxford University Press, 1964), pp. 243–246.

11. Frederick Douglass, *My Bondage and My Freedom,* ed. William L. Andrews (Urbana: University of Illinois Press, 1987), p. 93.

12. Ibid., pp. 94–95.

13. *St. Méry's American Journey,* pp. 59–60.

14. Norfolk *American Beacon,* July 18, 1835.

15. Ibid., July 21, 1849.

16. CCEM61.

17. Parramore, *Norfolk,* p. 149; Forrest, *Historical and Descriptive Sketches,* p. 156; Wertenbaker, *Norfolk,* pp. 156–164.

18. Norfolk's population had grown slowly. Its white population actually shrank between 1810 and 1820 but increased slowly to 5,100 by 1830. The slave population followed the same pattern, falling slightly in 1820 but rising to 3,750 by 1830. Although an 1805 Virginia law required newly emancipated blacks to leave the state within twelve months, the statute was largely ignored, and emancipated blacks, many of them from the surrounding countryside, illegally swelled the town's population. Between 1810 and 1830 the number of free blacks increased from 392 to 928. For a variety of reasons, including the demand for domestic help in the town, female slaves outnumbered male slaves by about four to three (similar imbalances could be found in many other Southern cities).

19. Charles Augustus Murray, *Travels in North America during the Years 1834, 1835, & 1836,* 2 vols. (London: Richard Bentley, 1839), 1: 176; James Silk Buckingham, *The Slave States of America,* 2 vols. (London: Fisher, Son, 1842), 2: 455–456.

20. Unknown diarist, probably a member of the Roe family, entry for March 13, 1844, American Antiquarian Society, Worcester, Mass.; Frederick Law Olmsted, *A Journey in the Seaboard Slave States in the Years 1853–1854, with Remarks on Their Economy* (New York: G. P. Putnam's, 1904), pp. 150–151.

21. Parramore, *Norfolk,* pp. 111, 113; Glenn had moved to Norfolk shortly after the turn of the century and opened the Eagle Tavern in Market Square. Two sources list Glenn as the operator of the Eagle Tavern in 1806, perhaps a dozen years before Minkins was born: an 1806 "List of Licenses Granted by the Court of the Borough of Norfolk to Tavern keepers," where Thomas Glenn's name appears among a dozen others (entry dated February 25, Norfolk Borough Land and Property Tax Book, 1806, Virginia State Library, Richmond, inserted at the end); and *Norfolk Directory, 1806–1807,* p. 16.

22. Rev. W. H. T. Squires, "Norfolk in By-Gone Days," *Norfolk Ledger-Dispatch,* November 16, 1939, Squires Scrapbook, Norfolk Public Library.

23. Norfolk *American Beacon*, July 21, 1832.

24. *Norfolk Directory, 1806–1807;* Squires, "Norfolk in By-Gone Days," *Norfolk Ledger-Dispatch*, November 19, 1939, Squires Scrapbook, Norfolk Public Library.

25. Norfolk *Southern Argus*, December 18, 1848.

26. "Market Square, later Commercial Place, in Norfolk in 1865," print from German edition of *Frank Leslie's Weekly*, Norfolk Public Library.

27. Anne Royall, *The Black Book; or, A Continuation of Travels in the United States*, 2 vols. (Washington, D.C.: privately printed, 1828), 1: 255.

28. Population schedules of the Fifth Census of the United States (1830), Norf 431 Norfolk. Twenty whites are listed at the hotel, but how many were guests and how many Glenn family members is not specified.

29. Royall, *Black Book*, 1: 255.

30. Frederick Law Olmsted, *Slavery and the South, 1852–1857*, vol. 2 of *The Papers of Frederick Law Olmsted*, ed. Charles E. Beveridge and Charles Capen McLaughlin (Baltimore: Johns Hopkins University Press, 1981), pp. 150–151.

31. Slaves' culture has been a leading topic of study for many years. See Sobel, *The World They Made Together*, esp. pp. 100–153; and the great studies by Eugene Genovese, *Roll, Jordan, Roll: The World the Slaves Made* (New York: Pantheon, 1974); and Herbert G. Gutman, *The Black Family in Slavery and Freedom, 1750–1925* (New York: Vintage, 1976).

32. Gutman, *The Black Family*, pp. 261–267; Charles Joyner, *Down by the Riverside: A South Carolina Slave Community* (Urbana: University of Illinois Press, 1984), pp. 231–233.

33. Gerald Mullin, *Flight and Rebellion: Slave Resistance in Eighteenth-Century Virginia* (Oxford: Oxford University Press, 1972), pp. 141–157; Douglass R. Egerton, *Gabriel's Rebellion: The Virginia Slave Conspiracies of 1800 and 1802* (Chapel Hill: University of North Carolina Press, 1993), pp. 67–68, 98–99.

34. Egerton, *Gabriel's Rebellion*, pp. 123–139; Bogger, "Black Community in Norfolk," pp. 120–122; Parramore, *Norfolk*, pp. 119–124, 128–131; A. G. Roeber, ed., "A New England Woman's Perspective on Norfolk, Virginia, 1801–1802: Excerpts from the Diary of Ruth Henshaw Bascom," *Proceedings of the American Antiquarian Society*, 88 (October 1978), 307, 316; Herbert Aptheker, *American Negro Slave Revolts* (1943; reprint, New York: International Publishers, 1969), pp. 41–45, 162–226; Stephen B. Oates, *The Fires of Jubilee: Nat Turner's Fierce Rebellion* (New York: Harper & Row, 1975), pp. 15–20.

35. Oates, *Fires of Jubilee*, pp. 150–151.

36. Ibid., pp. 98–100, 106–108.

37. Harriet Jacobs, *Incidents in the Life of a Slave Girl, Written by Herself* (Cambridge, Mass.: Harvard University Press, 1987), pp. 63–64.

38. Oates, *Fires of Jubilee*, pp. 110–111. The governor chastised the mayor's action as reflecting "cowardly fears." As Oates points out, the governor was angry on two counts: not only was Norfolk left virtually defenseless, but also, and perhaps more importantly, federal troops had become involved in what was regarded as an internal affair of Virginia, setting an unwelcome precedent.

39. Norfolk *Southern Argus*, August 26, September 1–2, 1831.

40. Norfolk *American Beacon*, August 26, 1831.

41. Deborah Shea, "Spreading Terror and Devastation Wherever They Have Been:

A Norfolk Woman's Account of the Southampton Slave Insurrection," *Virginia Magazine of History and Biography,* 95 (January 1987), 69.

42. Willard B. Gatewood, Jr., ed., *Free Man of Color: The Autobiography of Willis Augustus Hodges* (Knoxville: University of Tennessee Press, 1982), p. 26.

43. Norfolk *Southern Argus,* September 30, 1831.

44. Oates, *Fires of Jubilee,* pp. 135–141.

45. Norfolk *Southern Argus,* November 8, 1831.

46. Oates, *Fires of Jubilee,* pp. 99–100; Moses Grandy, *Narrative of the Life of Moses Grandy, Late a Slave in the United States of America* (Boston: Oliver Johnson, 1844), pp. 26–27.

47. Norfolk *American Beacon,* August 17–19, 11, 12, 15, 21; September 5; December 5, 1835.

48. June Purcell Guild, *Black Laws of Virginia: A Summary of the Legislative Acts of Virginia concerning Negroes from Earliest Times to the Present* (1936; reprint, New York: Negro Universities Press, 1969), pp. 106–110, 175–176.

49. Norfolk City Order Book, microfilm, 29 (1829–1832): 284, Virginia State Library; Bogger, "Black Community in Norfolk," p. 149.

50. Bogger, "Black Community in Norfolk," pp. 146–150. Ira Berlin, *Slaves without Masters: The Free Negro in the Antebellum South* (New York: Oxford University Press, 1974), pp. 192–249; and Wade, *Slavery in the Cities,* pp. 273–277, discuss the pressures that blacks increasingly faced in the decades before the Civil War, including competition from white immigrants from Ireland and Germany.

51. Bogger, "Black Community in Norfolk," p. 150; see also Marie Tyler McGraw, "Richmond Free Blacks and African Colonization, 1816–1832," *Journal of American Studies,* 21, no. 2 (1987), 207–224.

2. "Horses and Men, Cattle and Women, Pigs and Children"

1. Norfolk *Southern Argus,* October 27, 1851.

2. Frederick Douglass, *Narrative of the Life of Frederick Douglass, an American Slave, Written by Himself* (1845; reprint, New York: New American Library, 1968), p. 57.

3. Glenn died on Saturday, July 14, 1832, according to the obituary published in the Norfolk *American Beacon,* July 21, 1832.

4. Norfolk *American Beacon,* December 15, 1832, and January 1, 1833. An advertisement at the end of 1832 reveals that Ann Glenn had found a renter for the tavern building, now renamed the Virginia and North Carolina Hotel.

5. Ibid., December 29, 1836.

6. Norfolk County Audit Books, microfilm, 8 (1835–1842): 91, Virginia State Library, Richmond. The will was read on January 23, 1837.

7. Norfolk *American Beacon,* February 13 and November 21, 1834.

8. Norfolk County Audit Books, 8: 212.

9. Ibid.

10. Claudia Dale Goldin, *Urban Slavery in the American South, 1820–1860* (Chicago: University of Chicago Press, 1976), pp. 21–22, 45. Later figures show that Norfolk's customs inspector owned or hired as many as forty slaves, the Norfolk Draw Bridge Company twenty-two, and one brickmason, forty. Goldin's figures come from

the 1860 census, when slave use appears to have declined overall in the city, but still may be regarded as indicative of long-standing patterns. For other descriptions of the hiring practices in urban settings, see Richard C. Wade, *Slavery in the Cities: The South, 1820–1860* (New York: Oxford University Press, 1964), pp. 38–54; Tommy Lee Bogger, "The Slave and Free Black Community in Norfolk, 1775–1865" (Ph.D. diss., University of Virginia, 1976), pp. 161–191; David R. Goldfield, *Urban Growth in the Age of Sectionalism: Virginia, 1847–1861* (Baton Rouge: Louisiana State University Press, 1977), pp. 133–138; and Barbara Jeanne Fields, *Slavery and Freedom on the Middle Ground: Maryland during the Nineteenth Century* (New Haven: Yale University Press, 1985), pp. 27–28, 47–49.

11. Norfolk *American Beacon*, April 22, 1854.

12. Norfolk County Audit Books, 8: 207.

13. Ibid., p. 336.

14. Norfolk *American Beacon*, March 22 and October 14, 1828.

15. Ibid., January 1, 1829; Inventory of the estate of Richard S. Hutchings, December 2, 1828, Norfolk County Audit Books, 6 (1826–1831): 138–141.

16. Norfolk County Audit Books, 6: 141. The accounts also list several other children, who were apparently too young to work. Over the next several years Max, Sukey, Jack, and Charlotte were hired out for annual wages varying from $10 for Charlotte to $60 for Max. In January 1832 the accounts list an expense of $23.37 "for nursing Sukey," probably related to the birth of her child about this time; ibid., 8: 78.

17. "SALE OF NEGROES," signed "Martha Hutchings, administratrix," Norfolk *American Beacon*, August 26, 1834; Norfolk County Audit Books, 7 (1832–1834): 80.

18. By the Civil War Virginia would still have the largest slave population—nearly half a million—but by then seven other states had at least 250,000 slaves, and four of these more than 400,000; Table 6, "Negro Population, Slave and Free, at Each Census by Division and States: 1790–1860," in U.S. Bureau of the Census, *Negro Population in the United States, 1790–1915* (1918; reprint, New York: Arno Press, 1968), p. 57.

19. Norfolk *Southern Argus*, April 4, 1850.

20. James Silk Buckingham, *The Slave States of America*, 2 vols. (London: Fisher, Son, 1842), 2: 185.

21. Benjamin Drew, *A North-Side View of Slavery; The Refugee: or the Narratives of Fugitive Slaves in Canada, Related by Themselves, with an Account of the History and Condition of the Colored Population of Upper Canada* (Boston: John P. Jewett, 1856), p. 248.

22. See, for example, ibid., pp. 224–225, 239, 271, 280–281.

23. George Teamoh, *God Made Man, Man Made the Slave: The Autobiography of George Teamoh*, ed. F. N. Boney, Richard L. Hume, and Rafia Zafar (Macon, Ga.: Mercer University Press, 1990), pp. 8, 87–89.

24. Dickson J. Preston, *Young Frederick Douglass: The Maryland Years* (Baltimore: Johns Hopkins University Press, 1980), p. 76.

25. Moses Grandy, *Narrative of the Life of Moses Grandy, Late a Slave in the United States of America* (Boston: Oliver Johnson, 1844), pp. 29–31. In 1844 Grandy was still trying desperately to raise the $500 asked for his daughter Betsy, then held in slavery "a little way from Norfolk" but in danger of disappearing, too, into the Deep South market.

26. Solomon Northup, *Twelve Years a Slave*, ed. Sue Eakin and Joseph Logsdon (1853; reprint, Baton Rouge: Louisiana State University Press, 1988), pp. 42, 48–49.

27. Norfolk County Audit Books, 8: 336, 375, 206.

28. Ibid., 8: 206, 373, 374; 9 (1843–1845): 153.

29. Ibid., 7: 336–337. William's position with the navy is referred to in court papers when Robert came of age and received his portion of the estate.

30. Norfolk County Audit Books, 7: 298. Susan may have been the "Negro Woman, a Cook, Washer, &c. 40 years of age" that a Nash & Co. advertisement offered for sale on February 28; Norfolk *American Beacon*, February 27, 1843.

31. Norfolk County Audit Books, 9: 297.

32. Teamoh, *God Made Man*, p. 74.

33. Norfolk County Audit Books, 8: 373.

34. According to the entry, R. H. Glenn received $121.90 for "his portion of slaves divided under Decree of Court"; January 24, 1842, ibid., 9: 64.

35. Notes of R. H. Dana, Jr., U.S. v. Morris, 1st trial, p. 7, Dana legal papers, American Antiquarian Society, Worcester, Mass.; Norfolk *Southern Argus*, February 29, 1860.

36. William S. Forrest, *Historical and Descriptive Sketches of Norfolk and Vicinity, including Portsmouth and the Adjacent Counties, during a Period of Two Hundred Years* (Philadelphia: Lindsay and Blakiston, 1853), p. 214; Norfolk City Common Law Order Book, 2, June Term 1849, Norfolk City Hall.

37. Norfolk *American Beacon*, July 19–21, 1849. The notice also appeared in the Norfolk *Herald*.

38. According to the account of John DeBree's later testimony in the Boston *Commonwealth*, June 18, 1851, the purchase took place in November 1849. The same article reports DeBree as saying that he had known Minkins about a month when he purchased him. If this is true, then Higgins may have hired Minkins out from July through October.

39. *Register of the Commissioned and Warrant Officers of the Navy of the Confederate States, to January 1, 1863* (Richmond: MacFarlane & Fergusson, 1862), pp. 12–13.

40. Norfolk *American Beacon*, February 26, 1831.

41. Ibid., October 5, 1835; June 29, 1836.

42. *Register of Commissioned and Warrant Officers*, p. 12; copy of receipt dated February 1, 1862, Scrapbook for 1861–1865, Norfolk and Portsmouth Documents, Portsmouth Public Library.

43. More than a dozen property transactions are recorded in the Norfolk City General Index to Deeds, vol. 3 (1833–1850); and Land Book, State Assessment, Circuit Court of the City of Norfolk, Clerk's Office, vol. 1 (1850–1853), Norfolk City Hall.

44. In the 1960s the decaying neighborhood was razed in a massive urban renewal project.

45. William F. Ainsley, Jr., "Changing Land Use in Downtown Norfolk, Virginia: 1680–1930" (Ph.D. diss., University of North Carolina, 1976), p. 101; Rev. W. H. T. Squires, "Norfolk in By-Gone Days," *Norfolk Ledger-Dispatch*, June 27, 1935, Squires Scrapbook, Norfolk Public Library; William S. Forrest, *Norfolk Directory for 1851–1852* (Norfolk, 1851).

46. Notes of R. H. Dana, Jr., U.S. v. Hayden (trial), p. 5, Dana legal papers; Population Schedules of the Seventh United States Census (1850), Norf 115 Norfolk; Slave Schedule, Norfolk City, p. 167.

47. John DeBree to Capt. H. H. Cocke, July 9 and April 4, 1864, Cocke Family Papers, Virginia Historical Society, Richmond.

48. Forrest, *Norfolk Directory for 1851–1852*, p. 37. However, Bogger, "Black Community in Norfolk," p. 222, states that "two black churches were established in Norfolk during the ante-bellum era," citing Luther Porter Jackson, "Religious Development of the Negro in Virginia from 1760–1860," *Journal of Negro History*, 16 (April 1931), 168–239. On black religion in Southern cities, see Wade, *Slavery in the Cities*, pp. 161–172.

49. Norfolk *Southern Argus*, September 8, 1857; Norfolk *American Beacon*, September 18, 1852.

50. Norfolk *American Beacon*, September 1 and 22, 1852.

51. If angry letters to the editors of Norfolk's newspapers can be believed, there were many occasions when revival meetings and other activities and services took place without the presence of any whites; Norfolk *Southern Argus*, June 12 and 15, 1849.

52. Forrest, *Historical and Descriptive Sketches*, p. 420; Ira Berlin, *Slaves without Masters: The Free Negro in the Antebellum South* (New York: Oxford University Press, 1974), pp. 306–308; Norfolk *Southern Argus*, April 14, 1859; February 29, 1860.

53. *Boston Traveller*, reprinted in Norfolk *Southern Argus*, June 26, 1854; Norfolk *Southern Argus*, August 24, 1848.

54. Norfolk *American Beacon*, December 25, 1851.

55. Wade, *Slavery in the Cities*, pp. 177–179; Norfolk *Southern Argus*, October 24, 26, 28, 31, and November 7, 1850. According to the *Argus*, the party attracted nearly 200 blacks from as far away as Richmond and Baltimore, and rumors circulated that invitations had even been sent to blacks in New York and Philadelphia. At midnight, "the very zenith of their enjoyment," a band of "incensed citizens" attacked the "scene of festivity and gaiety, and dispersed the unlawful assembly."

56. Norfolk *Southern Argus*, October 13, 1852.

57. Norfolk *American Beacon*, August 10, 1852.

58. Ibid., July 7 and February 27, 1852.

59. Norfolk *Southern Argus*, July 21, 1851.

60. Ibid., May 3, 1860.

61. Wade, *Slavery in the Cities*, pp. 253–255.

62. Thomas C. Parramore, with Peter C. Stewart and Tommy L. Bogger, *Norfolk: The First Four Centuries* (Charlottesville: University Press of Virginia, 1994), p. 156; Marie Tyler McGraw, "Richmond Free Blacks and African Colonization, 1816–1832," *Journal of American Studies*, 21, no. 2 (1987), 220–223; Norfolk *Southern Argus*, April 3, 1848.

63. Norfolk *American Beacon*, June 24, 1850; November 17, 1851; April 20, 1852.

64. Bogger, "Black Community in Norfolk," pp. 272–273; Parramore, *Norfolk*, pp. 155–156; E. Lee Shepard, Frances S. Pollard, and Janet B. Schwarz, comps., " 'The Love of Liberty Brought Us Here': Virginians and the Colonization of Liberia," *Virginia Magazine of History and Biography*, 102 (January 1994), 90–99.

65. Grandy, *Narrative*, pp. 11–22.

66. Christopher L. Tomlins, "In Nat Turner's Shadow: Reflections on the Norfolk Dry Dock Affair of 1830–1831," *Labor History*, 33 (February 1992), 494–517.

67. Luther Porter Jackson, *Free Negro Labor and Property Holding in Virginia, 1830–1860* (1942; reprint, New York: Atheneum, 1969), pp. 153–154. Jackson calculated that if Norfolk had had the same rate of increase in black propertyholding as Richmond and Petersburg, the city should have had seventy-five free black propertyholders in 1860 instead of only thirteen.

68. Still, as late as 1851 a telegraphic dispatch from Boston would claim that "his right name is Sherwood"; *Voice of the Fugitive*, February 26, 1851. Although this may simply mean that Minkins told someone that his name *had* been Sherwood, it may also mean that Minkins still went by the name occasionally.

3. "The Silver Trump of Freedom"

1. Fletcher Webster, ed., *The Private Correspondence of Daniel Webster*, 2 vols. (Boston: Little, Brown, 1856), 2: 319.

2. Quoted in Sydney Nathans, *Daniel Webster and Jacksonian Democracy* (Baltimore: Johns Hopkins University Press, 1973), p. 33.

3. Webster, *Private Correspondence*, 2: 319.

4. Ibid., p. 320; Robert F. Dalzell, Jr., *Daniel Webster and the Trial of American Nationalism, 1843–1852* (Boston: Houghton Mifflin, 1973), pp. 166–167; Norma Lois Peterson, *Littleton Waller Tazewell* (Charlottesville: University Press of Virginia, 1983), pp. 260–261.

5. Peter Harvey, *Reminiscences and Anecdotes of Daniel Webster* (Boston: Little, Brown, 1877), pp. 310–315.

6. Herbert G. Gutman, *The Black Family in Slavery and Freedom, 1750–1925* (New York: Vintage, 1976), p. 265; Larry Gara, *The Liberty Line: The Legend of the Underground Railroad* (Lexington: University of Kentucky Press, 1961), pp. 43–44; Tommy Lee Bogger, "The Slave and Free Black Community in Norfolk, 1775–1865" (Ph.D. diss., University of Virginia, 1976), p. 248.

7. George Teamoh, *God Made Man, Man Made the Slave: The Autobiography of George Teamoh*, ed. F. N. Boney, Richard L. Hume, and Rafia Zafar (Macon, Ga.: Mercer University Press, 1990), pp. 68, 96.

8. William Still, *The Underground Railroad* . . . (Philadelphia: Porter and Coates, 1872), pp. 255, 412, 430.

9. Ibid., p. 430. Armstead arrived in 1857.

10. Benjamin Drew, *A North-Side View of Slavery; The Refugee: or the Narratives of Fugitive Slaves in Canada, Related by Themselves, with an Account of the History and Condition of the Colored Population of Upper Canada* (Boston: John P. Jewett, 1856), p. 113. Another example is a Norfolk slave named William who had been supporting his family at oystering for many years before his escape. He hired his own time, operating essentially as if he were free, except that the majority of his wages had to be turned over to support his master rather than his own family. Exasperation with this arrangement led him to escape.

11. Francis Jackson, "Treasurer's Accounts: The Boston Vigilance Committee Appointed at the Public Meeting in Faneuil Hall October 21, 1850, to Assist Fugitive

Slaves," MB (facsimile, Boston: Bostonian Society, n.d.); Wilbur H. Siebert, *The Underground Railroad from Slavery to Freedom* (New York: Macmillan, 1898).

12. Gara, *Liberty Line*, pp. 42–51; James Oliver Horton, *Free People of Color: Inside the African American Community* (Washington, D.C.: Smithsonian Institution Press, 1993), pp. 62–63.

13. See, for example, interview with Virginia ex-slave William I. Johnson in Charles L. Perdue, Jr., Thomas E. Barden, and Robert K. Phillips, eds., *Weevils in the Wheat: Interviews with Virginia's Ex-Slaves* (Charlottesville: University Press of Virginia, 1976), p. 167.

14. *Liberator*, March 31, 1854; *Savannah Republican*, in *Anti-Slavery Bugle*, July 14, 1854.

15. William Still, whose Philadelphia Vigilance Committee records provide the most extensive documentation of the fugitive traffic, seems to have taken few precautions when sending fugitives from Philadelphia northward, and many of those mentioned in his records apparently remained in the Philadelphia area.

16. Discussion of fugitive routes is based on Siebert's *Underground Railroad* and my own research in contemporary antislavery newspapers as well as local newspapers from Virginia, Maryland, Massachusetts, Pennsylvania, and Ohio.

17. *Congressional Globe*, 31st Cong., 1st sess., app., p. 79, quoted in Stanley Campbell, *The Slave Catchers: Enforcement of the Fugitive Slave Law, 1850–1860* (1968; New York: W. W. Norton, 1972), p. 6; Allan Nevins, *Fruits of Manifest Destiny, 1847–1852*, vol. 1 of his 4-volume *Ordeal of the Union* (New York: Charles Scribner's Sons, 1947), p. 243.

18. Barbara Jeanne Fields, *Slavery and Freedom on the Middle Ground: Maryland during the Nineteenth Century* (New Haven: Yale University Press, 1985), p. 16; figures "compiled from official sources for the year ending June 1, 1851," listed 249 fugitives from Maryland, 89 from Virginia; Boston *Commonwealth*, November 27, 1851.

19. Norfolk *American Beacon*, April 20 and March 31, 1854.

20. Norfolk *Southern Argus*, May 22, 1854.

21. Undated clipping from New York *Journal of Commerce*, reprinted in *Montreal Witness*, March 26, 1856. A letter to the editor of the Norfolk *American Beacon*, April 25, 1854, claimed that even $500,000 was a conservative estimate, but this assertion is farfetched and may have been the result of a misplaced decimal point.

22. Bogger, "Black Community in Norfolk," pp. 133–136; Francis Jackson, *Liberty Bell*, reprinted in Boston *Commonwealth*, December 25, 1851; Herbert Aptheker, "Maroons within the Present Limits of the United States," *Journal of Negro History*, 24 (1939), 167–184; Ira Berlin, *Slaves without Masters: The Free Negro in the Antebellum South* (New York: Oxford University Press, 1974), p. 158.

23. Still, *Underground Railroad*, pp. 45, 47, 215, 273, 313, 402; Bogger, "Black Community in Norfolk," pp. 256–257.

24. Norfolk *American Beacon*, March 1, 1855.

25. Wilbur Siebert scrapbooks, vol. 14, HL.

26. Irving H. Bartlett, "Abolitionists, Fugitives, and Imposters in Boston, 1846–1847," *New England Quarterly*, 55 (March 1982), 101.

27. Ibid., p. 103. Because his mother's address in New York was known to others, he soon went on to Boston.

28. See, for example, Still, *Underground Railroad*, pp. 325–327.

29. See, for example, ibid., pp. 225, 226, 228, 257; Norfolk *Southern Argus*, January 31, 1860; *New York Tribune*, December 30, 1857. Many fugitives went on to Canada.

30. Norfolk *American Beacon*, April 25, 1854; Thomas C. Parramore, with Peter C. Stewart and Tommy L. Bogger, *Norfolk: The First Four Centuries* (Charlottesville: University Press of Virginia, 1994), p. 125. Of the known fugitives from Norfolk, one was an oysterman and one a corn measurer who presumably worked around the port; Norfolk *American Beacon*, March 31, 1851; Norfolk *Southern Argus*, January 31, 1860.

31. Davis S. Cecelski, "The Shores of Freedom: The Maritime Underground Railroad in North Carolina, 1800–1861," *North Carolina Historical Review*, 71 (April 1994), 197–199.

32. A Virginia law passed in 1856 required licensed pilots to inspect all vessels leaving Virginia waters and to certify them free of fugitives within twelve hours of sailing. Vessels caught sailing without a certificate could be fined up to $500 even if they were found to harbor no fugitives. The penalties for being caught with fugitives were much greater. Undoubtedly the law made escape more difficult, but Philadelphia records of fugitive slave arrivals from Norfolk from 1856 through 1859 show that it did not shut off the flow. Because inspections could be made up to twelve hours before sailing, many intervening hours were left for fugitives to climb safely aboard; George W. Munford, *Code of Virginia*, 2nd ed. (Richmond: Ritchie, Dunnavant, 1860), pp. 792–793; Still, *Underground Railroad*, pp. 380 ff.

33. Still, *Underground Railroad*, p. 589.

34. Siebert scrapbooks, vol. 14, HL.

35. Still, *Underground Railroad*, pp. 260–261.

36. Ibid., pp. 301, 217, 309; Bogger, "Black Community in Norfolk," p. 252.

37. Works Progress Administration, *The Negro in Virginia* (1940; reprint, New York: Arno Press, 1969), p. 137.

38. Still, *Underground Railroad*, pp. 561–562.

39. Ibid., pp. 111–112, 160, 269, 587; Norfolk City Order Book, 37: 94; WPA, *Negro in Virginia*, p. 136.

40. William S. Forrest, *Norfolk Directory for 1851–1852* (Norfolk, 1851), p. 18.

41. Still, *Underground Railroad*, pp. 163–164, 559–562.

42. Gara, *Liberty Line*, pp. 50–52.

43. WPA, *Negro in Virginia*, pp. 136–137; Still, *Underground Railroad*, p. 269; Bogger, "Black Community in Norfolk," pp. 261–262.

44. WPA, *Negro in Virginia*, p. 136.

45. Still, *Underground Railroad*, pp. 330–331.

46. Norfolk *Southern Argus*, April 22, 1854.

47. See, for example, Norfolk *American Beacon*, August 2, 1848; December 9, 1852; January 31 and May 16, 1854; Norfolk *Southern Argus*, October 8, 1849; January 28, 1850; August 8, 1854.

48. Norfolk *American Beacon*, April 25, 1854; Norfolk *Southern Argus*, June 23, 1855.

49. A good, succinct account of the shifting political balance is David Herbert Donald, *Liberty and Union* (Boston: Little, Brown, 1978), pp. 3–58; see also Holman

Hamilton, *Prologue to Conflict: The Crisis and Compromise of 1850* (Lexington: University of Kentucky Press, 1964).

50. For discussion of the Compromise debate, the main sources are Nevins, *Fruits of Manifest Destiny,* pp. 219–314; William W. Freehling, *Secessionists at Bay, 1776–1854,* vol. 1 of *The Road to Disunion* (New York: Oxford University Press, 1990), pp. 487–510; and Dalzell, *Webster and Trial of American Nationalism,* pp. 156–195.

51. Thomas D. Morris, *Free Men All: The Personal Liberty Laws of the North, 1780–1861* (Baltimore: Johns Hopkins University Press, 1974), pp. 71–129. At the same time that the Supreme Court upheld Pennsylvania's law, it asserted that federal fugitive slave laws always took precedence over state laws.

52. Campbell, *The Slave Catchers,* pp. 15–16; Morris, *Free Men All,* pp. 130–147. Morris believes that Webster's proposed amendments were an afterthought, put forward simply to quiet his critics.

53. Campbell, *The Slave Catchers,* pp. 16–23; Freehling, *Road to Disunion,* pp. 500–505.

54. Campbell, *The Slave Catchers,* p. 18.

55. Dalzell, *Daniel Webster and Trial of American Nationalism,* pp. 177–188.

56. Nevins, *Fruits of Manifest Destiny,* pp. 291–292.

57. John Greenleaf Whittier, *Complete Poetical Works* (Boston: Houghton Mifflin, 1894), pp. 186–187.

58. *The Journals and Miscellaneous Notebooks of Ralph Waldo Emerson,* ed. William H. Gilman et al., 16 vols. (Cambridge, Mass.: The Belknap Press of Harvard University Press, 1960–1982), 11 (1848–1851): 346.

59. Daniel Webster to Peter Harvey, August 7, 1850, *DWC,* 7: 132.

60. Allan Nevins viewed Webster's March 7 speech as the turning point in securing the Compromise measures and saving the Union. After it, according to Nevins, disunionist fervor "rapidly subsided"; *Fruits of Manifest Destiny,* p. 297.

61. James Silk Buckingham, *The Slave States of America,* 2 vols. (London: Fisher, Son, 1842), 2: 486; *Revised Ordinances of the City of Norfolk* (Norfolk: Norfolk Councils, 1852), p. 135.

62. Advertisements and "Marine Journal," Norfolk *Southern Argus,* May 5–18, 1850; Still, *Underground Railroad,* p. 560.

63. Still, *Underground Railroad,* p. 313.

64. *Cincinnati Gazette,* in *Montreal Witness,* November 17, 1858.

65. Norfolk *American Beacon,* August 2, 1848.

66. *Liberator,* March 21, 1851.

67. Siebert, *Underground Railroad,* p. 81; *Liberator,* June 24, 1859.

68. Asa J. Davis, "The Two Autobiographical Fragments of George W. Latimer," *Journal of the Afro-American Historical and Genealogical Society,* 1 (Summer 1980), 9.

69. Still, *Underground Railroad,* pp. 63–64.

70. *Montreal Witness,* September 14, 1859.

71. Gutman, *The Black Family,* p. 265.

72. Still, *Underground Railroad,* pp. 325–327. Although Rebecca Jones located her husband in Boston, their reunion did not prove successful. Six months later she wrote Still that she had decided to accept an invitation to go with her children to California. In 1854 a seaman named Minkins (possibly a relative of Shadrach Mink-

ins) who worked aboard the *City of Richmond* was reportedly assisting fugitives; Still, *Underground Railroad*, p. 63.

4. "Cradle of Liberty"?

1. Peter R. Knights, *The Plain People of Boston, 1830–1860: A Study in City Growth* (New York: Oxford University Press, 1971), p. 35.

2. *Salem Gazette*, February 28, 1851.

3. Boston *Commonwealth*, January 16, 1851, which noted that 126 girls had been arrested in a single week.

4. Lorenzo Johnston Greene, *The Negro in Colonial New England* (1942; reprint, New York: Atheneum, 1968), pp. 15–49; William D. Peirsen, *Black Yankees: The Development of an Afro-American Subculture in Eighteenth-Century New England* (Amherst: University of Massachusetts Press, 1988), pp. 1–9.

5. John Daniels, *In Freedom's Birthplace: A Study of the Boston Negroes* (Boston: Houghton Mifflin, 1914), p. 457. Why Boston's black population followed this pattern of stagnation is a topic too complex to be fully addressed here. Probably the American Revolution scattered some of Boston's blacks. In the early nineteenth century Boston's great distance from the South, its lack of a large black population to act as a magnet, and its lack of opportunities would have made cities such as Philadelphia, Pittsburgh, and New York more attractive to free blacks and fugitive slaves.

6. Knights, *Plain People of Boston*, p. 16.

7. Oscar Handlin, *Boston's Immigrants, 1790–1880: A Study in Acculturation*, rev. ed. (Cambridge, Mass.: Harvard University Press, 1979), p. 106.

8. *Boston Daily Evening Traveller*, quoted in Philadelphia *Public Ledger*, May 6, 1851.

9. Leonard P. Curry, *The Free Black in Urban America, 1800–1850: The Shadow of the Dream* (Chicago: University of Chicago Press, 1981), p. 24.

10. In 1838 Susan Paul, a black woman, was unable to find affordable housing in the black neighborhoods. When she rented a small building in a street occupied entirely by whites, "the neighbors assured her that the family would not be allowed to remain there in comfort and safety"; Lydia Maria Child to Jonathan Phillips, January 23, 1838, in *Lydia Maria Child: Selected Letters, 1817–1880*, ed. Milton Meltzer and Patricia G. Holland (Amherst: University of Massachusetts Press, 1982), pp. 69–70. In 1847 South Boston residents boasted that "not a single colored family" lived among them; Handlin, *Boston's Immigrants*, p. 98; Curry, *Free Black*, p. 54.

11. *Liberator*, March 16, 1860, quoted in Leon F. Litwack, *North of Slavery: The Negro in the Free States, 1790–1860* (Chicago: University of Chicago Press, 1961), p. 110.

12. The east–west streets were May, Southac (Phillips), and Cambridge; the north–south streets were Garden, Belknap, West Cedar, and Butolph. There were also small concentrations of black homes along two streets in the North End near the wharves, and scattered residences elsewhere; Curry, *Free Black*, pp. 70–71; Handlin, *Boston's Immigrants*, p. 97; Boston "Streets" Tax ledgers, 1850–1852, Boston Public Library.

13. Leonard Curry believes that Boston's unusually low number of blacks per residence (1.27, the third lowest among the fifteen cities he studied) points to a preponderance of this type of house; *Free Black*, pp. 50, 54.

14. Beth Bower et al., "The African Meeting House, Boston, Massachusetts: Summary Report of Archeological Excavations, 1975–86," pp. 43–54, Museum of Afro-American History, Boston. Bower and her associates documented over a dozen residents between 1806 and 1860.

15. Population Schedules of the Seventh United States Census (1850), Suff 402 Boston 6.

16. James Oliver Horton and Lois E. Horton, *Black Bostonians: Family Life and Community Struggle in the Antebellum North* (New York: Holmes & Meier, 1979), pp. 16–18; James Oliver Horton, *Free People of Color: Inside the African American Community* (Washington, D.C.: Smithsonian Institution Press, 1993), pp. 29–32.

17. Carol Buchalter Stapp, *Afro-Americans in Antebellum Boston: An Analysis of Probate Records* (New York: Garland, 1993), p. 82. Stapp's survey of Boston's black community, based primarily on a painstaking analysis of probate documents, identifies a rich interaction among a tiny group of relatively prosperous, literate blacks, including clothing dealer John E. Scarlett, hairdresser Thomas Cole, gentleman/clothing dealer William Riley, and clothing dealer John Robinson. Although all these men died in the 1840s, before Shadrach Minkins arrived in Boston, their records mention other blacks with whom they interacted who lived into the 1850s, and thus imply a sustained interactive pattern. See also Horton and Horton, *Black Bostonians*, esp. pp. 15–25, 53–66; Horton, *Free People of Color*, pp. 29–39; George A. Levesque, *Black Boston: African American Life and Culture in Urban America, 1750–1860* (New York: Garland, 1994); and Adelaide M. Cromwell's somewhat dated but still useful dissertation recently published as *The Other Brahmins: Boston's Black Upper Class, 1750–1950* (Fayetteville: University of Arkansas Press, 1994), pp. 33–37.

18. William Still, *The Underground Railroad . . .* (Philadelphia: Porter and Coates, 1872), p. 558.

19. Testimony of William H. Parks, Boston *Commonwealth*, June 8, 1852.

20. Frederick Douglass, *Life and Times of Frederick Douglass, Written by Himself: His early life as a slave, his escape from bondage, and his complete history to the present time*, rev. ed. (Boston: DeWolf, Fisk, 1892), p. 209.

21. Scrapbook G70, Bostonian Society; "Cornhill Coffee House" scrapbook, Boston Athenaeum. By October 1850 the business was being listed as Young's Cornhill Coffee House, but the purchase may have taken place before or during the time Minkins worked there.

22. Figures for black occupations are taken from Handlin, *Boston's Immigrants*, table XIII, pp. 250–251. For slightly different figures see Charles H. Wesley, *Negro Labor in the United States, 1850–1925: A Study in American Economic History* (New York: Russell & Russell, 1927), p. 48.

23. According to Leonard Curry, barely 6 percent of Boston's black workers fell into artisan categories; *Free Black*, p. 28. Of large Northern cities, only Pittsburgh, which had a larger number of recent immigrant blacks than any other major city, had a lower index. For every trade in which blacks were employed, at whatever disadvantage, there were two trades that employed no blacks. Boston in 1850 had no black plumbers, coopers, sawyers, roofers, caulkers, chandlers, or other maritime workers and no black apprentices working at these trades. Frederick Douglass, a skilled caulker by trade, was forced to seek work in New Bedford as a common laborer at half

the pay; *My Bondage and My Freedom,* ed. William L. Andrews (Urbana: University of Illinois Press, 1987), p. 213. As one Southerner pointed out, Northern blacks who tried to earn a living driving a hack or dray (a common black occupation in Southern cities) found that the other carters would "run over them, [and] break their carriages"; *Charleston Mercury,* March 12, 1851; Litwack, *North of Slavery,* p. 159.

24. Professional and trade skills were no guarantee of equal opportunity. As Frederick Douglass noted with regard to black professionals, "white people will not employ them to the obvious embarrassment of their causes, and the blacks, taking their cue from the whites, have not sufficient confidence in their abilities to employ them." The result, Douglass concluded bitterly, was that "educated colored men, among the colored people, are at a very great discount"; *Life and Times of Douglass,* pp. 285–286.

25. One in four barbers in antebellum Boston was black. Litwack, *North of Slavery,* p. 157, says that blacks were preferred because they made it possible for whites to "assume aristocratic airs."

26. Black seamen probably accounted for an even greater percentage of black workers because they were easily missed in the census and because racial origin of at least a quarter of all seamen was not known.

27. Handlin, *Boston's Immigrants,* pp. 250–251; Samuel Eliot Morison, *The Maritime History of Massachusetts, 1783–1860* (1921; reprint, Boston: Houghton Mifflin, 1961), p. 353. Seafaring, with its own rigorous codes of status and behavior, had always offered blacks an alternative society, one in which color typically brought far fewer disadvantages than on land. Bostonians like Joseph Jacobs, brother of writer Harriet Jacobs and the model for the character Benny in her narrative, shipped out to sea when racial prejudices encountered on land became intolerable; Harriet Jacobs, *Incidents in the Life of a Slave Girl, Written by Herself* (Cambridge, Mass.: Harvard University Press, 1987), pp. xvi, 186, 287, n. 2. But as noted by both Morison and W. Jeffrey Bolster (" 'To Feel like a Man': Black Seamen in the Northern States, 1800–1860," *Journal of American History,* 76 [March 1990], 1174–75, 1193–99), seafaring in the mid-nineteenth century was no longer the route to the middle class that it had been early in the century.

28. Half of the entire Irish-born working population (7,007) were identified in the 1850 census as laborers.

29. *Boston Pilot,* November 2, 1850; March 15, 1851.

30. Of 3,249 domestic servants, only 48 are listed in the census as being black. This figure, representing less than 10 percent of the black working population and only 1.5 percent of the domestic servants, is probably the result of blacks' displacement by Irish and English immigrants. The process was accelerated by the willingness of thousands of Bridgetts and Marys to work for low wages. By 1850, according to one conservative estimate, 2,227 young Irish girls tended the homes of Boston's upper classes, outnumbering the entire black population of the city; Handlin, *Boston's Immigrants,* p. 61. Additionally, young blacks probably shared the American distaste for the social inequalities of life in service. The newly arrived Irish had more European, class-ingrained acceptance of menial positions.

Many black newcomers or transients who worked as waiters could easily have been missed in the census and city directory, especially if they did not maintain separate households in the city.

31. Boston *Commonwealth*, June 8, 1852; Population Schedules of the Seventh United States Census (1850), Suff 15 Boston 7; and *Boston Daily Evening Traveller*, February 18, 1851, which states that Minkins was commonly called "Frederick" while in Boston. Frederick Douglass notes that "Johnson" was a common name adopted by fugitives; *Narrative of the Life of Frederick Douglass, an American Slave, Written by Himself* (1845; reprint, New York: New American Library, 1968), p. 114.

32. According to Joseph H. Willard, *Half a Century with Lawyers* (Boston: Houghton Mifflin, 1895), p. 239, George Young sometimes received advance warning from a friend who worked at the Court House if one of his workers was sought as a fugitive slave, but that arrangement was apparently in place much later in the decade.

33. Boston *Commonwealth*, June 8, 1852.

34. *Boston Pilot*, November 2, 1850.

35. *Boston Congregationalist*, quoted in the *Montreal Witness*, July 9, 1859.

36. William Chambers, *Things as They Are in America* (London: W. Edinburg & R. Chambers, 1854), p. 356.

37. Douglass, *My Bondage and My Freedom*, p. 368.

38. W. C. Nell to Editor, *Liberator*, December 16, 1853, reprinted in Carter G. Woodson, ed., *The Mind of the Negro as Reflected in Letters Written during the Crisis, 1800–1860* (Washington, D.C.: Associated Publishers, 1926), p. 345.

39. Quoted in Clifton Joseph Furness, "Walt Whitman Looks at Boston," *New England Quarterly*, 1 (July 1928), 356.

40. Nell, in Woodson, *Mind of the Negro*, p. 346.

41. Horton and Horton, *Black Bostonians*, pp. 68–70; Levesque, *Black Boston*, pp. 133–135.

42. Levesque, *Black Boston*, pp. 181–229; for documents and commentary on the case of Sarah C. Roberts v. City of Boston (1849), an important unsuccessful lawsuit to open Boston's public schools, see Leonard W. Levy and Douglass L. Jones, eds., *Jim Crow in Boston: The Origins of the Separate but Equal Doctrine* (New York: Da Capo Press, 1974).

43. Gary L. Collison, "Antislavery, Blacks, and the Boston Elite: Notes on the Reverend Charles Lowell and the West Church," *New England Quarterly*, 61 (September 1988), 419–429.

44. Roy E. Finkenbine, "Boston's Black Churches: Institutional Centers of the Antislavery Movement," in *Courage and Conscience: Black and White Abolitionists in Boston*, ed. Donald M. Jacobs (Indianapolis: Indiana University Press, 1993), pp. 169–189; Robert C. Hayden et al., *The African Meeting House in Boston: A Celebration of History* (Boston: Museum of African American History, 1987). In the 1980s the building, which was a synagogue for part of the twentieth century, was renovated as part of the Boston African-American historic site.

45. Facts about Boston's black churches are taken from the *Pennsylvania Freeman*, August 25, 1853; Finkenbine, "Boston's Black Churches," pp. 169–189; Levesque, *Black Boston*, pp. 263–313; Horton and Horton, *Black Bostonians*, pp. 39–52; and Robert C. Hayden, *Faith, Culture and Leadership: A History of the Black Church in Boston* (Boston: Boston NAACP, 1983).

46. Horton and Horton, *Black Bostonians*, p. 39. The Hortons' list draws on classic studies of the black church by Charles V. Hamilton, *The Black Preacher in America*

(New York: Morrow, 1972); and E. Franklin Frazier, *The Negro Church in America* (New York: Schocken Books, 1963).

47. William H. Hester, *One Hundred and Five Years by Faith* (Boston: Twelfth Baptist Church, 1946), pp. 9–18; Charles Emory Stevens, *Anthony Burns: A History* (Boston, 1856), pp. 203–210. The departure of many fugitive slaves in the months after the Fugitive Slave Law took effect depleted church coffers, with the result that the building would be left unfinished for several years.

48. Cromwell, *The Other Brahmins*, pp. 40–41; Horton, *Free People of Color*, pp. 41–51, 125–133. According to Horton, the reasons for the minimal impact of skin tone include the small size of the black community, the great distance from the South, and greater residential segregation than was common in Southern cities.

49. Greene, *Negro in Colonial New England*, pp. 216–217; Levesque, *Black Boston*, pp. 138–152; Horton and Horton, *Black Bostonians*, pp. 70–74.

50. Quoted in Vincent Harding, *There Is a River: The Black Struggle for Freedom in America* (1981; New York: Vintage Books, 1983), p. 86.

51. *Liberator*, December 12, 1845, quoted in William F. Cheek, *Black Resistance before the Civil War* (Beverly Hills: Glencoe Press, 1970), p. 184; Horton and Horton, *Black Bostonians*, pp. 41, 47–48.

52. Stanley J. and Anita W. Robboy, "Lewis Hayden, From Fugitive Slave to Statesman," *New England Quarterly*, 46 (December 1973), 595–597; *BAP*, 4: 268–269. See also R. J. M. Blackett, *Beating against the Barriers: Biographical Essays in Nineteenth-Century Afro-American History* (Baton Rouge: Louisiana State University Press, 1986), pp. 91–95.

53. Austin Bearse, *Reminiscences of Fugitive-Slave Law Days in Boston* (Boston: Warren Richardson, 1880), p. 8.

54. *BAP*, 3: 307–308n; Robert P. Smith, "William Cooper Nell: Crusading Black Abolitionist," *Journal of Negro History*, 55 (July 1970), 183–199; Dorothy Porter Wesley, "Integration versus Separatism: William Cooper Nell's Role in the Struggle for Equality," in Jacobs, *Courage and Conscience*, pp. 207–224; *Dictionary of American Biography*, 13: 413.

55. *BAP*, 3: 305–306, 155–156, 304–305. Watkins returned to Boston in 1861.

56. Stevens, *Anthony Burns*, p. 208; *New York Independent*, in *Pennsylvania Freeman*, August 25, 1853; Notes of R. H. Dana, Jr., U.S. v. Wright, item 3, Dana legal papers, American Antiquarian Society, Worcester, Mass.; Boston *Commonwealth*, November 8, 1851.

5. "A New Reign of Terror"

1. Daniel Webster to Franklin Haven, September 12, 1850, *DWC*, 7: 144.

2. Quoted in Allan Nevins, *Fruits of Manifest Destiny, 1847–1852*, vol. 1 of his 4-volume *Ordeal of the Union* (New York: Charles Scribner's Sons, 1947), pp. 343–344; Holman Hamilton, *Prologue to Conflict: The Crisis and Compromise of 1850* (Lexington: University of Kentucky Press, 1964), pp. 166–167.

3. Harriet Jacobs, *Incidents in the Life of a Slave Girl, Written by Herself* (Cambridge, Mass.: Harvard University Press, 1987), p. 191. Although Jacobs objected to having her freedom purchased, as did many fugitives, she finally gave in to her employer's importunities and allowed herself to be purchased for $300. Once

officially free, she felt an immense relief. "I was no longer afraid to unveil my face and look at people as they passed," she wrote (p. 200).

4. *Boston Daily Advertiser,* September 28, in *Montreal Witness,* October 7, 1850; Benjamin Quarles, *Black Abolitionists* (New York: Oxford University Press, 1969), pp. 199–200.

5. *Pittsburgh Saturday Visiter,* October 26, 1850.

6. *Western Citizen,* November 5, 1850.

7. *Pennsylvania Freeman,* September 26 and October 3, 1850. The report not only gives the exaggerated percentage but lists Boston's black population at 8,900, thereby confusing the number of Boston fugitives with the total black population of Massachusetts.

8. *Centenary Edition [The Works of Theodore Parker],* 15 vols. (Boston: American Unitarian Association, 1907–1911), 11: 335.

9. Nevins, *Fruits of Manifest Destiny,* p. 385; *Liberator,* October 4, 1850.

10. Henry Clay to "a numerous committee in New York," Ashland, October 3, in *Liberator,* November 1, 1850.

11. Harriet Beecher Stowe to Catharine Beecher, December 1850, quoted in Annie Fields, ed., *Life and Letters of Harriet Beecher Stowe* (Boston: Houghton Mifflin, 1899), pp. 130–131.

12. *Liberator,* October 4, 1850. Unless otherwise noted, all facts about and quotations from this meeting are taken from this source.

13. "Declaration of Sentiments of the Colored Citizens of Boston on the Fugitive Slave Bill," Library of Congress, reprinted in James Oliver Horton and Lois E. Horton, *Black Bostonians: Family Life and Community Struggle in the Antebellum North* (New York: Holmes & Meier, 1979), insert following p. 80; *Liberator,* October 4 and 11, 1850. Philip Foner's *History of Black Americans: From the Compromise of 1850 to the End of the Civil War* (Westport, Conn.: Greenwood Press, 1983), though useful, contains numerous errors in the sections on Boston.

14. Theodore Parker, speech at October 14 meeting, quoted in *Liberator,* October 18, 1850.

15. Dateline October 5, in *Hartford Courant,* October 8, 1850.

16. David Herbert Donald, *Charles Sumner and the Coming of the Civil War* (1960; reprint, Chicago: University of Chicago Press, 1981), p. 188.

17. Dateline October 2, in *Hartford Courant,* October 4, 1850; *Liberator,* October 11 and 25, 1850.

18. *Boston Evening Transcript,* October 2, in *Liberator,* October 4, 1850; *Boston Atlas,* in *Liberator,* October 11, 1850.

19. *Springfield Republican,* in *Hartford Courant,* October 4, 1850.

20. *Boston Daily Evening Traveller,* October 7, in *New York Daily Tribune,* October 9, 1850.

21. Caroline Healey Dall, Journal, October 20, 1850, microfilm, reel 34, Dall Papers, MHS.

22. *Liberator,* October 18, 1850. Lowell's words are reported to be "substantially as follows." Unless otherwise noted, all facts about and quotations from the meeting are from the *Liberator* account.

23. Ibid.; *National Anti-Slavery Standard,* October 24, 1850, reprinted in *The Frederick Douglass Papers; Series One: Speeches, Debates, and Interviews,* ed. John

W. Blassingame et al., 5 vols. (New Haven: Yale University Press, 1982–1992), 2: 243–248. The "dead kidnappers" quotation comes from Douglass' speech at the Free Soil Convention in Pittsburgh, August 11, 1852, ibid., p. 390. Douglass recommended the same remedy in his speech at Syracuse on January 7, 1851, ibid., p. 277.

24. *Boston Morning Post*, October 15, 1850, quoted in Allen Chamberlain, "Old Passages of Boston's Underground Railroad," *Magazine of History*, 31, no. 4 (1926), 217–218.

25. Wilbur H. Siebert, "The Vigilance Committee of Boston," in *Proceedings of the Bostonian Society, Annual Meeting, January 27, 1953* (Boston: Old State House for the Society, 1953), pp. 22–45.

26. Letter of October 19, *Philadelphia Bulletin*, in Norfolk *American Beacon*, November 12, 1850.

27. Stanley W. Campbell, *The Slave Catchers: Enforcement of the Fugitive Slave Law, 1850–1860* (1968; New York: W. W. Norton, 1972), pp. 49–55; Quarles, *Black Abolitionists*, pp. 201–202.

28. *Boston Daily Evening Traveller*, September 25, 1850, in *Liberator*, October 4, 1850.

29. For the meetings and actions of the Vigilance Committee, see "Records of the Vigilance Committee, Boston," BPL; Siebert, "Vigilance Committee"; Gary L. Collison, "The Boston Vigilance Committee: A Reconsideration," *Historical Journal of Massachusetts*, 12 (June 1984), 104–116.

30. Francis Jackson, "Treasurer's Accounts: The Boston Vigilance Committee Appointed at the Public Meeting in Faneuil Hall October 21, 1850, to Assist Fugitive Slaves," BPL (facsimile, Boston: Bostonian Society, n.d.).

31. Austin Bearse, *Reminiscences of Fugitive-Slave Law Days in Boston* (Boston: Warren Richardson, 1880), pp. 34–37; Sidney Kaplan, "The *Moby Dick* in the Service of the Underground Railroad," *Phylon*, 12, no. 2 (1951), 173–176.

32. Occupations are taken from George Adams, comp., *The Boston Directory for 1850–51* (Boston: Adams, 1850).

33. Thomas Wentworth Higginson, *Cheerful Yesterdays* (Boston: Houghton Mifflin, 1899), pp. 139–140.

34. Ibid., p. 148; Deborah Weston to Anne W. Weston, April 15, 1851, BPL.

35. George Teamoh, *God Made Man, Man Made the Slave: The Autobiography of George Teamoh*, ed. F. N. Boney, Richard L. Hume, and Rafia Zafar (Macon, Ga.: Mercer University Press, 1990), p. 114.

36. Jackson, "Treasurer's Accounts," pp. 8, 10, 18, 20, 26, 30.

37. *Boston Daily Bee*, in *Liberator*, October 25, 1850.

38. *Boston Daily Courier*, in *Liberator*, October 11, 1850. Except for a little-known, unverified failed attempt in Hartford, New England fugitives had thus far been immune from the operations of the new law; *Liberator*, October 18, 1850.

39. Stephen B. Oates, *The Fires of Jubilee: Nat Turner's Fierce Rebellion* (New York: Harper & Row, 1975), pp. 129–136.

40. *Baltimore Sun*, in Norfolk *American Beacon*, November 1, 1850.

41. Leonard W. Levy, "The 'Abolition Riot': Boston's First Slave Rescue," *New England Quarterly*, 25 (March 1952), 85–92.

42. Asa J. Davis, ed., "The Two Autobiographical Fragments of George W. La-

timer," *Journal of the Afro-American Historical and Genealogical Society,* 1 (Summer 1980), 9.

43. Horton and Horton, *Black Bostonians,* p. 99; *Proceedings of the Citizens of the Borough of Norfolk, on the Boston Outrage, in the Case of the Runaway Slave George Latimer* (Norfolk: Broughton and Son, 1843), pp. 11–12.

44. *Address of the Committee Appointed by a Public Meeting Held at Faneuil Hall, September 24, 1846, for the Purpose of Considering the Recent Case of Kidnapping from Our Soil* (Boston, 1846); Irving H. Bartlett, "Abolitionists, Fugitives, and Impostors in Boston, 1846–1847," *New England Quarterly,* 55 (March 1982), 97–112.

45. Daniel Webster to Millard Fillmore, November 5, 1850, *DWC,* 7: 178.

46. Webster to Fillmore, October 14, 1850, *DWC,* 7: 162. To Choate, it was folly to think that "mere feelings . . . of a sense of right" could "try a grand complex polity, embracing a multitude of interests and conflicting desires and duties"; quoted in Jean M. Matthews, *Rufus Choate: The Law and Civic Virtue* (Philadelphia: Temple University Press, 1980), p. 199.

47. Webster to Fillmore, October 24, 1850, *DWC,* 7: 165.

48. *New Orleans Daily Picayune,* November 2, 1850.

49. Fillmore to Webster, October 17, 1850, *DWC,* 7: 162.

50. Charles Pelham Curtis to Daniel Webster, October 15, 1850, mDW, reel 23; Webster to Fillmore, October 19, 1850, mDW, reel 23 (copy).

51. *Liberator,* November 8, 1850.

6. "Much Excitement Prevails"

1. John Knight to Editor, Macon *Journal and Messenger,* November 11, 1850, reprinted in Norfolk *American Beacon,* November 25, 1850; Albert S. Foley, *Dream of an Outcast: Patrick Healy, S.J.* (Tuscaloosa: Portals, 1976), p. 35.

2. John E. Talmadge, "Georgia Tests the Fugitive Slave Law," *Georgia Historical Quarterly,* 49 (1965), 57–64.

3. Robert Collins, "Essay on the Management of Slaves," *Southern Cultivator,* 12 (1854), 206. Collins' essay is reprinted in James O. Breeden, ed., *Advice among Masters: The Ideal in Slave Management in the Old South* (Westport, Conn.: Greenwood Press, 1980), pp. 16–27.

4. R. J. M. Blackett, "The Odyssey of William and Ellen Craft," in *Beating against the Barriers: Biographical Essays in Nineteenth-Century Afro-American History* (Baton Rouge: Louisiana State University Press, 1986), p. 88.

5. Discussion of William and Ellen Craft's escape is based on William Craft, *Running a Thousand Miles for Freedom; or, The Escape of William and Ellen Craft from Slavery* (1860; reprint, New York: Arno Press, 1969); Blackett, "Odyssey of William and Ellen Craft," pp. 87–90.

6. Manufacturing Schedules of the Seventh United States Census, Boston.

7. The account of Hughes's attempts to obtain warrants against the Crafts is taken from Hughes's letter of November 21, 1850, Macon *Telegraph,* reprinted in Norfolk *American Beacon* and Boston *Daily Chronotype,* December 2, 1850; Knight, letter, November 11, 1850; George T. Curtis to Daniel Webster, November 23, 1850, reprinted in Norfolk *American Beacon,* December 9, 1850.

8. *Boston Daily Evening Transcript,* December 6, 1895.

9. Willis Hughes, 2nd letter (undated), Columbus, Ga., *Times*, reprinted in *National Anti-Slavery Standard*, January 2, 1851.

10. Norfolk *American Beacon*, October 29, 1850.

11. Theodore Parker wrote in his journal that according to J. B. Smith, warrants for two Parker House employees had been issued; John Weiss, *Life and Correspondence of Theodore Parker*, 2 vols. (New York: D. Appleton, 1864), 2: 95.

12. *Boston Atlas*, October 26, 1850.

13. Norfolk *American Beacon*, October 29, 1850.

14. Hughes, letter, November 21, 1850.

15. *Boston Daily Evening Traveller*, October 25, in *New York Daily Tribune*, October 28, 1850.

16. Hughes, letter, November 21, 1850.

17. Knight, letter, November 11, 1850; dateline October 31, *New York Daily Tribune*, in *Montreal Pilot*, November 7, 1850; Richard Henry Dana to Edmund T. Dana, November 12, December 14, 1850, and January 2, 1851 (one letter), MHS.

18. A detailed statement by the deputy who made this arrest was printed in the *National Anti-Slavery Standard*, October 28, 1850.

19. Dana to Dana, November 12, 1850–January 2, 1851.

20. *New York Daily Tribune*, November 2, 1850; Dana to Dana, November 12, 1850–January 2, 1851; on the writ *de homine replegiando*, see Thomas D. Morris, *Free Men All: The Personal Liberty Laws of the North, 1780–1861* (Baltimore: Johns Hopkins University Press, 1974), pp. 11–12.

21. *National Anti-Slavery Standard*, October 31, 1850.

22. Daniel Webster to Millard Fillmore, November 15, 1850, *DWC*, 7: 181. Attorney General John Crittenden, called on by Fillmore to investigate Devens' conduct, concluded "there does not sufficiently appear any cause for the censure [of the federal officers] . . . or removal of the Marshal from office"; J. J. Crittenden to Millard Fillmore, November 25, 1850, in *National Anti-Slavery Standard*, December 5, 1850.

23. Weiss, *Theodore Parker*, 2: 96.

24. Norfolk *American Beacon*, November 4, 1850. A letter from R. H. Dana, Jr., to J. Thomas Stevenson, October 28, 1850, MHS, shows that it was Stevenson who led the offer to purchase the Crafts' freedom and that Stevenson asked Dana to act as agent.

25. *New York Daily Tribune*, October 31, 1850.

26. Ibid., November 2, 1850; *Pennsylvania Freeman*, October 31, 1850.

27. Blackett, "Odyssey of William and Ellen Craft," p. 92; George W. Putnam to Wilbur Siebert, December 27, 1893, typed copy, Siebert scrapbooks, vol. 13, HL; Weiss, *Theodore Parker*, 2: 95.

28. Weiss, *Theodore Parker*, 2: 97.

29. Ibid.

30. Gamaliel Bailey to Charles Sumner, November 27, 1850, Microfilm Papers of Charles Sumner, ed. Beverly Palmer, Letters to Charles Sumner, 85 reels (Alexandria, Va.: Chadwyck-Healey, 1988), reel 7.

31. Webster to Fillmore, November 15, 1850, *DWC*, 7: 180.

32. Craft, *Running a Thousand Miles*, pp. 91, 101–107; Blackett, "Odyssey of William and Ellen Craft," pp. 96–108; *BAP*, 4: 36–37; Boston *Daily Chronotype*, November 9, 1850.

33. Webster to Fillmore, November 15, 1850, pp. 180–181.

34. Caroline Healey Dall, Journal, November 15, 1850, microfilm, reel 34, Dall Papers, MHS; detailed reports of the meeting from a variety of Boston Whig papers were reprinted in the *Liberator*, November 22, 1850.

35. Caroline Dall thought that the police were never called, but she had been far from the platform and may have been confused by the darkness and the noise.

36. Norfolk *American Beacon*, November 20, 1850.

37. George T. Curtis "for the Committee" to George G. Smith, November 18, 1850, MHS; George T. Curtis, Samuel L. Lewis, et al. to J. C. Warren, November 20, 1850, MHS.

38. David D. Van Tassel, "Gentlemen of Property and Standing: Compromise Sentiment in Boston in 1850," *New England Quarterly*, 23 (September 1950), 313.

39. Benjamin R. Curtis, Jr., *A Memoir of Benjamin Robbins Curtis, LL.D., with Some of His Professional and Miscellaneous Writings*, 2 vols. (Boston: Little, Brown, 1879), 1: 136; *Proceedings of the Constitutional Meeting at Faneuil Hall, Nov. 26, 1850* (Boston: Beale & Green, 1850); *National Anti-Slavery Standard*, December 12, 1850.

40. William Gillette, "Benjamin R. Curtis," in *The Justices of the United States Supreme Court, 1789–1969: Their Lives and Major Opinions*, ed. Leon Friedman and Fred L. Israel, 5 vols. (New York and London: Chelsea House/R. R. Bowker, 1969–1978), 2: 900–904.

41. Daniel Webster to Millard Fillmore, November 5, 1851, *DWC*, 7: 178.

42. Daniel Webster to [Thomas B. Curtis], December 8, 1850, mDW, reel 23 (probably written to George T. rather than Thomas B. Curtis).

43. Daniel Webster to Peter Harvey, November 29, 1850, *DWC*, 7: 186.

44. Webster to Fillmore, November 5, 1850, p. 178; *Boston Daily Advertiser*, November 27 or 28, 1851, quoted in *DWC*, 7: 179n.

45. Webster to Fillmore, November 5, 1850, p. 178.

46. Knight, letter, November 11, 1850.

47. *National Anti-Slavery Standard*, December 5, 1850.

48. Edward Everett to Daniel Webster, December 9, 1850, mDW, reel 23; Everett papers, MHS.

49. Millard Fillmore to Robert Collins, November 9, 1850, in Norfolk *Southern Argus*, November 21, 1850.

50. *Essex County Freeman*, November 6, 1850.

51. *Baltimore Sun*, in Norfolk *American Beacon*, November 9, 1850.

52. *Boston Daily Evening Traveller*, February 17, 1851.

53. Norfolk *Southern Argus*, December 7, 1850.

54. Ibid.

55. The Vigilance Committee financial records show that on February 28, 1851, a man named Charles Mahoney received five dollars "for passage of Cornelius Sparrow" (p. 10); "Fugitive Slaves aided by the Vigilance Committee since the passage of the Fugitive Slave Bill, 1850," Garrison Collection, BPL.

56. Boston *Commonwealth* and *Boston Post*, February 17, 1851; William S. Forrest, *Norfolk Directory for 1851–1852* (Norfolk, 1851), pp. 66, 73.

57. Boston *Commonwealth*, February 17, 1851.

58. Ibid., January 31, 1851; *New York Daily Tribune*, February 1, 1851.

59. Wendell Phillips, "Surrender of Sims" speech before the Massachusetts Anti-Slavery Society, January 30, 1852, in *Speeches, Lectures, and Letters* (1863; Boston: Lee and Shepard, 1894), 1: 56–57; Boston *Commonwealth*, January 31, in *New York Daily Tribune*, February 1, 1851. Blakeley may have been the same person as a dark mulatto woman just escaped from slavery who was introduced at an earlier Boston antislavery rally. In an electrifying moment recorded by visiting Swedish novelist Frederika Bremer, the woman was led forward onto the stage by young Lucy Stone. Bremer remembered the contrast between the woman's dark skin and Stone's simple white dress and how Stone had placed her hand on the woman's head and called her "sister"—all this being carried out as if part of some ancient sacred ceremony. "A beautiful sight," Bremer concluded, obviously moved; Frederika Bremer, *Homes of the New World* (New York: Harper & Bros., 1853), p. 195.

60. Boston *Commonwealth*, January 31, 1851.

61. *Fayetteville* (N.C.) *Carolinian*, in Raleigh, N.C., *Semi-Weekly Standard*, reprinted in *National Anti-Slavery Standard*, January 16, 1851.

62. These counts, derived from my research in more than sixty newspapers published across the North and Upper South, should be considered minimal figures. Many attempts on fugitives were never reported or else were reported only in obscure local newspapers.

63. Almost no information is available about the Bedford case. For an incomplete list of early attempts on fugitives, see Campbell, *The Slave Catchers*, pp. 199–200.

64. *Liberator*, January 17 and 31, 1851; *New York Daily Tribune*, January 7, 1851.

65. Campbell, *The Slave Catchers*, p. 199; *Liberator*, January 1, 1851.

66. For example, see the discussion of kidnapping operations in the Philadelphia area ca. 1825–1826 in Julie Winch, "Philadelphia and the Other Underground Railroad," *Pennsylvania Magazine of History and Biography*, 111 (January 1987), 3–25.

67. Gerald Eggert, "The Impact of the Fugitive Slave Law on Harrisburg: A Case Study," *Pennsylvania Magazine of History and Biography*, 109 (October 1985), 537–569.

7. "A Thing . . . or a Man?"

1. Wendell P. Garrison and Francis J. Garrison, *William Lloyd Garrison, 1805–1879: The Story of His Life Told by His Children*, 4 vols. (New York: Century, 1885–1889), 3: 119n.

2. Caphart was one of six Norfolk constables in 1851, according to William S. Forrest, *Norfolk Directory for 1851–1852* (Norfolk, 1851), p. 87.

3. Norfolk *Southern Argus*, June 2, 1849; George Teamoh, *God Made Man, Man Made the Slave: The Autobiography of George Teamoh*, ed. F. N. Boney, Richard L. Hume, and Rafia Zafar (Macon, Ga.: Mercer University Press, 1990), pp. 175–176, n. 20.

4. Norfolk *Southern Argus*, May 3, 1859.

5. Norfolk *American Beacon*, August 16 and November 7, 1834.

6. Boston *Commonwealth*, June 19, 1851, from Caphart's testimony in the trial of Robert Morris.

7. Teamoh, *God Made Man*, p. 74.

8. Richard Henry Dana, Jr., to Edmund T. Dana, March 2, 1851, MHS; Caphart quoted in Richard Henry Dana, Jr., to Harriet Beecher Stowe, November 25, 1852, copy MHS.

9. Dana to Stowe, November 25, 1852.

10. Broadside Collection, Rare Books Division, BPL; a slightly different version appeared in the Boston *Commonwealth*, February 21, 1851.

11. Boston *Commonwealth*, February 19, 1851.

12. Harriet Beecher Stowe to Richard Henry Dana, Jr., November 9, 1852, MHS.

13. William H. Hoyt, Diary, February 15, 1851, BPL.

14. "Deposition of Patrick Riley," February 17, 1851, *Boston Daily Evening Traveller*, February 17, 1851. Unless otherwise noted, the account of the arrest presented in the text is taken from this source.

15. Boston *Commonwealth*, June 8, 1852.

16. *Boston Daily Evening Transcript*, February 9, 1886.

17. Frederick Douglass, *My Bondage and My Freedom*, ed. William L. Andrews (Urbana: University of Illinois Press, 1987), p. 207.

18. William S. McFeely, *Frederick Douglass* (New York: W. W. Norton, 1991), p. 144. Nathan Irwin Huggins, *Slave and Citizen: The Life of Frederick Douglass* (Boston: Little, Brown, 1980), pp. 33–35, discusses the controversy surrounding the purchase.

19. Bigelow later alleged that the marshal "had made no request for assistance" but had merely "communicated the fact of the arrest"; *Boston Daily Bee*, February 18, 1851, which contains statements by both Bigelow and Tukey.

20. *Report of the Proceedings at the Examination of Charles G. Davis, on a Charge of Aiding and Abetting in the Rescue of a Fugitive Slave, Held in Boston, in February, 1851* (Boston: White & Potter, 1851), p. 13; *Boston Daily Evening Transcript*, February 9, 1886.

21. *Boston Daily Mail* and *Boston Daily Times*, February 17, 1851.

22. *Examination of Charles G. Davis*, p. 17.

23. Charles Francis Adams, *Richard Henry Dana: A Biography*, 2 vols. (Boston: Houghton Mifflin, 1890), 1: 183.

24. Boston *Commonwealth*, November 8, 1851.

25. *Boston Daily Advertiser*, February 18, 1851.

26. Boston *Commonwealth*, February 17, 1851.

27. Ibid.

28. See Thomas D. Morris, *Free Men All: The Personal Liberty Laws of the North, 1780–1861* (Baltimore: Johns Hopkins University Press, 1974), pp. 8–10, for a brief history of the use and interpretation of habeas corpus in the United States.

29. Leonard W. Levy, *The Law of the Commonwealth and Chief Justice Shaw: The Evolution of American Law, 1830–1860* (1957; New York: Harper & Row, 1967), pp. 65–66.

30. Ibid., p. 91.

31. *Eleventh Annual Report, Presented to the Massachusetts Anti-Slavery Society, by Its Board of Managers, January 25, 1843* (Boston, 1843), pp. 69–71.

32. *The Journal of Richard Henry Dana, Jr.*, ed. Robert F. Lucid, 3 vols. (Cambridge, Mass.: Harvard University Press, 1968), 2: 410–412.

33. Ibid., p. 412.

34. *Boston Daily Evening Traveller*, February 21, 1851.

35. *Boston Daily Times,* February 17, 1851.

36. When asked later how many men he had had in the courtroom, Riley said "fifteen or twenty" but noted that he had never counted. He listed the names of only eleven officers, including some city constables; *Boston Daily Journal,* February 18, 1851.

37. *Boston Daily Times,* February 17, 1851. This story is corroborated by numerous witnesses during later hearings and trials.

38. Morris, *Free Men All,* pp. 114–115.

39. *Boston Daily Evening Transcript,* February 17, 1851.

40. *Boston Daily Times,* February 27, 1851.

41. Boston *Commonwealth,* February 17, 1851.

42. Ibid., June 7, 1851.

43. Ibid., February 17, 1851.

44. Ibid., February 18, 1851.

45. *Boston Daily Courier,* March 11, 1851.

46. *Boston Post,* March 11, 1851.

47. Boston *Commonwealth,* May 9 and November 6, 1851.

48. *Boston Daily Journal,* March 5, 1851.

49. *Boston Daily Courier,* March 6, 1851.

8. "Plucked as a Brand from the Burning"

1. The chapter title is taken from William Lloyd Garrison, editorial, *Liberator,* as quoted in Austin Bearse, *Reminiscences of Fugitive-Slave Law Days in Boston* (Boston: Warren Richardson, 1880), p. 18.

2. *Boston Daily Evening Traveller,* February 15, 1851; *Boston Daily Mail,* February 20, 1851.

3. Boston *Commonwealth,* November 8, 1851.

4. Ibid., May 29, 1851; *Boston Daily Evening Traveller,* February 28, 1851.

5. Vincent Y. Bowditch, *Life and Correspondence of Henry Ingersoll Bowditch,* 2 vols. (Boston: Houghton Mifflin, 1902), 1: 212–213; John A. Andrew to James Freeman Clark, March 5, 1851, quoted in Clark, *Memorial and Biographical Sketches* (Boston: Houghton, Osgood, 1878), p. 17.

6. *Report of the Proceedings at the Examination of Charles G. Davis, on a Charge of Aiding and Abetting in the Rescue of a Fugitive Slave, Held in Boston, in February, 1851* (Boston: White & Potter, 1851), p. 14; *Boston Daily Evening Traveller,* February 21, 1851.

7. *Boston Post,* February 20, 1851.

8. *Boston Globe,* April 7, 1889. Samuel Gridley Howe also asserted that the rescuers had been armed, although the source of his information is unknown; Laura E. Richards, ed., *Letters and Journals of Samuel Gridley Howe,* 2 vols. (Boston: Dana Estes, 1909), 2: 340. Charles Sumner claimed that the rescue was by "a very few unarmed negroes," but the source of his information seems to have been secondhand; Charles Sumner to Horace Mann, February 19, 1851, in *Selected Letters of Charles Sumner,* ed. Beverly Wilson Palmer, 2 vols. (New York: Columbia University Press, 1990), 1: 322.

9. *Boston Daily Evening Traveller,* February 22, 1851.

10. Ibid., February 19, 1851.

11. *Boston Post*, February 19, 1851.

12. At some point before the assault Riley apparently sent for aid to City Marshal Tukey, but Tukey alleged that Riley had asked only for "spare" men, of which, he claimed, he had none (contrary to the *Transcript* charge that upward of forty officers were assembled in Tukey's office at the time of the assault). According to Tukey, his specific instructions from Mayor Bigelow were to "prevent any breach of the peace outside the Court House," and in obedience to those instructions he had sent men "from time to time to [see] that all was quiet"; *Boston Daily Evening Transcript*, February 17, 1851.

13. Boston *Commonwealth*, November 8, 1851.

14. *Boston Daily Evening Journal*, February 18, 1851.

15. *Boston Daily Times*, February 17, 1851.

16. *Boston Daily Evening Journal*, February 19, 1851.

17. *Boston Daily Evening Traveller*, February 28, 1851.

18. *Boston Post* and *Boston Daily Mail*, February 19, 1851.

19. *Boston Daily Times*, February 17 and 27, 1851; and *Boston Daily Evening Traveller*, February 27, 1851.

20. Cheney testimony, Boston *Commonwealth*, November 6, 1851.

21. Snowden testimony, ibid., November 8, 1851.

22. Charles Francis Adams, *Richard Henry Dana, a Biography*, 2 vols. (Boston: Houghton Mifflin, 1890), 1: 182.

23. Boston *Commonwealth*, June 2, 1851.

24. Richard Henry Dana, Jr., to Edmund T. Dana, March 2, 1851, MHS.

25. Ibid.; *Boston Daily Evening Traveller*, February 21, 1851.

26. Dana to Dana, March 2, 1851.

27. Joseph H. Willard, *Half a Century with Lawyers* (Boston: Houghton Mifflin, 1895), p. 239; Boston *Commonwealth*, November 8, 1852.

28. *Boston Daily Courier*, March 4, 1851; *Boston Daily Evening Traveller*, March 3, 1851; Boston *Commonwealth*, November 8 and 11, 1851. Another, uncorroborated account says that the cab took them to the corner of Garden and Southac, where they disembarked.

29. Boston *Commonwealth*, November 6 and 8, 1851; Ellis Wright testified that the crowd seemed to stop at the corner of Grove Street.

30. *Boston Daily Courier*, March 4, 1851; also *Boston Daily Evening Traveller*, March 3 and June 12, 1851; Boston *Commonwealth*, June 10, 1851.

31. *Boston Daily Mail* and *Boston Daily Journal*, February 19, 1851; *Boston Daily Courier*, February 17, 1851.

32. Boston *Commonwealth*, June 13, 1851, from the report of Lewis Hayden's trial.

33. *Boston Daily Evening Traveller*, June 12, 1851; Boston *Commonwealth*, June 13, 1851.

34. Boston *Commonwealth*, November 8, 1851.

35. *Boston Daily Times*, February 17, 1851, which claims that while at Hayden's, Minkins was dressed in women's clothing as a disguise before being smuggled out of the city.

36. *Boston Globe*, April 7, 1889; Southac Place, which was entered just above 78 Southac Street, was built over in 1902.

37. *Boston Daily Evening Traveller,* June 12, 1851; Boston *Commonwealth,* June 13, 1851.

38. Boston *Commonwealth,* June 11, 1851; *Boston Courier,* March 4, 1851.

39. Testimony of Wm. C. Reed, Boston *Commonwealth,* June 14, 1851.

40. Boston *Commonwealth,* November 8, 1851.

41. In some newspaper reports, Murray's testimony mentions three men, not two, in his cab.

42. *Boston Globe,* April 7, 1889.

43. Ibid.

44. John Daniels, *In Freedom's Birthplace: A Study of the Boston Negroes* (Boston: Houghton Mifflin, 1914), p. 57.

45. A summary of the rescue, with the note "copied from Miss Fannie P. Gates' notebook marked 'General Topics,' " Leominster Public Library, claims that from Watertown Minkins was driven to Concord by a William A. White, possibly meaning William Abijah White, temperance advocate, reformer, and abolitionist; *BAP,* 3: 422, n. 5.

46. *Boston Globe,* April 7, 1889.

9. "Never Was a Darker Day"

1. See, for example, *Springfield Republican* and *Cincinnati Republican,* February 17, 1851.

2. Curtis, quoted in *New York Herald,* March 9, 1851.

3. Vincent Y. Bowditch, *Life and Correspondence of Henry Ingersoll Bowditch,* 2 vols. (Boston: Houghton Mifflin, 1902), 1: 212; John Weiss, *Life and Correspondence of Theodore Parker,* 2 vols. (New York: D. Appleton, 1864), 2: 103; Wendell P. Garrison and Francis J. Garrison, *William Lloyd Garrison, 1805–1879: The Story of His Life Told by His Children,* 4 vols. (New York: Century, 1885–1889), 3: 324.

4. William H. Hoyt, Journal, February 14 and 15, 1851, BPL.

5. John Watterston Smith, Journal, February 15, 1851, Boston Athenaeum.

6. *Boston Daily Journal,* February 16, 1851.

7. *Liberator,* February 28, 1851.

8. John Watterston Smith, Journal, February 16, 1851.

9. *Anti-Slavery Bugle,* March 22, 1851; *Liberator,* March 28, 1851.

10. *Boston Daily Courier,* February 17, 1851.

11. Quoted in *Boston Daily Bee,* February 18, 1851.

12. *Boston Daily Advertiser,* February 19, 1851; *Boston Herald,* February 17, 1851; *Boston Investigator,* February 26, 1851.

13. *Boston Daily Times,* February 17, 1851.

14. Ibid., February 18, 1851; "Bobalition of Slavery," broadside (1830), reproduced in James Oliver Horton and Lois E. Horton, *Black Bostonians: Family Life and Community Struggle in the Antebellum North* (New York: Holmes & Meier, 1979), between pp. 80–81; and "Grand Bobalition, or 'Great Annibersary Fussible,' " broadside (1820), reproduced in Bernard F. Reilly, Jr., "The Art of the Antislavery Movement," in *Courage and Conscience: Black and White Abolitionists in Boston,* ed. Donald M. Jacobs (Indianapolis: Indiana University Press, 1993), p. 53.

15. *New York Express,* February 17, 1851; *New York Herald,* February 18, 1851.

16. *New York Herald,* February 17, 1851.

17. Quoted in the *Liberator,* April 11, 1851.

18. *Boston Daily Advertiser,* February 17, 1851; *Richmond Examiner,* February 22, 1851; *Louisville Daily Journal,* March 14, 1851; *New York Commercial Advertiser,* February 22, 1851.

19. Daniel Webster to Charles Devens, Jr., February 18, 1851, *DWC,* 7: 206; Benjamin R. Curtis, Jr., *A Memoir of Benjamin Robbins Curtis, LL.D., with Some of His Professional and Miscellaneous Writings,* 2 vols. (Boston: Little, Brown, 1879), 2: 490.

20. Daniel Webster to Peter Harvey, February 17, 1851, *DWC,* 7: 204.

21. Daniel Webster to G. T. Curtis, February 17, 1851, and G. T. Curtis to Webster, February 18, 1851, printed in *New York Herald,* March 9, 1851; *Boston Daily Evening Transcript,* February 25, 1851.

22. "It is, strictly speaking, an act of treason," wrote Webster to Moses Taylor et al., February 20, 1851, on the occasion of New York's celebration of Washington's birthday; draft, mDW 32591, reprinted in Curtis, *Memoir of Benjamin Robbins Curtis,* 2: 490–491; *Boston Pilot,* June 7, 1851, quoting Webster's speech in Albany.

23. *Congressional Globe,* February 18, 1851, 31st Cong., 2nd sess., p. 59. Moncure Daniel Conway, *Autobiography, Memories, and Experiences,* 2 vols. (Boston: Houghton Mifflin, 1904), 1: 92, had the impression that this speech, before it was printed in the *Congressional Globe,* was "considerably manipulated" (as was common practice).

24. William Wetmore Story to Charles Sumner, February 19, 1851, Sumner Papers, HL.

25. *Congressional Globe,* February 18, 1851, 31st Cong., 2nd sess., p. 598.

26. Robert J. Rayback, *Millard Fillmore: Biography of a President* (Buffalo: Henry Stewart, 1959), pp. 270–271; *Baltimore Sun,* April 12, 1851.

27. Norfolk *American Beacon,* November 5, 1850; Millard Fillmore to Daniel Webster, October 28, 1850, *DWC,* 7: 172.

28. Report of February 19 by the Washington correspondent of the *New Orleans Daily Picayune,* March 2, 1851. The writer believed that Attorney General Crittenden took a more moderate position because he hoped to be the vice-presidential candidate on the ticket with General Winfield Scott.

29. *Boston Daily Evening Traveller,* February 21, 1851.

30. "A Proclamation of the President of the United States," February 18, 1851, reprinted in *DWC,* 7: 207.

31. Letters from the respective secretaries, dated February 17, went out to Commodore John Downes, commandant of the navy yard at Boston, and to Brevet Major George A. Thomas, commanding officer of Fort Independence in Boston Harbor; *New York Herald,* February 27, 1851.

32. James D. Richardson, ed., *A Compilation of the Messages and Papers of the Presidents, 1789–1897,* 10 vols. (Washington, D.C.: U.S. Government Printing Office, 1869–1899), 5: 101–106.

33. Webster to Moses Taylor et al., February 20, 1851, reprinted in Curtis, *Memoir of Benjamin Robbins Curtis,* 2: 490–491.

34. Amos A. Lawrence to Samuel A. Eliot, February 18, 1851, copy MHS.

35. *Boston Daily Evening Transcript,* February 18, 1851; *Boston Daily Mail,* February 22, 1851.

36. Boston *Commonwealth*, February 18, 1851. On the opinions of Boston's conservative Whig businessmen and their uneasiness with the Fugitive Slave Law, see Richard H. Abbott, *Cotton and Capital: Boston Businessmen and Antislavery Reform, 1850–68* (Amherst: University of Massachusetts Press, 1991), pp. 23–28. Abbott goes too far, however, in asserting that "no one in Massachusetts defended the [fugitive slave] law" (p. 23).

37. *Boston Daily Mail*, February 19, 1851; *Boston Daily Journal*, February 18, 1851.

38. *Boston Daily Evening Transcript*, February 18, 1851; *Boston Daily Journal*, February 18, 1851; *Boston Daily Evening Traveller*, February 18, 1851.

39. *Boston Daily Mail* and Boston *Commonwealth*, February 20, 1851.

40. Boston *Commonwealth*, February 20, 1851.

41. *Boston Daily Times*, February 20, 1851.

42. *Boston Daily Journal*, February 21, 1851; *Boston Daily Mail*, February 22, 1851; *Boston Daily Courier*, March 3, 1851.

43. Philadelphia *Public Ledger*, February 20, 1851.

44. The fullest account of the hearing is the anonymous *Report of the Proceedings at the Examination of Charles G. Davis, Esq., on a Charge of Aiding and Abetting in the Rescue of a Fugitive Slave* (Boston: White & Potter, 1851), which appears to have been taken primarily from the *Commonwealth* columns and may have been written by Elizur Wright.

45. For George Lunt, see James Grant Wilson and John Fiske, eds., *Appleton's Cyclopedia of American Biography*, 7 vols. (New York: D. Appleton, 1894–1901), 4: 55; James Freeman Clarke, *Anti-Slavery Days: A Sketch of the Struggle which Ended in the Abolition of Slavery in the United States* (New York: John W. Lovell, 1883), pp. 103–104.

46. Richard Henry Dana, Sr., to William C. Bryant, March 6, 1851, MHS.

47. Lunt himself privately called the evidence "somewhat circumstantial"; George Lunt to John J. Crittenden, February 22, 1851, Record Group 60, Attorney Generals' Papers, letters received (Mass. 1813–1864), National Archives, Washington, D.C.

48. *Examination of Charles G. Davis*, pp. 10–11.

49. Ibid., pp. 11–12.

50. Ibid., pp. 12, 14.

51. Ibid., p. 12.

52. Ibid., p. 35. Dana's closing is reprinted in his *Speeches in Stirring Times and Letters to a Son*, ed. Richard H. Dana III (Boston: Houghton Mifflin, 1910), pp. 178–209.

53. *The Journal of Richard Henry Dana, Jr.*, ed. Robert F. Lucid, 3 vols. (Cambridge, Mass.: Harvard University Press, 1968), February 23, 1851, 2: 414–415.

54. *Examination of Charles G. Davis*, pp. 41–42.

55. Richard Henry Dana, Jr., to Edmund T. Dana, March 2, 1851, MHS.

56. Richard Henry Dana, Sr., to William C. Bryant, March 6, 1851, MHS.

57. Dana to Dana, March 2, 1851.

58. *Boston Daily Journal*, February 21, 1851; Boston *Commonwealth*, March 13, 1851. Three years later, when Hayes had become Boston's chief of police, he gained considerable celebrity in abolitionist circles by resigning rather than be forced to assist in the Anthony Burns fugitive slave case.

59. *Boston Daily Evening Transcript,* February 21, 1851.

60. *Boston Daily Journal,* February 21, 1851; *Boston Daily Courier,* February 22, 1851; *Salem Register,* February 24, 1851; *Essex County Freeman,* February 26, 1851; *Salem Gazette,* February 22, 1851.

61. "Indictment of Andrew J. Burton," U.S. District Court, Case Papers, March Term 1851, Federal Archives, Waltham, Mass. On the back of one of the documents in the court records is a statement by U.S. Marshal Charles Devens, dated March 15, that "the body of the within named Burton" could not be found.

62. Boston "Streets" Tax Ledgers, 1850 and 1851, Fifth Ward, BPL. Tax records list him as a laborer in 1850 and a seaman in 1851, when his name is given as Andrew G., at the same address. Vigilance Committee records show, however, that near the end of April Burton was given $23 and then $9.50 "for passage," and on May 15 another $20 was paid out of the treasury for "assisting Andrew J. Burton & family"; Francis Jackson, "Treasurer's Accounts: The Boston Vigilance Committee Appointed at the Public Meeting in Faneuil Hall October 21, 1850, to Assist Fugitive Slaves," BPL (facsimile, Boston: Bostonian Society, n.d.), pp. 16, 18.

63. Lunt to Crittenden, February 22, 1851, Record Group 60, Attorney Generals' Papers, letters received (Mass. 1813–1864), National Archives.

64. *Boston Daily Journal,* February 22, 1851.

65. Burton later filed suit for $10,000 for having been arrested "maliciously, and without any just and probable cause" (Boston *Commonwealth,* February 28, 1851; *National Era,* March 6, 1851). Later the charge against Lunt was dismissed. Ten years later Burton sued a Boston theater for denying him admission because of his color. A similar suit brought a few years before by black barber Julian McCrea had lost, and Burton's suit fared no better; Alexander Burton v. John C. Scherpf, *Reports . . . Supreme Judicial Court of Massachusetts,* 1 Allen (1861), 134–136, quoted in George Levesque, "Black Boston: Negro Life in Garrison's Boston, 1800–1860" (Ph.D. diss., State University of New York at Binghamton, 1976), pp. 124–125.

For many years Burton lived in Lowell, operating a popular barbershop. When he died of typhoid fever on December 20, 1885, at the age of fifty-four, the December 22 *Lowell Morning Mail* acknowledged his passing in an unusually lengthy obituary. Noting that he had been born in Le Havre, France, and had come to the United States at an early age, the *Mail* called him "a man of some intelligence and education, speaking three languages—French, Spanish, and English."

66. *Boston Daily Journal* and *Boston Daily Mail,* February 22, 1851; *Boston Daily Courier,* March 1, 3, and 4, 1851; *Boston Daily Bee,* March 1 and 3, 1851.

67. Boston *Commonwealth,* June 13, 1851; *Boston Daily Courier,* February 24, 1851; Boston *Commonwealth,* June 11, 1851 (testimony of George Greenleaf).

68. *Boston Daily Courier,* March 4–6, 1851.

69. *Boston Daily Evening Transcript,* February 21, 1851.

70. Boston *Commonwealth,* February 20, 1851; *Boston Daily Evening Transcript,* February 18, 1851.

71. *Boston Post,* February 19, 1851.

72. A. A. Lawrence to Samuel A. Eliot, February 18, 1851, copy MHS.

73. Wendell Phillips to Elizabeth Pease, March 9, 1851, quoted in Garrison and Garrison, *William Lloyd Garrison,* 3: 323.

74. Phillips, quoted in ibid., p. 324.

75. "Records of the Boston Vigilance Committee" (1851–1859), February 28, 1851, BPL. Two persons were named to the second group initially, but no further reference appears in the sketchy Vigilance Committee records. Whether its ranks were filled out or how often it was called into operation is unknown.

76. *Boston Daily Evening Traveller,* February 24, 1851.

77. Jackson, "Treasurer's Accounts," p. 10. This may refer to John P. Armstead, who was married in Boston in 1844 and fled to Canada without his wife, Mary L., who raised money to purchase her husband's freedom. He deserted her in 1853; William H. Mulligan, Jr., "The Pressure of Uncertain Freedom: A Documentary Note on the Antebellum Black Family," *Negro History Bulletin,* 42 (October–December 1979), 107.

78. Jackson, "Treasurer's Accounts," p. 10, probably referring to St. John, New Brunswick.

79. Abby Alcott to S[amuel J. May], February 28, 1851, HL.

80. Theodore Parker wrote that "Hayden wants a place for his wife—still a slave—I should take her, & should tonight—but have another lodger in the spare chamber"; "Memorandum of the Troubles in Boston Occasioned by the Infamous Fugitive Slave Law," entry for March 16, 1851, BPL.

81. Phillips to Pease, March 9, 1851, in Garrison and Garrison, *William Lloyd Garrison,* 3: 323. "Many families are made wretched by the flight of some important member," wrote one Boston correspondent of the *Newburyport Herald* (quoted in the *Salem Gazette,* February 28, 1851). Phillips noted that he had even been approached by a terrified freeborn seventy-year-old black woman who wanted to know if she, too, should flee.

82. *Newburyport Herald,* in *Salem Gazette,* February 28, 1851.

83. Alcott to S[amuel J. May], February 28, 1851.

10. North Star

1. E. W. Emerson, "Notes on the Underground Railway . . . made in 1892 from memory of a talk with old Mrs. Bigelow," typescript copy, Thoreau Society Archives, Concord Free Public Library.

2. On Concord's blacks in the 1840s and 1850s, see Joan Trumbull, "Concord and the Negro" (Master's thesis, Vassar College, 1944). According to the Seventh U.S. Census (1850), only twenty-nine blacks lived in Concord. As many recent studies have shown, blacks actively assisted fugitive slaves in many cities and larger towns; see, for example, James Oliver Horton, "Links to Bondage: Free Blacks and the Underground Railroad," chap. 2 of his *Free People of Color: Inside the African American Community* (Washington, D.C.: Smithsonian Institution Press, 1993), pp. 53–74; and William and Aimee Lee Cheek's depiction of Cincinnati blacks' activism in *John Mercer Langston and the Fight for Black Freedom, 1829–65* (Urbana: University of Illinois Press, 1989).

3. Mary Brooks is characterized in Ann Warren Weston to Deborah Weston, September 16, 1841, *Concord Saunterer,* 17 (December 1984), 48.

4. Autograph notes enclosed in Mrs. Ann Damon to Wilbur Siebert, December 1, 1893, Siebert Collection, Ohio Historical Society, Columbus.

5. Moncure Conway, *Autobiography, Memories, and Experiences,* 2 vols. (Boston:

Houghton Mifflin, 1904), 1: 141; Walter Harding, *The Days of Henry Thoreau* (New York: Alfred A. Knopf, 1970), pp. 314–317.

6. Charles W. Flint to *Boston Daily Evening Transcript*, February 10, 1886, quoted in Nina Moore Tiffany, "Stories of the Fugitive Slaves. I. Shadrach," *New England Magazine*, n.s., 2 (1890), 282.

7. Undated letter "from a Leominster lady," in ibid.

8. Mrs. W. S. Robinson, ed., *"Warrington" Pen-Portraits: A Collection of Personal and Political Reminiscences, from 1848 to 1876, from the Writings of William S. Robinson* (Boston: Lee and Shepard, 1877), p. 72.

9. George M. Brooks, "Nathan Brooks," in *Memoirs of the Social Circle in Concord: Second Series from 1795 to 1840* (Cambridge, Mass.: privately printed, 1888), pp. 207–208.

10. Emerson, "Notes on the Underground Railway."

11. Damon to Siebert, December 1, 1893.

12. Theron J. Damon, "Inside History of Shadrach Fugitive Slave Case," American Antiquarian Society, Worcester, Mass.

13. Quoted in M. M. Fisher to W. H. Siebert, October 23, 1893, Siebert Collection, Ohio Historical Society; *Boston Globe*, April 7, 1889.

14. *Liberator*, April 6, 1851.

15. *The Writings of Henry D. Thoreau: Journal*, ed. John C. Broderick et al., 5 vols. to date (Princeton: Princeton University Press, 1990–), February 16, 1851, 3: 194.

16. Theodore Parker, "The New Crime against Humanity," reprinted in *The Rights of Man in America*, ed. F. B. Sanborn, vol. 12 of the *Centenary Edition* [*The Works of Theodore Parker*] (Boston: American Unitarian Association, 1909), pp. 255, 287.

17. Henry David Thoreau, "Slavery in Massachusetts," in *The Writings of Henry D. Thoreau: Reform Papers*, ed. Wendell Glick (Princeton: Princeton University Press, 1973), p. 108.

18. Thoreau, *Journal*, 4: 113.

19. *The Journal of Richard Henry Dana, Jr.*, ed. Robert F. Lucid, 3 vols. (Cambridge, Mass.: Harvard University Press, 1968), 2: 513–514; "List of jurors sworn 22 Oct. 1852," U.S. Circuit Court, Case Papers, Federal Archives, Waltham, Mass.

20. Ann Bigelow thought her husband drove Minkins to Leominster by way of Sudbury, but she may have been mistaken.

21. Charles Francis Adams, *Richard Henry Dana*, 2 vols. (Boston: Houghton Mifflin, 1890), 1: 217–218. Adams claimed that authorities in Fitchburg had been alerted by telegram that Minkins would be aboard the train from Boston, but he gives no source for his information.

22. *Boston Daily Evening Transcript*, January 18, 1897. Further corroboration comes from Franklin B. Sanborn, a Concord resident and friend of Emerson. Sanborn recounted hearing Francis Bigelow tell him the outline of the events, including the stop in Leominster, "about 1867 when he was putting some hinges on my gate"; Sanborn to Wilbur H. Siebert, February 1, 1896, Siebert scrapbooks, vol. 41, HL; essentially the same information may be found in Sanborn's note in Laura E. Richards, ed., *Letters and Journals of Samuel Gridley Howe*, 2 vols. (Boston: Dana Estes, 1909), 2: 340.

23. Frances H. Drake to Theodore Parker, September 2, 1854, BPL.

24. Boston *Commonwealth,* February 19, 1851.

25. Ibid., June 13, 1851.

26. *Leominster Daily Enterprise,* June 21, 1928.

27. Further evidence of the legendary character of this story appears in an 1895 letter to Siebert claiming that Minkins did not flee immediately to Canada but remained "near Boston for several weeks disguised in women's attire"; Addis H. Brainerd to W[ilbur H]. Siebert, October 21, 1895, Siebert scrapbooks, vol. 41, HL. A modern local history illustrates this legendary story with a crude pen-and-ink rendering of Minkins in outlandish widow's garb being ushered in at the door of the meeting, the man at his elbow looking nervously over his shoulder; Doris Kirkpatrick, *The City and the River* (Fitchburg: Fitchburg Historical Society, 1971), p. 261.

28. Frances H. Drake to William Lloyd Garrison, February 19, 1851, in *Liberator,* February 28, 1851.

29. Testimony of James Buffum, June 12, quoted in Boston *Commonwealth,* June 13, 1851.

30. Chicago *Western Citizen,* in *Burlington* (Iowa) *Hawkeye,* March 20, 1851.

31. Item dated February 15, 1851, and marked "copied from Miss Fannie P. Gates' notebook marked 'General Topics,' " Leominster Public Library.

32. Wilbur H. Siebert, *The Underground Railroad in Massachusetts* (Worcester, Mass.: American Antiquarian Society, 1936), p. 35. Another source gives the name Alvin Ward instead of Mr. Wood; Gates's notebook, Leominster Public Library.

33. *Fitchburg Daily Sentinel,* October 31, 1888, in Siebert scrapbooks, vol. 14, HL.

34. Wilbur Siebert conjectures: "Probably at Keene . . . he boarded the Cheshire train for Canada"; *The Underground Railroad in Massachusetts,* p. 46.

35. Boston *Daily Chronotype,* October 5, 1850. Although the census reported sixty-two blacks in Burlington, there were sixty-seven others in nearby St. Albans and small numbers scattered elsewhere through northwestern Vermont; U.S. Bureau of the Census, *The Seventh Census of the United States: 1850* (Washington, D.C.: U.S. Government Printing Office, 1853), pp. 35–36.

36. Wilbur H. Siebert, *Vermont's Anti-Slavery and Underground Railroad Record, with a Map and Illustrations* (Columbus: Spahr and Glenn, 1937), pp. 81–82; Joshua Young to Wilbur Siebert, April 21, 1893, Siebert scrapbooks, vol. 41, HL; C. E. Edson, "U.S. History 13 Special Report 8," 1887–1888, Siebert scrapbooks, vol. 41, which contains the notation "Sources: original authorities." However, although Young claimed to know "the particulars of the rescue of Shadrach," he was still living in Boston at the time (he did not move to Burlington until 1852) and thus presumably meant the *Boston* details.

37. Samuel Gridley Howe to Charles Sumner, [March?] 18, [1851], in Richards, *Letters and Journals of Howe,* 2: 340.

38. Henry D. Thoreau, *A Yankee in Canada with Anti-Slavery and Reform Papers* (1892: reprint, New York: Greenwood Press, 1969), p. 8.

39. Robin Winks, *The Blacks in Canada: A History* (New Haven: Yale University Press, 1971), pp. 168–174. However, several fugitive slaves were later returned to the United States through the carelessness of civil authorities.

11. "Please to Remember Me Kindly"

1. James Bryce Brown, *Views of Canada and the Colonists, Embracing the Experience of an Eight Years' Residence; Views of the Present State, Progress, and Prospects of the Colony; with Detailed and Practical Information for the Intending Emigrant,* 2nd ed. (Edinburgh: A. and C. Black, 1851), pp. 116–117.

2. The manuscript censuses, Canada East, Montreal, 1842 and 1851, Public Archives of Canada, Ottawa, are of little help. The former gives the names of heads of households only, and the house-to-house records for the latter were almost entirely destroyed.

3. Robin Winks, *The Blacks in Canada: A History* (New Haven: Yale University Press, 1971), pp. 233–240, 493–494.

4. Michael Wayne, "The Myth of the Fugitive Slave: The Black Population of Canada West on the Eve of the Civil War" (manuscript, University of Toronto).

5. Daniel G. Hill, *The Freedom Seekers: Blacks in Early Canada* (Agincourt, Ontario: Book Society of Canada, 1981), p. 54; Winks, *Blacks in Canada,* p. 245. The 1851 manuscript census for Canada West reported 353 blacks living in Chatham (an 1852 estimate multiplied this number fivefold). In 1852 one visitor found more than 200 black families living in the Windsor-Sandwich area; Winks, p. 245.

6. Hill, *The Freedom Seekers,* p. 52.

7. Winks, *Blacks in Canada,* pp. 48, 156, 178.

8. In his 1898 *Underground Railroad* Wilbur Siebert claimed that Montreal was a center of fugitive activity. Siebert's unsubstantiated assertion was echoed in the July 1984 *National Geographic,* which contains a map showing the migration routes of fugitive slaves with a giant arrow swinging up to Montreal; Hill, *The Freedom Seekers,* p. 29; *Montreal Pilot,* January 26, 1850; dateline Montreal, October 31, Norfolk *Southern Argus,* November 4, 1850.

9. The traffic was clearly sporadic, but on occasion it seems to have been considerable even in the 1840s; see Fayette Shipherd to "Brother Hicks," November 20, 1840, Siebert scrapbooks, vol. 41, HL.

10. David Brown to [William Lloyd Garrison], March 8, 1853, in *Liberator,* April 29, 1853. The Philadelphia Vigilance Committee sent dozens of fugitives to Toronto and nearby St. Catharines; William Still, *The Underground Railroad . . .* (Philadelphia: Porter and Coates, 1872), pp. 42, 57–59, 64–65, etc. Many fugitives were assisted by Still's friends and agents in Syracuse, St. Catharines, and Toronto. Two deacons from Boston's Twelfth Baptist Church who fled to Canada West, possibly Toronto, returned to Boston after funds were raised for their purchase; William H. Hester, *One Hundred and Five Years by Faith* (Boston: Twelfth Baptist Church, 1946), pp. 17–18.

11. Caroline H. Dall to Wilbur Siebert, October 30, 1893, Siebert scrapbooks, vol. 41, HL; report of the *Tribune'*s special commissioner, reprinted in *National Anti-Slavery Standard,* October 31, 1857.

12. "Proceedings of a Meeting of Toronto Blacks . . . 13 January 1838," Toronto *Christian Guardian,* January 17, 1838, reprinted in *BAP,* 5: 68–70; correspondence of the *New York Tribune,* dateline Toronto, January 9, 1852, reprinted in *Liberator,* January 23, 1852.

13. "Incredible as it may appear, travellers can now reach Boston from Montreal in fourteen or fifteen hours"; *Montreal Gazette,* June 3, 1851.

14. Record of Inventories, Appraisements, & Account Sales, vol. 2 (November 21, 1871), Norfolk County Court House.

15. Quoted in *Boston Daily Evening Transcript*, February 22, 1851.

16. Boston *Commonwealth*, February 24, March 4, and April 15, 1851; *Louisville Daily Journal*, March 15, 1851.

17. Donald George Simpson, "Negroes in Ontario from Early Times to 1870" (Ph.D. diss., University of Western Ontario, 1971), p. 552. Simpson's source is not clear.

18. Boston *Commonwealth*, March 29, 1859. An identical copy of the letter is printed in Frederick Douglass' *North Star* for April 10.

19. But apparently he continued to use "Frederick" on occasion. The *Montreal Directory* for 1865–66 listed him as "Frederick."

20. *Census of the Canadas, 1851–1852: Personal Census, Vol. 1* (Québec City: John Lovell, 1853). How many blacks there were in Montreal when Shadrach Minkins arrived is impossible to determine, since most of the manuscript census of 1850–51 has been destroyed. A few other contemporary records—notably the *Montreal Directory* (various publishers, 1842–1900, sometimes prefaced by *McKay's* or *Lovell's*) and local tax records—do not identify individuals by race. The blacks mentioned here have been identified from newspaper stories or from working backward in city directories and municipal tax records from the 1861 manuscript census. A few additional blacks have been identified by working forward from the manuscript census, Canada East, Montreal, 1842.

21. Registre d'état civil, St. Paul's (Methodist) Church, April 3, 1843, National Archives of Québec, Montreal.

22. *Montreal Directory*, 1847–48.

23. CCEM61, no. 4494; Anne Arundel County, Maryland, Certificates of Freedom Index, 1797–1845 (Md HR 947), p. 243, and 1845–1864 (Md HR 951), p. 91, Maryland Hall of Records, Annapolis; interview with Robert Jones of St. Hubert, June 29, 1992.

24. Manuscript census, Canada East, Montreal, 1842; *Montreal Directory*, 1850–51; Montreal property tax books, 1850, 1851, Hotel de Ville, Montreal.

25. Half of the individual blacks counted in 1842 were males and half females. Because most were living as members of households headed by white businessmen and craftsmen, it is likely that they were either domestic servants or apprentices.

26. Sherwood Healy entered the Sulpician Seminary in 1852, and later that year the youngest Healy sisters, Eliza and Josephine, were brought to Montreal to be raised in the Convent of Saint Jean; Albert S. Foley, S.J., *Bishop Healy, Beloved Outcaste: The Story of a Great Man Whose Life Has Become a Legend* (New York: Farrar, Straus and Young, 1954), pp. 41–50.

27. Herbert Gutman points out that in the cycle of slave life, the destruction of kin networks by sale, which produced tremendous pain and dislocation, also inevitably meant that the separated persons would construct new social and kin networks to supplement old ones; *The Black Family in Slavery and Freedom, 1750–1925* (New York: Vintage, 1976), p. 138.

28. *Montreal Gazette*, February 2, 1853.

29. *Montreal Pilot*, January 26, 1850.

30. See especially *Le Canadien*, October 9 and 21 and November 6, 1850; *Le*

Moniteur canadien, May 9, 1851; *La Minerve,* October 17, 21, 24, November 4 and 21, 1850; January 13, 1851.

31. *Montreal Courier,* October 23, 1850.

32. *Montreal Witness,* quoted in *Montreal Pilot,* October 17, 1850.

33. Winks, *Blacks in Canada,* p. 251.

34. Jason H. Silverman, *Unwelcome Guests: Canada West's Response to American Fugitive Slaves, 1800–1865* (Millwood, N.Y.: Associated Faculty Press, 1985), pp. 151–157; Samuel Ringgold Ward to Henry Bibb and James Theodore Holly, October 1852, *Voice of the Fugitive,* November 4, 1852, reprinted in *BAP,* 5: 225. Silverman mistakenly attributes the quotation to Bibb. Ward's letter appeared in Bibb's *Voice* as the third piece in a series, "Canadian Negro Hate."

35. *Montreal Courier,* October 3 and 7, 1850. The latter nevertheless claimed to "rejoice" over the escape of fugitives and to be ready to "aid them to secure the rewards of industry in this haven." Winks, *Blacks in Canada,* p. 249, records an example of similar "helpful advice" in a newspaper editorial of 1855 from Canada West, an indication that this thinly disguised racist argument was widespread.

36. Letter of Toronto correspondent, April 3, in *Montreal Courier,* April 11, 1851.

37. *Montreal Gazette,* March 31, 1852.

38. Ibid., March 12, 14, 16, 1851; *Montreal Pilot,* March 15, 1851; *Montreal Transcript,* March 6, 1851.

39. *Montreal Transcript,* March 11, 1851. Another advertisement requested a "situation" for "A woman of Colour" who "would be happy to find a situation as COOK, in a Private Family, or in a Hotel. She is an excellent hand at WASHING and IRONING"; ibid., March 6, 1851.

40. *Montreal Pilot,* March 8 and April 5, 1851.

41. *First Annual Report Presented to the Anti-Slavery Society of Canada by Its Executive Committee, March 24, 1852* (Toronto, 1852), copy in Siebert scrapbooks, vol. 1, HL; Samuel Ringgold Ward to Henry Bibb, October 16, 1851, *Voice of the Fugitive,* November 5, 1851, reprinted in *BAP,* 2: 177–179, where "D. S. Janes" is given as "D. P. Jones."

42. For basic biographical information on Gould, see Gerald J. J. Tulchinsky, *The River Barons: Montreal Businessmen and the Growth of Industry and Transportation, 1837–53* (Toronto: University of Toronto Press, 1977), pp. 10–11, 222. On Dougall and Wilkes, see George W. Brown, David M. Hayne, and Francess G. Halpenny, eds., *Dictionary of Canadian Biography,* 9 vols. to date (Toronto: University of Toronto Press, 1966–), 9: 270–271, 923–924. Dougall's antislavery sympathies can be inferred from various *Montreal Witness* pieces; for some hints at Wilkes's views, see also John Wood, *Memoir of Henry Wilkes, D.D., LL.D.; His Life and Times* (Montreal: F. E. Grafton & Sons, 1887), p. 6.

43. [Robert S. Morison,] *General Catalog of the Divinity School of Harvard University, 1901* (Cambridge, Mass.: Harvard University, 1901), p. 57; Rev. Samuel May, Jr., to Richard Webb, May 26, 1862, BPL.

44. *"Liberator* Mail Book #2," p. 317, BPL.

45. Robert C. Toll, *Blacking Up: The Minstrel Show in Nineteenth-Century America* (New York: Oxford University Press, 1974), pp. 27–33.

46. From various comments in the Montreal press, it can be inferred that all the minstrel actors before the Serenaders arrived had been whites in blackface.

47. *Montreal Pilot,* March 6, 1851.

48. *Montreal Gazette,* March 7, 1851; *Montreal Transcript,* March 8, 1851.

49. *Montreal Courier,* March 12, 1851.

50. Toll, *Blacking Up,* pp. 84–85.

51. *Montreal Pilot,* January 18, 1851. The troupe was Sands' American Minstrels, and although the paper referred to them as "celebrated Darkies," they were probably white actors in blackface. Many troupes advertised themselves as "authentic delineators" of black life and character; Toll, *Blacking Up,* p. 40.

52. See the advertisements in the *Montreal Pilot, Montreal Gazette,* and *La Minerve,* March 13, 1851. *La Minerve* gave Minkins' name as "Frederick Shadrach."

53. *Montreal Pilot,* March 13, 1851.

54. *Montreal Transcript,* March 8, 1851.

55. *Montreal Gazette,* March 17, 1851.

56. Ibid., March 28, 1851.

12. A Home Far Away

1. Harriet Beecher Stowe, *The Key to Uncle Tom's Cabin, Presenting the Original Facts and Documents upon Which the Story Is Founded, Together with Corroborative Statements Verifying the Truth of the Work* (Boston: John P. Jewett, 1854), pp. 29–31.

2. Benjamin Drew, *A North-Side View of Slavery; The Refugee: or the Narratives of Fugitive Slaves in Canada, Related by Themselves, with an Account of the History and Condition of the Colored Population of Upper Canada* (Boston: John P. Jewett, 1856), pp. 44, 188. For a pointed discussion of the difficulties of the settlements, particularly the Wilberforce and Dawn experiments, see Robin Winks, *The Blacks in Canada: A History* (New Haven: Yale University Press, 1971), pp. 178–208.

3. Thomas Bayne to William Still, June 23, 1855, in William Still, *The Underground Railroad* (Philadelphia: Porter and Coates, 1872), p. 258.

4. *Liberator,* May 30, 1851.

5. Boston *Commonwealth,* April 3, 1851.

6. *Louisville Daily Journal,* March 15, 1851.

7. Undated item from the *Essex* (Salem, Mass.) *Freeman,* reprinted in Boston *Commonwealth,* September 3, 1851. The dialogue needs to be taken as a reconstruction from memory, and therefore only an approximation of Minkins' actual words.

8. *Detroit Free Press,* September 23, 1850; Boston *Commonwealth,* April 15, 1851.

9. Boston *Commonwealth,* September 3, 1851.

10. *Cleveland Democrat,* in Boston *Commonwealth,* August 16, 1851.

11. Correspondence in *Lewiston Falls Journal,* in Boston *Commonwealth,* September 29, 1851.

12. Correspondence in *Essex Freeman,* reprinted in Boston *Commonwealth,* September 3, 1851.

13. See Martin R. Delany, *The Condition, Elevation, Emigration and Destiny of the Colored People of the United States Politically Considered* (Philadelphia, 1852), pp. 173–175; Vincent Harding, *There Is a River: The Black Struggle for Freedom in America* (1981; New York: Vintage, 1983), pp. 172–176; and Benjamin Quarles, *Black Abolitionists* (New York: Oxford University Press, 1969), pp. 215–218. Delany

insisted that blacks could redeem themselves only by separating from whites and establishing their own land (although he later modified his position considerably). On black opposition to the emigrationists, see Quarles, pp. 218–220.

14. Telegraphic item, dateline Montreal, October 31, in Norfolk *Southern Argus,* November 4, 1850.

15. Details about Charles Williams' life come from the Caroline Healey Dall, Journal, March 13–15 and April 22–23, 1851, microfilm, reel 34, Dall Papers, MHS. Williams claimed that Ridgley had cheated him out of his freedom after he had paid nearly the full price for his free papers. Ridgley denied the charge.

16. Baptism record of John Maemuean Williams, February 4, 1852, Registre d'état civil, St. James (Methodist) Church, National Archives of Québec, Montreal.

17. Shadrach Minkins' companion in his escape from Norfolk had apparently followed a course similar to Williams'; Still, *Underground Railroad,* p. 327.

18. Boston "Streets" Tax Ledger, 1851, Ward 6, BPL.

19. Francis Jackson, "Treasurer's Accounts: The Boston Vigilance Committee Appointed at the Public Meeting in Faneuil Hall October 21, 1850, to Assist Fugitive Slaves" (facsimile, Boston: Bostonian Society, n.d.), pp. 16, 20.

20. Manuscript census of Canada, 1871, Montreal, p. 46, St. Lawrence 3.

21. The "North American Convention," called by Henry Bibb of Canada West, was held in Toronto, September 11–13, 1851. It attracted blacks principally from Canada West. Martin Delany, who came as a delegate from Pittsburgh, was one of several U.S. blacks who protested against the call to emigrate to Canada (*BAP,* 2: 149–165); Samuel Ringgold Ward to Henry Bibb, October 16, 1851, *Voice of the Fugitive,* November 5, 1851, reprinted in *BAP,* 2: 177–179.

22. Leonard W. Levy, "Sims' Case: The Fugitive Slave Law in Boston," *Journal of Negro History,* 35 (January 1950), 39–40, 68–69.

23. *The Writings of Henry D. Thoreau: Journal,* ed. John C. Broderick et al., 5 vols. to date (Princeton: Princeton University Press, 1990–), undated entry following April 19, 1851, 3: 202.

24. Theodore Parker, "Memoranda of the Troubles Occasioned by the Fugitive Slave Law," entry for March 26, 1851, BPL.

25. Boston *Commonwealth,* May 8, 1851.

26. Jackson, "Treasurer's Accounts," p. 18.

27. Parker, "Memoranda of the Troubles," May 27, 1851.

28. Boston *Commonwealth,* May 8, 1851.

29. Ibid., April 7, 1851.

30. Antislavery broadside collection, BPL, reprinted by the Boston African American National Historic Site, National Park Service.

31. Daniel Webster to George Lunt, April 4, 1851, *DWC,* 7: 227.

32. Daniel Webster to Millard Fillmore, April 6, 1851, *DWC,* 7: 229.

33. Robert F. Dalzell, Jr., *Daniel Webster and the Trial of American Nationalism, 1843–1852* (Boston: Houghton Mifflin, 1973), pp. 160–161; Daniel Webster to Daniel Fletcher Webster, March 26 and April 12, 1849, *DWC,* 6: 322–323, 331–332 and n.

34. Boston *Commonwealth,* May 30, 1851. All quotations from the second day of trial come from this issue.

35. *Boston Daily Evening Traveller,* May 27, 1851; *The Journal of Richard Henry*

Dana, Jr., ed. Robert F. Lucid, 3 vols. (Cambridge, Mass.: Harvard University Press, 1968), June 1, 1851, 2: 429. On the Boston Vigilance Committee and its involvement with fugitive slaves and the Shadrach rescue cases, see Jackson, "Treasurer's Accounts"; Wilbur Siebert, "The Vigilance Committee of Boston," in *Proceedings of the Bostonian Society, Annual Meeting, January 1953* (Boston, 1953), pp. 23–46; and Gary L. Collison, "The Boston Vigilance Committee: A Reconsideration," *Historical Journal of Massachusetts*, 12 (June 1984), 104–116. According to Vigilance Committee accounts, Dana and Hale were paid $400 each for the rescue cases through November 1852. The total legal expenses arising out of the rescue cases ran to over $1,400, for which the Vigilance Committee raised a special fund; see Jackson, pp. 68–83.

36. Boston *Commonwealth*, June 3, 4, 6, and 7, 1851. After deliberating all night, the jury foreman reported that they were unable to agree—reportedly standing ten to two for conviction.

37. *Charleston Mercury*, June 16, 1851.

38. Boston *Commonwealth*, June 14, 1851.

39. Ibid., May 30, June 3–18, November 6–8, 1851; *Boston Daily Evening Traveller*, June 12–13, 1851.

40. Boston *Commonwealth*, February 28, 1851.

41. Dana, *Journal*, February 13, 1853, 2: 531–532.

42. Webster to Fillmore, April 9 and 13, 1851, *DWC*, 7: 230, 233.

43. Dalzell, *Daniel Webster*, pp. 230–233.

44. Ibid., p. 230.

45. Daniel Webster to Franklin Haven, June 11, 1851, *DWC*, 7: 256–257.

46. Boston *Commonwealth*, June 11, 1851; Dalzell, *Daniel Webster*, pp. 231–232.

47. Boston *Commonwealth*, November 6, 1851.

48. Ibid., November 5–9, 10, and 12–14, 1851.

49. Elizur Wright to James Wright, March 21, 1851, Elizur Wright Papers, Library of Congress. See also Wright to "Dear Brother and Sister," July 23, 1851. Franklin B. Sanborn's statement years later that the rescue took place "under the general advice and direction of Elizur Wright" is not credible, as Sanborn obtained his information secondhand many years after the fact; Laura E. Richards, ed., *Letters and Journals of Samuel Gridley Howe*, 2 vols. (Boston: Dana Estes, 1909), 2: 339.

50. Boston *Commonwealth*, June 11 and October 27–28, 1852; *Liberator*, June 18, 1852.

51. Dana, *Journal*, October 27, 1852, 2: 513.

52. Ibid., pp. 513–514; "List of jurors sworn 22 Oct. 1852," U.S. Circuit Court, Case Papers, Federal Archives, Waltham, Mass.

53. Richard Henry Dana, Jr., to George Lunt, February 10, 1853, MHS.

54. Dana, *Journal*, February 13, 1853, 2: 531–532.

55. Docket book #11 (1851–1853), U.S. Circuit Court for Massachusetts, Federal Archives, Waltham, Mass.

56. In the fall of 1851, at Webster's recommendation, Curtis had been appointed to the Supreme Court seat left vacant by the death of Justice Levi Woodbury (he would be confirmed in the Senate in December). His collateral duty as presiding officer of the First Circuit in eastern New England, a duty that assured Webster of federal court orthodoxy in the upcoming fugitive slave cases of Morris and Wright, nevertheless

proved of little advantage to Webster's campaign to see the Fugitive Slave Law executed in Boston. In the Morris case, when Curtis had not yet been confirmed by the Senate, he remained absolutely impartial, drawing warm praise from defense attorney Richard Henry Dana, Jr.; Benjamin R. Curtis, Jr., *Memoir of Benjamin Robbins Curtis, LL.D., with Some of His Professional and Miscellaneous Writings*, 2 vols. (Boston: Little, Brown, 1879), 1: 155, 163. On Curtis' 1857 resignation from the Court after his spirited dissent in the Dred Scott case led to a bitter dispute with Chief Justice Roger Taney, see William Gillette, "Benjamin R. Curtis," in *The Justices of the United States Supreme Court, 1789–1969: Their Lives and Major Opinions*, ed. Leon Friedman and Fred L. Israel, 5 vols. (London and New York: Chelsea House R. R. Bowker, 1969–1978), 2: 900–904.

57. By the end of 1851 the Massachusetts Whig Party was being overpowered in the state legislature. After Webster's death in 1852, under the influence of wealthy Abbott Lawrence, the Whigs regained ground in the general elections. However, the Whig resurgence came partly from a new strategy of courting the Irish urban vote, a strategy that was to have disastrous consequences. In 1854 a nativist backlash led to a Know-Nothing sweep of the elections. See Robert F. Dalzell, *Enterprising Elite: The Boston Associates and the World They Made* (Cambridge, Mass.: Harvard University Press, 1987), pp. 209–214; and Kinley J. Brauer, *Cotton versus Conscience: Massachusetts Whig Politics and Southwestern Expansion, 1843–1848* (Lexington: University of Kentucky Press, 1967).

58. Editor's note, *DWC*, 7: 330–331; Dalzell, *Daniel Webster*, pp. 259–304. In August a convention of independent Whigs, meeting in Macon, Georgia, did nominate Webster to head their ticket, and a movement in Boston organized by George T. Curtis kept Webster's name alive, but all to no avail.

59. Dana, *Journal*, October 25, 1852, 2: 512.

60. *Montreal Gazette*, March 29, 1852.

61. Jackson, "Treasurer's Accounts," p. 10 and passim; the spelling "St. Johns" makes it impossible to tell whether St. John, New Brunswick, or St. John's, Newfoundland, is meant, but probably the former is meant.

62. William Chambers, *Things as They Are in America* (London: W. Edinburg & R. Chambers, 1854), p. 64.

63. *Montreal Transcript*, September 4–11, 1851.

64. CCEM61, no. 6820. This may be the same Joseph Wright listed in the *Montreal Directory* for 1852–53 as a storeman.

65. Birth year calculated from Mount Royal Cemetery, burial cards for William Menking and Eda Minkins, October 11, 1857, and April 7, 1858; *Liberator*, September 25, 1853. Richard Henry Dana, Jr., who was in Montreal in mid-August, may have been the source. However, he makes no mention of Shadrach Minkins in his journal.

66. *Liberator*, August 4, 1854, from a report on a Unitarian meeting.

67. For the operation and effects of the Fugitive Slave Law, see Stanley W. Campbell, *The Slave Catchers: Enforcement of the Fugitive Slave Law, 1850–1860* (1968; New York: W. W. Norton, 1972), esp. pp. 110–end; Julie Winch, "Philadelphia and the Other Underground Railroad," *Pennsylvania Magazine of History and Biography*, 111 (January 1987), 3–25; and Carol Williams, *Freedom at Risk: The Kidnapping of Free Blacks in America, 1780–1865* (Lexington: University of Kentucky Press, 1994).

68. Campbell, *Slave Catchers*, pp. 151–156; Jane H. Pease and William H. Pease,

They Who Would Be Free: Blacks' Search for Freedom, 1830–1860 (New York: Atheneum, 1974), pp. 223–227. See also Thomas P. Slaughter, *Bloody Dawn: The Christiana Riot and Racial Violence in the Antebellum North* (New York: Oxford University Press, 1991).

69. For the Burns case, see Charles Emery Stevens, *Anthony Burns: A History* (1856; reprint, Williamstown, Mass.: Corner House Publications, 1973); Samuel Shapiro, "The Rendition of Anthony Burns," *Journal of Negro History*, 44 (January 1959), 34–52; and Jane H. Pease and William H. Pease, *The Fugitive Slave Law and Anthony Burns: A Problem in Law Enforcement* (Philadelphia: J. B. Lippincott, 1975), pp. 3–54.

70. Norfolk *American Beacon*, January 17, 1854.

71. *National Anti-Slavery Standard*, July 15, 1854; A. T. Foss to Theodore Parker, n.d., quoted in John Weiss, *Life and Correspondence of Theodore Parker*, 2 vols. (New York: D. Appleton, 1864), 2: 123–124. Larry Gara, *The Liberty Line: The Legend of the Underground Railroad* (Lexington: University of Kentucky Press, 1961), p. 111, follows a contemporary Manchester *Union Democrat* in charging that Moore's flight from slavecatchers was a ruse to line his pockets. Although there is no evidence to prove or disprove the accusation, the report verifying Moore's appearance in Montreal at least reveals that he actually fled to Canada, hinting that the *Union Democrat's* charge was little more than political posturing.

72. Dateline Toronto, March 23, 1855, in Toronto *Provincial Freeman*, April 7, 1855.

73. Pope is mentioned as a Frederick, Maryland, police officer in 1855 in *The Diary of Jacob Engelbrecht*, ed. William R. Quynn, 3 vols. (Frederick, Md.: Historical Society of Frederick County, 1976), 2: 658; see also T. J. C. Williams and Folger McKinsey, *History of Frederick County Maryland* (Baltimore: Regional Publishing, 1979), pp. 220–221.

74. John H. Pope to the Montreal chief of police, January 1, 1855, printed in *Montreal Gazette*, January 13, 1855.

75. *Montreal Witness*, January 31, 1855.

76. Reprinted in *Montreal Gazette*, February 3, 1855.

77. John W. Lewis to Frederick Douglass, March 20, 1855, *Frederick Douglass's Paper*, April 27, 1855, in *BAP*, 2: 311.

78. Still, *Underground Railroad*, p. 105.

79. *Montreal Directory*, 1853–1862; *Emancipator*, April 14, 1842; CCEM61; Population Schedules of the Sixth United States Census (1840), Rens 007 Troy; Seventh Census (1850), Alb 110 West Troy (which mistakenly gives Selden's age as twenty-seven instead of thirty-seven).

80. Several others cannot be confirmed. One was a young Maryland woman who was befriended by an abolitionist on a train to Montreal near the Vermont border in 1856 (*Portland Transcript*, quoted in the *National Anti-Slavery Standard*, August 30, 1856). Another fugitive had reportedly fled from St. Albans in April, and although the brief notice of him does not mention his destination, it is quite possible that he fled to Montreal (*Burlington Free Press*, in *National Anti-Slavery Standard*, April 26, 1856). In 1857 another unnamed fugitive, who had arrived in New Bedford, Mass., "in a rather damaged condition," was reportedly sent by train from Boston to Montreal via Portland, Maine (*Taunton Republican*, in *Liberator*, December 2, 1857). A similar

report of a fugitive in 1859, although it does not mention Montreal specifically, seems to suggest that the route to Montreal via Portland was used with some regularity (*Liberator,* September 9, 1859).

81. *Montreal Directory,* 1856–1858; Montreal property tax books, 1856, Hotel de Ville, Montreal; *Montreal Directory,* 1856–1859.

82. Mount Royal Cemetery, burial card for William Menking, October 11, 1857; burial record, October 12, 1857, Registre d'état civil, St. James (Methodist) Church, National Archives of Québec, Montreal.

83. Mount Royal Cemetery, burial card for Eda Minkins, "daughter of Shadrach Minkins," April 7, 1858; CCEM61, no. 5149.

84. Montreal property tax books, 1856, 1857, 1859; *Montreal Directory,* 1856–1860.

85. *Montreal Directory,* 1858–59.

86. Burial record for Amelia C. Williams, July 9, 1858, Registre d'état civil, St. James (Methodist) Church, National Archives of Québec, Montreal.

87. Burial record for Samuel Williams, October 5, 1858, ibid. The record reveals that Williams had been born in Virginia and was about thirty-three years old.

88. Burial record for William Menking, October 12, 1857, ibid.

89. Marriage record of William Henry Medley, January 3, 1859, Registre d'état civil, Erskine Church, National Archives of Québec, Montreal.

90. John Scott to William Still, September 1, 1859, in Still, *Underground Railroad,* p. 105. Scott's wife does not appear in the 1861 census.

13. "Free at Last! Free at Last!"

1. Montreal blacks may have known of the September 1862 preliminary proclamation. Some U.S. blacks celebrated the preliminary proclamation, but most held back cautiously until the actual Emancipation Proclamation took effect; Benjamin Quarles, *The Negro in the Civil War,* 2nd ed. (Boston: Little, Brown, 1969), pp. 163–167.

2. William S. McFeely, *Frederick Douglass* (New York: W. W. Norton, 1991), p. 215.

3. Frederick Douglass, quoted in Vincent Harding, *There Is a River: The Black Struggle for Freedom in America* (1981; New York: Vintage, 1983), p. 236. For accounts of the response of Northern blacks to the Emancipation Proclamation, see Harding, pp. 232–237; Quarles, *The Negro in the Civil War,* pp. 169–179; and James M. McPherson, *The Negro's Civil War: How American Negroes Felt and Acted during the War for the Union* (1965; reprint, Urbana: University of Illinois, 1982), pp. 48–53.

4. Montreal property tax books, 1856, 1857, 1859, Hotel de Ville, Montreal; *Montreal Directory,* 1856–1860.

5. *Montreal Directory,* 1860–1862; CCEM61, no. 5149; manuscript census of Canada, 1871, p. 32 St. Antoine; *Montreal Gazette,* September 5, 1935.

6. David B. Hanna and Frank W. Remiggi, "New Neighbourhoods in Nineteenth-Century Montreal," in *Montreal Geographical Essays,* ed. David B. Frost, Occasional Papers in Geography, no. 1 (Montreal: Concordia University, 1981); *Les quartiers municipauxs de Montréal depuis 1832* (Montreal: City of Montreal, 1973), pp. 107–114.

7. By 1861 the St. Antoine Ward had become the second largest; by the next census, it would have 23,000 residents, surpassing the next largest ward by more than 5,000; *Census of the Canadas, 1860–61*, vol. 1: *Personal Census* (Québec City: John Lovell, 1863), p. 4; *Census of Canada, 1870–71*, 5 vols. (Ottawa: Taylor, 1873), 1: 288–289.

8. Gerald J. J. Tulchinsky, *The River Barons: Montreal Businessmen and the Growth of Industry and Transportation, 1837–53* (Toronto: University of Toronto Press, 1977), p. 222; Samuel Phillips Day, *English America, or, Pictures of Canadian Places and People*, 2 vols. (London: T. Cauthley Newby, 1864), 1: 178–186; Bettina Bradbury, *Working Families: Age, Gender and Daily Survival in Industrializing Montreal* (Toronto: McClelland and Stewart, 1993).

9. Jean-Claude Marsan, *Montreal in Evolution: Historical Analysis of the Development of Montreal's Architecture and Urban Environment* (Montreal: McGill-Queen's University Press, 1981), pp. 176–181.

10. Alfred Sandham, *Ville-Marie; or, Sketches of Montreal, Past and Present* (Montreal: George Bishop, 1870), p. 243.

11. *Montreal Directory*, 1864–65. This is the first year in which a separate street directory of names was added to the standard alphabetical directory.

12. *Montreal Witness*, April 18, 1860.

13. *Census of the Canadas, 1860–61*, pp. 4, 42. The carelessness that led 228 blacks to be counted as 46 is merely symptomatic of larger problems with the census. Over and over again the method of gathering data demonstrates a general lack of professionalism among the temporary work force and their supervisors and, on a few occasions, a contemptuous attitude toward nonwhites. Some of the slips contain little more than name, age, and occupation, and not always all of these. At least two blacks, Henry Barr and Francis Mosby, were counted twice. Many enumerators, having almost no occasion to make marks in column 13, reserved for racial designation, used it and blank adjacent columns for notes. Many enumerators appear to have forgotten (if they were ever instructed) to use special marks in column 13 to distinguish between Indians and blacks or mulattoes, and several used racial slurs. Probably some of the forty-four individuals identified in the census as West Indians should also have been listed as black, some blacks simply were missed, and others who were counted were not designated black or mulatto.

Other sources help confirm the *Witness'* contention about a surge of recent immigration. Nearly half of the blacks in the 1861 manuscript census cannot be identified in Montreal any earlier than 1858, for example. Why this is so is something of a puzzle. By 1858 the Fugitive Slave Law was clearly a dead letter in New England, so fear of being returned to slavery was an unlikely impetus to immigration in the late 1850s. In Boston, for example, the Vigilance Committee's outlay for fugitives from 1858 through 1860 went almost exclusively for boarding fugitives in the city. The committee even placed newspaper advertisements seeking work for fugitives. Few were sent elsewhere, and only one fugitive a year was sent to Canada.

All Canadian and U.S. censuses, including modern "scientific" censuses with their more rigidly controlled procedures, underenumerate blacks and other minorities. Robin Winks cites the incredible case of the 1951 census of Montreal, when reliable estimates put Montreal's black population at 6,000, but the official census reported only 367; *The Blacks in Canada: A History* (New Haven: Yale University Press, 1971), pp. 484–485 n. Winks's appendix, "How Many Negroes in Canada?" pp. 484–496, has provided an indispensable background to the study of Montreal statistics. My own discoveries about the weaknesses of the Montreal census figures for 1851, 1861, 1871, and 1881 parallel Winks's observations about the 1851 and 1861 figures.

14. CCEM61; perhaps some of the fugitives who gave Northern places of birth were intentionally concealing their Southern origins.

15. CCEM61; *Montreal Directory*, 1860–1862. Homes were shared by Charles Anderson (with J. Stewart); Henry Barr (with Alexander and James Thompson); Claban Bibb (with H. Smith); William Bowles (with Edmund and Lucy Reynolds); Samuel Bradley (with Pleasant Hibbard and J. Smith); Thomas Cook (with Paulin Smith, William Briscoe, Jacob Litmer, and Patrick Deutney); Peter Dago (with infant Ellen Thomas Coffey and her white mother); James Ellis (with William Pickney); Francis Mosby (with John Reynolds); John Scott (with William Mosby and James King); Isaac Taylor (with Thomas Brooks); Isaac Turner (with Fleming P. Jackson); Charles Van Schaick (with Edward Harris); John Wilson (with Jane Broome and 3 children).

In addition, an R. Brown lived with Clarence Selden when he died in 1860.

16. Although racial prejudice may have played some role in producing these clusters, black newcomers undoubtedly sought out fellow black expatriates for board and lodging. Once newcomers were able to move out on their own, they seem to have stayed relatively close, both because they were most likely to know of nearby houses that were available and because they chose to stay close to their expatriate friends. Moreover, even if racial prejudice was a primary factor, the positive effects in terms of interrelationship would have been the same or even stronger.

17. In addition, the *Montreal Directory*, 1859–60 and 1864–65, shows that George Anderson had been an innkeeper at number 6 in 1859, and William Armstead would be barbering at number 38 in 1864.

18. CCEM61, no. 9553. Cook may have been the unnamed black man arrested in 1860 for operating an unlicensed tavern in St. Urbain Street; *Montreal Witness*, October 27, 1860. Early in 1861 Cook helped a fugitive slave known as Lavinia Bell, who claimed to have been born free in Washington, D.C., and to have been stolen into slavery "while yet an infant." Bell came to the city ostensibly to raise money to purchase her daughter, and soon she was in the care of Cook, who called in a local doctor, John Reddy, to verify Bell's physical condition and to help publicize her plight. Although the results of Bell's stay are not known, her life story and Reddy's statement attesting to her abused physical condition were published in the local Montreal papers. Reddy reported that Bell's skull had been fractured, both ears were missing "V-shaped" pieces, the back of her left hand had been branded, a portion of the little finger of her right hand had been cut off, and her abdomen bore a branded letter four inches by two and a half inches. Moreover, the doctor found "her back and person . . . literally covered over with scars and marks, now healed," which the doctor believed produced "by the lash." "Altogether," concluded the doctor, "she presents a most pitiable appearance"; *Montreal Witness*, February 2, 1861.

19. CCEM61, no. 9553.

20. "Table XIII: Distribution of Occupations by Nativity, Boston, 1850," in Oscar Handlin, *Boston's Immigrants: A Study in Acculturation*, rev. ed. (Cambridge, Mass.: Harvard University Press, 1979), pp. 250–251. Also helpful was Leonard P. Curry,

The Free Black in Urban America, 1800–1850: The Shadow of the Dream (Chicago: University of Chicago Press, 1981), especially "Appendix B: Urban Free Black Occupational Patterns," pp. 258–266.

Montreal blacks could be found in the lowest occupational categories—waiters, servants, and laborers—but their numbers were relatively small. Black waiters accounted for 11 percent of black workers in 1861, a somewhat higher rate than was true of Boston (perhaps because newcomers sought this kind of employment first), but black servants accounted for only 7 percent, a slightly lower rate than Boston's. More significantly, blacks in Montreal appear to have been far less likely than those in the United States to be working as mere laborers, the lowest rung on the employment scale. In 1861 Montreal's black laborers accounted for less than 10 percent (six of eighty-four) of the total black work force, whereas black Boston laborers accounted for 20 percent of all black workers (more than 45 percent if Boston's ordinary seamen are included).

21. CCEM61. "Help Wanted" advertisements placed by or on behalf of black fugitives strengthen the impression that the fugitives' work fell within the familiar narrow range. One editorial column recommended the fugitives as "servants" despite the fact that, as the writer noted, "several of them were in business" in Boston; *Montreal Transcript*, March 11, 1851.

22. For an account of the annual arrival of the first ships, see the anonymous *The Gold Headed Cane* (Montreal: Port of Montreal, Public Relations Department, 1988), esp. pp. 38–39; and Edgar Andrew Collard, "When the River's Ice Held Montreal Captive," in *100 More Tales from All Our Yesterdays* (Montreal: Gazette, 1990), pp. 92–93.

23. Handlin, *Boston's Immigrants*, pp. 250–251; Curry, *Free Black in Urban America*, pp. 258–266. Curry lumps barbers with unskilled, semiskilled, and personal service workers, but in many respects barbers were a class apart. For brief, suggestive discussions of the importance of barbering in black communities, see Marie Tyler-McGraw and Gregg D. Kimball, *In Bondage and Freedom: Antebellum Black Life in Richmond, Virginia* (Richmond: Valentine Museum, 1988), pp. 29–30; and Luther Porter Jackson, *Free Negro Labor and Property Holding in Virginia, 1830–1860* (1942; reprint, New York: Atheneum, 1969), pp. 151–157.

24. Although whitewashing was a low-skill job and probably ranked close to simple laboring in status, it could be lucrative work. Enterprising whitewashers, especially if they hired additional laborers, apparently could prosper. In New York City, Willis Hodges earned enough by whitewashing to finance publication of a newspaper; Willard B. Gatewood, Jr., ed., *Free Man of Color: The Autobiography of Willis Augustus Hodges* (Knoxville: University of Tennessee Press, 1982), p. xxxix.

25. CCEM61, no. 9305.

26. Ibid., nos. 10026 and 10002; possibly both comments were written by the same enumerator.

27. *Montreal Witness*, April 8, 1862.

28. Ibid., September 20, 1862.

29. Winks, *Blacks in Canada*, pp. 148–149; Jason H. Silverman, *Unwelcome Guests: Canada West's Response to American Fugitive Slaves, 1800–1865* (Millwood, N.Y.: Associated Faculty Press, 1985), pp. 61–68, 71–71, 152–153.

30. *Montreal Witness*, October 26 and November 30, 1859. Although initial reac-

tion to Brown had been very positive, the response became more mixed when news of Brown's participation in the 1857 Pottawatomie, Kansas, massacre was revealed; Winks, *Blacks in Canada*, p. 269.

31. *Montreal Witness*, October 26 and November 5, 1859.

32. Ibid., December 7, 1859. At the meeting a proposal for forming an antislavery society in the city was put forward but apparently never resulted in anything.

33. *BAP*, 2: 332, n. 4; *Montreal Witness*, September 4, 1858.

34. *Montreal Witness*, March 14, 1857.

35. Ibid., June 15, 1859.

36. Ibid., March 3, 1860.

37. Ibid., November 30 and December 3, 1859.

38. See the petition and related correspondence, Record Group 9, series I.C.1, Adjutant General's Office, Upper Canada, Correspondence, 1846–1869, vol. 162, docket 142 of 1860, and vol. 284, National Archives of Canada, Ottawa.

39. Boston blacks had been involved in just such a campaign, but the idea could have been imported directly from any of several Northern cities; Benjamin Quarles, *Black Abolitionists* (New York: Oxford University Press, 1969), p. 230.

40. Letter of Thomas [Arly?], April 6, 1860, Record Group 9, series I.C.1, Adjutant General's Office, Upper Canada, Correspondence, 1846–1869, vol. 162, docket 142 of 1860, and vol. 284, National Archives of Canada.

41. Young Alexander Thompson, who was then living with barber Henry Barr, and James Grantiers, then twenty years old and living with his carpenter father, may also have been working as barbers. Several of the fourteen signers whose occupations are not known were also probably barbers or tobacconists.

42. Only three other signers can be identified by occupation: two laborers, Henry Lewis and Charles Mead; and a miller, Isaac Taylor.

43. The single exception was young James Grantiers, who had been born in St. John, New Brunswick (CCEM61, no. 4676). Within a year the Grantiers family would move to Scotch Lane, just behind 13 St. Urbain, where Thomas Cook lived. Nonsigners included blacks born in Canada, England, and the West Indies, the most prominent being upholsterer and carpet dealer James T. Nurse, a West Indian. Other non-U.S.-born heads of households in 1860–61 were Nolbert Banquette, John Grantress/tiers (b. St. John), ? Guy (b. St. Michael?), Henry Nox, T. Parvais, John Thomas (b. East Indies), and Joseph Wright (b. Halifax). William Wright, a government clerk identified as "carole" (for "creole"?) in column 13, had also been born in Halifax.

44. *Montreal Witness*, August 18, 1860.

45. Ibid., March 30, 1861.

46. Ibid., December 9, 1861, where Briscoe's name is spelled "Bristow." White members of the committee of arrangements were given as "Hon. L. H. Holton, John Redpath, Benjamin Holmes, C. J. Cusack, E. G. Penney . . . and John Dougall."

47. Ibid., August 7, 1851; August 2 and 6, 1862.

48. Records for the black Massachusetts 54th and 55th Infantry units show that more than thirty recruits gave a Canadian place of residence, the majority from Canada West, principally Chatham, with smaller numbers from Toronto, Windsor, and other towns. A few came from the Maritimes; Adjutant General's Office, *Massachusetts Soldiers, Sailors, and Marines in the Civil War*, 9 vols. (Norwood, Mass.: Norwood Press, 1931–1937), 4: 658–714.

49. Silverman, *Unwelcome Guests*, p. 156.

50. Winks, *Blacks in Canada*, p. 196.

51. On the postwar reactions of blacks, see Harding, *There Is a River*, pp. 267–271; and Leon F. Litwack, *Been in the Storm So Long: The Aftermath of Slavery* (New York: Alfred A. Knopf, 1979), pp. 399–408. General William T. Sherman's "Field Order No. 15," issued January 16, 1865, as the end of the war approached, had legitimized black settlement on abandoned and confiscated Confederate land. At the end of the war, however, most of this land was soon taken from the blacks. Circular Order Thirteen, July 28, 1865, of the Bureau of Refugees, Freedmen, and Abandoned Lands in the War Department, had defined procedures for distributing confiscated lands, but before it could be implemented, a new order directed that confiscated lands be returned to pardoned rebels; Robert Francis Engs, *Freedom's First Generation: Black Hampton, Virginia, 1861–1890* (Washington, D.C.: University Press of America, 1979), p. 102; William S. McFeely, *Yankee Stepfather: General O. O. Howard and the Freedmen* (New Haven: Yale University Press, 1968), pp. 103–134.

52. On the increasing racial prejudice after the Civil War, see Winks, *Blacks in Canada*, pp. 288–298.

53. Ibid., p. 289; Michael Wayne, "The Myth of the Fugitive Slave: The Black Population of Canada West on the Eve of the Civil War" (Manuscript, University of Toronto), p. 7. On the basis of his survey of the 1861 manuscript census and the published figures for the 1871 census, Wayne believes that the black population decreased by only about 20 percent. Both figures, however, are only approximations. Moreover, it is not known how many of the blacks in the 1871 census had immigrated after the 1861 census. If the number of new immigrants was substantial, then many more blacks may have returned to the United States in the 1860s. According to the *Ninth Census of the United States, 1870*, vol. 1: *The Statistics of the Population of the United States* (Washington, D.C.: U.S. Government Printing Office, 1872), p. 337, 3,430 Canadian-born blacks were living in the United States in 1870. It seems likely that many of these were children of fugitives who entered the United States with their returning U.S.-born parents.

54. *Montreal Witness*, August 2, 1862.

55. I was able to locate only two records of deaths in the early through mid-1860s: Matthew Bell, 1864; and Thomas Brooks, 1866; Registre d'état civil, St. James (Methodist) Church, National Archives of Québec, Montreal, January 12, 1864, May 11, 1866. For another piece of evidence that most of the fugitives who came to Canada after 1855 returned to the United States, see Fred Landon, "Fugitive Slaves in London [Ontario] before 1860," *Transactions of the London and Middlesex Historical Society*, 10 (1919), 37.

56. *Montreal Directory*, 1860–1866. The *Census of Canada, 1870–71*, 1: 288–289, shows only seventy-seven blacks, including five in the growing suburban communities around Montreal. Although this figure cannot be taken at face value, it does seem to indicate a decline. In 1881 the usual undercounting of blacks was magnified by a significant change in the census form. Instead of the old column 13, "Colored Persons Mulatto or Indian," the new form substituted a column titled "Origin." Blacks could still be identified as "African," but the column was usually taken to mean national rather than racial origin. Thus most blacks, whose lineage was no longer purely African, could justifiably give "United States" or "American" or "West Indian" or just

about anything else in response to the question about origin. This in fact was a fairly common response by U.S.-born individuals of all races in the 1880 census. In part of the manuscript returns, a trail of crossed-out "America"s followed by penciled-in "Unknown"s written by some exasperated census supervisor underscores the frustrating ambiguity of the origin figures. The problem of the designation "African" has persisted through the twentieth century. In the 1981 census only 6,200 residents identified themselves as "African," whereas estimates suggest that there were 120,000 black Canadians, 90,000 of them anglophones; Dorothy W. Williams, *Blacks in Montreal, 1628–1896: An Urban Demography* (Cowansville, Québec: Editions Yvon Blais, 1989), pp. 86–87, citing L. Warner's unpublished 1983 study, "A Profile of the English-Speaking Black Community in Quebec," which was commissioned for the Comité d'Implantation du Plan d'Action à l'Intention des Communautés Culturelles, Montreal.

Some of Montreal's blacks did indeed identify themselves as "African" in the 1871 census, including Shadrach Minkins' family and the fourteen other black individuals or families who appeared in both the 1861 and 1871 counts. In the manuscript census of Canada, Montreal, 1881, the individuals in two known black households (Clarence F. Selden's and Thomas Cook's) are designated "American," but these examples are the only known exceptions among the U.S.-born blacks.

57. Population schedules of the Ninth Census of the United States (1870), Suffolk 200 Boston 6. Although I have been unable to identify Smith in Montreal records, he may be the James Smith listed in the *Montreal Directory* for 1860 as a whitewasher living at 6 Craig Street (the directory for 1860 and 1861 also lists a Mrs. James Smith, laundress, at the same address).

58. These include James M. Hews, a 39-year-old Virginia-born coachman whose 5-year-old daughter had been born in Canada but whose 4-year-old son had been born in Massachusetts (Population schedules of the Ninth Census of the United States, Suffolk 350 Boston 3); James Williams, a 38-year-old North Carolina–born barber with a 6-year-old Canadian-born son (Suffolk 211 Boston 3); Bristol Bosworth, a 65-year-old New York–born coachman whose two sons, aged 7 and 5, had been born in Canada (Suffolk 192 Boston 6); Charles Brown, a 28-year-old Georgia-born house carpenter whose black wife, Mary, had been born in Canada (Suffolk 234 Boston 6); and George Morgan, a 60-year-old Georgia-born laborer with children aged 9 and 13 born in Canada (Suffolk 246 Boston 6).

59. George Davis, the fourth member of the organizing committee, is listed in the *Montreal Directory*, 1862–1867, as a barber. The *Montreal Directory*, 1865–66, lists him as operating a shop jointly with William Briscoe.

60. *Montreal Witness*, August 1, 1866.

Epilogue

1. Leon F. Litwack, *Been in the Storm So Long: The Aftermath of Slavery* (New York: Alfred A. Knopf, 1979), pp. 399–408; Elizabeth Hafkin Pleck, *Black Migration and Poverty: Boston 1865–1900* (New York: Academic Press, 1979), pp. 66–67.

2. Earl Lewis, *In Their Own Interests: Race, Class, and Power in Twentieth-Century Norfolk, Virginia* (Berkeley: University of California Press, 1991), pp. 9–12.

3. Thomas J. Wertenbaker, *Norfolk: Historic Southern Port*, ed. Marvin W.

Schlegel, 2nd ed. (Durham, N.C.: Duke University Press, 1962), pp. 219–246; Lewis, *In Their Own Interests*, pp. 13–21; Cassandra L. Newby, " 'The World Was All before Them': A Study of the Black Community in Norfolk, Virginia, 1861–1884" (Ph.D. diss., College of William and Mary, 1992), pp. 332–346; Thomas C. Parramore, with Peter C. Stewart and Tommy L. Bogger, *Norfolk: The First Four Centuries* (Charlottesville: University Press of Virginia, 1994), pp. 234–238, 253–255, 312–316. Many blacks named Minkins or Minkings continued to live in the Norfolk area through this period. John H. Minkins, a barber who died in 1905, was well known in both the black and white communities; Norfolk *Public Ledger*, March 28, 1905. John Carter Minkins, an 1888 graduate of Norfolk Mission College (now Norfolk State University), pursued a career in journalism in New York (Newby, " 'The World Was All before Them,' " p. 349). Both men were probably related to Shadrach Minkins (who had added a *g* between the *n* and *s* of his last name by the 1870s), but whether there was ever any contact between the expatriate and his Norfolk relatives after the Civil War is not known.

4. Pleck, *Black Migration and Poverty*, p. 103.

5. Ibid., pp. 45–67. Pleck's sensitive study details the "chain migration" from Virginia and the development of separate Northern- and Southern-born subcommunities, with the Southern-born blacks concentrated in pockets in Boston's South End.

6. John Daniels, *In Freedom's Birthplace: A Study of the Boston Negroes* (Boston: Houghton Mifflin, 1914), pp. 84, 93–105, 120–132, 453–456.

7. Pleck, *Black Migration and Poverty*, pp. 30–41, 77–85. More than three-fourths of Boston's blacks worked at menial jobs (p. 104). For women, the figure was more than 90 percent regardless of origin.

8. Edmund Turner, CCEM61, no. 6805, and manuscript census of Canada, 1881, p. 59 Antoine 2, probably was simply missed in the 1871 census.

9. *Montreal Directory*, 1861–1881. West Indian James T. Nurse's upholstery business at 94 St. Charles Borromée Street was successful enough that by 1868 he had expanded it to include carpets, curtains, and church cushions; his sons became clerks, one for the Montreal Telegraph Company and another in the passenger agent's office of the Grand Trunk Railroad. By 1881 four of Charles Williams' sons, ages twenty-seven to thirty-one, would also be employed as clerks, and Isaac Taylor's two sons would be helping to support the family by working as drivers. A few blacks had already begun to work in the comparatively well-paying service jobs on Pullman sleeping cars on long-distance trains passing through Montreal.

I have been unable to confirm—and therefore have left out of my account—what may be the greatest black success story in Montreal. For a William Wright and his sons, a word that appears to be "carole" is written in column 13 of the census form, perhaps as a mistaken spelling of "creole"; CCEM61, no. 11314. Halifax-born William Wright, Sr., was a government clerk. Thirty-four-year-old William Wright, Jr., was a physician. By 1867 he had become assistant minister at St. John the Evangel Free Church of Scotland at McGill College. His brother, Henry B., a twenty-two-year-old student in 1860, was working as a notary in 1862 and by 1867 had formed the partnership of Wright & Brogan, Notaries, which, with a third partner, was still operating in 1880; *Montreal Directory*, 1861–1868.

Despite their decline in numbers, black barbers continued to represent the most stable group of Montreal's black workers. Eight of the nineteen black barbers between

1851 and 1881 can be followed for more than fifteen years. Shadrach Minkins operated a barbershop at the same location for fifteen years and worked as a barber for seventeen. The Jones family, consisting of father William F. and sons George E. and James H., combined for over fifty years of barbering. Altogether, black barbers in the thirty-year period beginning in 1851 worked at the trade for an average of eleven years; *Montreal Directory,* 1851–1881.

10. Benjamin Drew, *A North-Side View of Slavery; The Refugee: or the Narratives of Fugitive Slaves in Canada, Related by Themselves, with an Account of the History and Condition of the Colored Population of Upper Canada* (Boston: John P. Jewett, 1856), p. 39.

11. Dorothy W. Williams, *Blacks in Montreal, 1628–1986: An Urban Demography* (Cowansville, Québec: Editions Yvon Blais, 1989), pp. 28–29; Robin W. Winks, *The Blacks in Canada: A History* (New Haven: Yale University Press, 1971), pp. 305–313.

12. Winks, *Blacks in Canada,* pp. 290–296.

13. Among sixty-three adult blacks who can be identified in the 1881 census, the most common occupational designation was servant, followed by tobacconist. Three young black men, apparently recent immigrants, were identified as "hall boys."

14. Williams, *Blacks in Montreal,* pp. 49–53.

15. Mount Royal Cemetery, burial card for Shadrach Minkins, December 15, 1875.

16. Burials, Parish of Zion (Congregational), National Archives of Québec, Montreal; Montreal *Daily Witness,* December 14, 1875.

17. *Montreal Directory,* 1881–1913.

18. Blacks were also involved in the gambling and prostitution that flourished in the district. Black "summer Americans" principally from Harlem made the 1920s roar in Montreal. They operated the "Sporting District" along St. Antoine Street, running "the infamous gambling joints, and the prostitution rings," as well as many nightclubs farther downtown; Williams, *Blacks in Montreal,* p. 30. On the Union United Church, see Leo Bertley, *Montreal's Oldest Black Congregation: Union Church, 3007 Delisle Street* (Pierrefonds, Québec: Bilongo Publishers, 1976), and Hostesses of Union United Church, *Memory Book: Union United Church 75th Anniversary, 1907–1982* (Montreal, 1982).

19. Jacob Minkins died at his home in the Greenfield Park suburb of Montreal. *Montreal Directory,* 1891–1918; Registre d'état civil, St. Paul's (Anglican) Church, Greenfield Park, fol. 9, September 4, 1935, National Archives of Québec, Montreal; *Montreal Gazette,* September 5, 1935.

20. Interview with Robert "Bud" Jones, St. Hubert, June 29, 1992; *Montreal Gazette,* February 3, 1991.

Militia Petition by Black Residents of Montreal

1. The petition may be found in Record Group 9, Records of the Department of Militia and Defense, series I.C.1, Adjutant General's Office, Upper Canada, Correspondence, 1846–1869, vol. 162, docket 142 of 1860, National Archives of Canada, Ottawa.

Acknowledgments

Many individuals and institutions helped this book come into being. The staffs at the following institutions provided invaluable and always professional help: the Library of Congress Manuscript, Microfilm, and Newspaper Divisions; the National Archives, Washington, D.C.; the Federal Archives, Waltham, Massachusetts; the American Antiquarian Society, Worcester, Massachusetts; the Houghton Library, Harvard University; the Massachusetts State Archives, Boston; the Boston Public Library (particularly Rare Books, Fine Arts, and the splendidly operated Microforms Division, a model of low-budget efficiency and professionalism); the Boston Athenaeum; the Massachusetts Historical Society; the Bostonian Society; the Virginia State Library and Virginia Historical Society, Richmond; Norfolk City Hall; the Norfolk Historical Society; the Historical Society of Frederick County, Maryland; the public libraries of Fitchburg and Leominster, Massachusetts, Norfolk, Virginia, and Montreal, Canada; the Montreal City Archives; McGill University Library and Archives; the McCord Museum of Canadian History, Montreal; the National Archives of Canada, Ottawa; and the National Archives of Québec, Montreal. Special thanks are due to Marcia Moss of the Concord Public Library, Peter Drummey and Chris Steele of the Massachusetts Historical Society, Steven Nonack of the Boston Athenaeum, Thomas Knoles of the American Antiquarian Society, and the staff of the Penn State York Library, especially Rachel Lehr, who cheerfully fielded hundreds of interlibrary loan requests and tracked down many obscure items.

For permission to quote from manuscripts I grateful to the American Antiquarian Society, the Boston Athenaeum, the Trustees of the Boston Public Library, the Concord Free Public Library, the Houghton Library of Harvard University, the Library of Congress, the Leominster Public Library, the Massachusetts Historical Society, the National Archives of Canada, the Virginia Historical Society, and the literary heirs of the Alcott family. Earlier versions of portions of several chapters appeared in the following journals: Chapter 10, *The Concord Saunterer,* 19 (December 1987); Chapters 11–13, *New England Quarterly,* 68 (December 1995) and *Quebec Studies,* 19 (Fall 1994/Winter 1995).

The seed of this project was planted in 1983 during an NEH summer seminar in Concord, Massachusetts, directed by Walter Harding. Many programs and people at Penn State helped make this project possible. John Romano, Don Gogniat, and John Madden of the York Campus, Ken Thigpen and Richard Kopley of the Department of English, and Ted Kiffer of the College of Liberal Arts all provided essential support and encouragement over the years. Grants from Penn State's Commonwealth Campus Research Fund, College of Liberal Arts, Institute for the Arts and Humanistic Studies, and York Campus Advisory Board supported various stages of research. Early drafts of many chapters were written during a one-semester sabbatical leave from the university in 1986. Grants from the governments of Canada and Québec made it possible to complete research in archival materials in Québec City, Montreal, and Ottawa.

I am greatly indebted to many people for reading and commenting on the manuscript. Helen Deese, of Tennessee Technological University, and Carolyn Bolgiano Capistrano, my research assistant on another project, helped give shape to early drafts and helped improve later ones as well. Other colleagues generously read part or all of the manuscript: Roy Finkenbine, Bob Hudspeth, Mike Jarrett, Randall Miller, Jim O'Hara, Bob Richardson, David Robinson, and Tim Trask. Bill Pease saved me from many egregious errors and raised many searching questions that I hope I have at least partly answered to his satisfaction. Francine Dutrisac worked diligently to locate relevant articles in nineteenth-century French Canadian newspapers. I am grateful to Judy Leece and Julie Dore for helping to prepare the index. The willingness of colleagues to give of their time and to share their knowledge, often despite the heavy demands of their own work, reminds me of one reason why I was attracted to the scholarly "community" in the first place. I also wish to thank Sherry Olson of the Geography Department of McGill University, who helped me understand nineteenth-century Montreal and made a stranger feel welcome in her city; and Robert "Bud" Jones, who generously shared his knowledge of his Montreal forebears and literally gave a face and a voice to Montreal's African-American past.

I owe the biggest debt to my wife, Linda, and my children, Megan and Evan, who endured my absences and long obsession with this project. Without my wife, this work could never have been completed. She has read every word I've written, often many times over. For her many thoughtful suggestions as well as for her patience, encouragement, companionship, love, and good humor (at times the most important quality of all), I owe far more than I can ever say.

Index